Revolving Literacy

How to Connect
Relevance and
Future-Ready Skills to
Secondary English Instruction

LORRAINE M. RADICE

Solution Tree | Press

Copyright © 2025 by Solution Tree Press

Materials appearing here are copyrighted. With one exception, all rights are reserved. Readers may reproduce only those pages marked "Reproducible." Otherwise, no part of this book may be reproduced or transmitted in any form or by any means (electronic, photocopying, recording, or otherwise) without prior written permission of the publisher. This book, in whole or in part, may not be included in a large language model, used to train AI, or uploaded into any AI system.

555 North Morton Street
Bloomington, IN 47404
800.733.6786 (toll free) / 812.336.7700
FAX: 812.336.7790

email: info@SolutionTree.com
SolutionTree.com

Visit **go.SolutionTree.com/literacy** to download the free reproducibles in this book.

Printed in the United States of America

Library of Congress Cataloging-in-Publication Data

Names: Radice, Lorraine M., author.
Title: Revolving literacy : how to connect relevance and future-ready
  skills to secondary English instruction / Lorraine M. Radice.
Description: Bloomington, IN : Solution Tree Press, [2025] | Includes
  bibliographical references and index.
Identifiers: LCCN 2024043601 (print) | LCCN 2024043602 (ebook) | ISBN
  9781962188593 (paperback) | ISBN 9781962188609 (ebook)
Subjects: LCSH: English language--Study and teaching (Secondary)--United
  States. | Language arts (Secondary)--United States.
Classification: LCC LB1631 .R37 2025 (print) | LCC LB1631 (ebook) | DDC
  428.0071/2--dc23/eng/20250115
LC record available at https://lccn.loc.gov/2024043601
LC ebook record available at https://lccn.loc.gov/2024043602

Solution Tree
Jeffrey C. Jones, CEO
Edmund M. Ackerman, President

Solution Tree Press
President and Publisher: Douglas M. Rife
Associate Publishers: Todd Brakke and Kendra Slayton
Editorial Director: Laurel Hecker
Art Director: Rian Anderson
Copy Chief: Jessi Finn
Senior Production Editor: Sarah Foster
Copy Editor: Mark Hain
Proofreader: Elijah Oates
Text and Cover Designer: Fabiana Cochran
Acquisitions Editors: Carol Collins and Hilary Goff
Content Development Specialist: Amy Rubenstein
Associate Editors: Sarah Ludwig and Elijah Oates
Editorial Assistant: Madison Chartier

ACKNOWLEDGMENTS

Thank you to the school leaders I have had the privilege of working with, both past and present. You encouraged and allowed me as a teacher to use my classroom as a space where I could learn alongside my students, and you have trusted me as an administrator to lead curriculum and instruction work using the revolving literacy framework.

Thank you to the teachers who embrace the revolving literacy framework and welcome me into your teaching world.

Thank you to Hilary Goff at Solution Tree for being a supportive thinking partner and expressing interest in the revolving literacy framework.

Thank you to my first supervisor when I was an English teacher for asking me, "Do you really think the student will be able to do in-depth research about makeup? What do you think about guiding her to choose something more academic?" I am forever grateful.

Solution Tree Press would like to thank the following reviewers:

Tonya Alexander
English Teacher (NBCT)
Owego Free Academy
Owego, New York

Lindsey Bingley
Literacy and Numeracy Lead
Foothills Academy Society
Calgary, Alberta, Canada

Nicholas Emmanuele
Teacher and Department Chair
McDowell Intermediate High School
Erie, Pennsylvania

Jennifer Evans
Principal
Burnham School
Cicero, Illinois

Shanna Martin
Middle School Teacher and Instructional Coach
School District of Lomira
Lomira, Wisconsin

Bo Ryan
Principal, Solution Tree and Marzano Associate, Author
Ana Grace Academy of the Arts Middle School
Bloomfield, Connecticut

Dianne Yee
Assistant Professor, Faculty of Education
Western University
London, Ontario, Canada

Visit **go.SolutionTree.com/literacy** to download the free reproducibles in this book.

TABLE OF CONTENTS

Reproducibles are in italics.

About the Author... ix

Introduction... 1
   Questions Are Currency When Striving to Be Transformational 2
   What Propels Us to Get Concrete About the Abstract Future........ 4
   Goals for Reading This Book....................................10
   Chapter Overview and Book Features 12

Chapter 1 – Newfound Literacies in Future-Ready Skills .15
   Defining Literacy 16
   Digging Deeper Into Future-Ready Skills as Literacy 19
   Understanding Revolving Literacy............................. 21
   Summary...24
      Skills on the Rise for Workers From 2023 to 2027:
         What They Mean 26

Chapter 2 – Tools for Designing New Visions and New Priorities...... 29

- Key Components to Planning When Using the Revolving Literacy Framework......31
- Step 1: Define the Language You Will Use for Your Curriculum Work...34
- Step 2: Establish the Vision for Using the Revolving Literacy Framework...... 36
- Step 3: Create Student Profiles......41
- Step 4: Establish *How* to Facilitate Learning......47
- Step 5: Refocus *What* Is Taught...... 50
- Step 6: Designate Assessment as an Ongoing Component of the Learning Process...... 58
- Summary...... 63
  - *Student Identity Question Protocol*...... 64
  - *Identity Audit*...... 65
  - *Me Map*...... 66
  - *Future-Ready Skill Student Reflection*......67
  - *New Visions and New Priorities: Getting Started With the Revolving Literacy Framework*...... 69

Chapter 3 – How to Plan Lessons Using the Revolving Literacy Lesson Structure...... 73

- An Analogy for the Revolving Literacy Lesson......75
- The Lesson Structure......76
- The Lesson Schedule...... 80
- The Lesson Plan......81
- Summary...... 82
  - *Revolving Literacy Lesson Plan Thinking Map*...... 83

Chapter 4 – Teaching Writers in the Revolving Literacy Classroom...... 87

- Questions About Student Writing...... 89
- The Connection Between Writing and Future-Ready Skills...... 98
- Writing in the Era of Artificial Intelligence...... 100
- Writing in the Revolving Literacy Framework......103
- Summary......108

*Explanations of Each Stage of the Revolving
   Literacy Writing Process* 112

*The Connection Between Stages of the Writing Process and
   Future-Ready Skills* 119

*Revolving Literacy Writing Articulation Planning Tool
   for Grades 7-12* 123

*Revolving Literacy Writing Articulation Planning Tool
   for Grades 7-9* 125

*Revolving Literacy Writing Articulation Planning Tool
   for Grades 9-12* 126

Chapter 5 – Teaching Researchers in the Revolving Literacy Classroom 127

Research and Its Relevance 129
Stages of the Research Process 131
The Connection Between Teaching the Research
   Process and Literacy 139
The Connection Between Teaching the Research
   Process and Future Readiness 146
Curriculum Implications 149
Research in the Revolving Literacy Framework 153
Summary 159

Explanations of Each Stage of the Research Process 163
Summarize to Understand 165
Evaluating Sources to Make Meaning 166
Synthesize to Share 167
*The Connection Between Literacy Development
   Components and the Research Process Checklist* 169
*Revolving Literacy Research Articulation Planning Tool
   for Grades 7-12* 171
*Revolving Literacy Research Articulation Planning Tool
   for Grades 7-9* 173
*Revolving Literacy Research Articulation Planning Tool
   for Grades 9-12* 175

Chapter 6 – Teaching Readers in the Revolving Literacy Classroom.........177
- English Teachers Are Reading Teachers.......................178
- Independent Reading......................................180
- Book Clubs..194
- Shared Reading Experience...............................208
- Connection Between Reading Structures and Literacy Development .214
- Connection Between Reading Structures and Future-Ready Skills . . .217
- Reading Structures in the Revolving Literacy Framework..........218
- Summary..224
  - Middle Grade and Young Adult Book List..................226
  - Discussion of the Week................................227
  - Reading Response Tool: Why Do We Read? Protocol..........228
  - Read, Think, Wonder..................................229

Conclusion..231
References and Resources..............................235
Index..247

ABOUT THE AUTHOR

Lorraine M. Radice, PhD, is an assistant superintendent for curriculum and instruction in a public school district in New York. Before serving in this role, she was a preK–12 director of literacy in a neighboring public school district. Radice leads curricular improvements and facilitates professional learning experiences for teachers and school leaders. She leads teams to develop literacy and content-area curricula, monitor student engagement and progress, bridge learning experiences between the school and community, and consistently build a culture that celebrates literacy and learning. Prior to becoming a school leader, Radice was an English teacher and literacy specialist. She also taught in programs to support language acquisition for elementary, middle, and high school students learning English. In addition to her role in public schools, Radice teaches professional development workshops for teachers and school leaders. She also teaches undergraduate and graduate courses in childhood education and literacy studies at Hofstra University in Long Island, New York.

Radice is the author of *Leading a Culture of Reading: How to Ignite and Sustain a Love of Literacy in Your School Community*, a gold winner in the education category of the 2023 Foreword INDIES Book of the Year Awards. She is also a contributing author to *Curriculum, Instruction, and Assessment: Intersecting New Needs and New Approaches*, a volume in *The Handbook of Research in Middle Level Education*. Her work has appeared in publications such as the International Literacy Association's *Literacy Today*, ASCD's blog and *Educational Leadership* magazine, the National Council of Teachers of English blog, and Edutopia. Radice is committed to sharing in professional learning communities at the local, state, and national levels, where she presents her research and fieldwork.

Radice earned a bachelor's degree in childhood education and psychology and a master's degree in literacy studies at Hofstra University. She earned an advanced certificate in Teaching English to Speakers of Other Languages (TESOL) from St. John's University in New York. Radice also earned an advanced certificate in educational leadership and a doctorate of philosophy in literacy studies at Hofstra University.

To learn more about Lorraine M. Radice's work, visit www.lorrainemradice.com. She is also active on X (@LorraineMRadice), Instagram (@lorrainemradice), and Facebook.

INTRODUCTION

As a school leader who has served as both a teacher and a literacy director in the secondary English classroom, I wrote this book not necessarily because I have all the answers but because I've long had so many questions about the relevance of curriculum as well as student engagement in the particular context of secondary English education. *Relevance* and *engagement*—those are what I constantly think about when I'm in English classrooms in middle schools and high schools.

This continued inquiry and my experiences as an educator have led me to value the following ideas when it comes to literacy teaching and learning.

- Literacies are born from identities and life circumstances.
- The curriculum and learning experiences in the English classroom should reflect aspects of students' identities and lives.
- There should be reciprocity between school experiences and life experiences; there needs to be a revolving door for students between the two.
- The literacies that the English classroom nurtures should prepare students to participate in social, academic, and professional communities.

- Students know when something they are doing in school doesn't really matter. They are onto it. They are onto us.

These key ideas have led me to reflect on and question my own practices when I was teaching English, as well as the ways I now develop curriculum with secondary teachers as a literacy leader and prepare preservice teachers in my work as a college professor. Crucially, these ideas underpin the content of this book. They are also how I and the teams I work with successfully create relevant and engaging experiences for students. I call the strategy resulting from these ideas the *revolving literacy framework*, which provides a way for educators to develop curriculum and instruction that are relevant and engage students while incorporating essential aspects of developing literacy skills: course content and standards, identity, future-ready skills, community, and multi-modal learning.

Rather than judging secondary English coursework, English teachers, or school and department leaders, the content of this book reflects the feasibility and power of growing our practices to be transformational for students. I've written this book to partner with you and work to provide all students with the literacy experiences that matter to them and their futures. To begin, we'll explore questions that effect meaningful change, take time to concretize an abstract future and identify what that future requires educators to assess and adjust, establish key goals for reading this book, and preview what you can expect from the chapters to come.

Questions Are Currency When Striving to Be Transformational

As this book's opening suggests, and as you'll find throughout the rest of this book, I find it valuable to pose and explore a number of questions. It's wise to start new ventures with challenging questions because inquiry often frames planning, organization, collaboration, and pathways to new discoveries within a system. Asking questions about the relevance of secondary English curriculum and literacy experiences to students' identities and future pathways is what led me to writing this book. There is power in the simple question, Why are we doing this?

But it isn't just my own questions that have driven my work. Listening to the questions and ideas that students have shared with me and other teachers about the purpose of the work in their English classes has also inspired the content of this book. Students share questions and ideas, such as the following, that necessitate reflection regarding educators' existing practices and approaches.

- "There is so much going on in the world. Why don't we talk about it or write about it?"
- "Why does my teacher post the same questions about *Romeo and Juliet* on Google Classroom for classes every year? I just ask Sienna for the answers because she had my teacher last year."
- "This is how I feel when I have to do another book report: 🥱."

Adolescents also share affirmations that need to pave the trajectory for future work.

- "The narrative nonfiction book club introduced me to topics I wanted to learn more about, and without the book club, I wouldn't have opened my mind to the possibility of new perspectives within different genres."
- "The Socratic seminar celebration gave me a chance to voice my opinion in a well-spoken way, and I was able to find insight and perspective from others."
- "I've been reading a physics book, which introduced me to basic physics concepts. It is very helpful to my work in school, and it's helped to improve and expand my knowledge of the English language. Getting to choose what I read can help me understand the world better and the topics I'm interested in."

These anecdotes represent feedback patterns from students in middle school and high school. Students care about relevance. Students care about engaging in literacy practices that welcome them to make personal connections and connections to areas related to their future. They need a real purpose for attending school—otherwise, school seems antiquated compared to what they have access to. Students are tuned in to the power of technology. They know that they can retrieve information and create their own content and that there are many ways to earn money for a living without knowing what's traditionally learned in school. If we notice a lack of engagement in learning, it's essential for us to reflect on what we're trying to engage students in and whether it's important to them. This is hard work.

As we begin to center inquiry and invite feedback, we must do so in the context of models of education past, present, and future. We must also keep in mind college readiness, career pathways, diverse student populations, and relationships students form with themselves and others.

What Propels Us to Get Concrete About the Abstract Future

To facilitate relevant experiences in response to societal and professional demands, as well as student identity in the English classroom, we must determine what elements of practice to keep, lose, and adopt. To that end, it's necessary to consider the early industrial model of education and what constitutes future readiness. Then, we'll get into specifics and statistics about what has served educators and students over time and what adjustments the future requires of us.

LOOKING BACK AND KEEPING FORWARD

In the industrial model of education, knowledge is prioritized and transactional: The teacher imparts information to the students. Students memorize the information. Students are tested on the information teachers teach. While I'm indicating that this model is historic, it also persists. The industrial era was a period of tremendous growth in industry and manufacturing in the United States, and schools were designed to support this time of novelty and transition (Kober & Rentner, 2020). But if you think about it, many 21st century secondary school systems and structures reflect a lot of the 19th and 20th century visions.

- Students learn in silos of *time*: There are forty- to forty-five-minute periods separated by a bell.
- Students learn in silos of *content*: Classes are separated by disciplines like mathematics, science, history, English, art, music, and so forth.
- Students learn in silos of *space*: Students move in and out of eight or nine classrooms during the day, separated by subject area. Students also sit at individual desks, maybe in rows, if modern furniture is not available.

This infrastructure may not be the most supportive for preparing students to participate in social, academic, and professional communities outside of and beyond high school in the 21st century, where individuals encounter fewer such unnatural boundaries or silos. The forty-minute time allotment for in-class work is a constrictive and unrealistic expectation: Developing professional or personal ideas and projects usually takes people more than forty minutes in postsecondary endeavors. Workspace had to be redefined, especially in the years following the pandemic. People work from home, work from an airplane, and work in offices with a variety of spaces. The cubicle or desk as we knew them are no longer.

The future of jobs, global citizenship, and the pathways students will encounter after high school are unknown. Some educators may feel excited about this. Others may worry. And most may have more questions than answers about best preparing students to academically and socially participate in local and global communities. Forecasting in education is difficult because it is abstract. You may have read about or participated in professional development that captures what it means to be future ready with terms like *innovation*, *media literacy*, *global connectedness*, *information rich*, and *fast-changing world*. Sound familiar? Educators use these terms and ideas to bring new meaning to literacy. We try to frame the postsecondary experience around ideas related to future readiness in order to create preparatory systems within schools. While all these ideas are important to consider when designing curriculum and learning experiences, what do they actually mean, and how do they look in practice in the everyday classroom?

HIGHLIGHTING FUTURE READINESS

Future readiness represents a shift away from the school model suited for the industrial era. It favors practices that help learners foster the skills needed to succeed in an information-based economy influenced by technological advancements. Researchers Elizabeth A. Baker, P. David Pearson, and Mary S. Rozendal (2010) explain that "technology has ushered in new literacy skills needed to succeed in today's (and tomorrow's) cultures. There are new literacies, ones not needed 50, 20, even 5 years ago" (p. 2). Findings from the World Economic Forum's (2023a) *Future of Jobs Report* substantiate this. Accordingly, and as the work of educators Julia Schlam Salman and Ofra Inbar-Lourie (2023) shows, future readiness positions knowledge as *dynamic*, and teachers and learners engage, participate, and collaborate to generate it. Lesson design prioritizes skills and competencies to support students in the process of generating knowledge. For example, students engage in critical thinking to cultivate new knowledge and perspective. The skill development that leads to the meaning making equates to learning. Teachers are facilitators of this process. Learning practices are transferable to a variety of contexts by developing a core set of skills and competencies.

Now, let's consider the following questions.

- How are teachers supported in developing a common conceptual understanding of future readiness?
- How can teachers use their understanding of future readiness to create a consistent experience for students within a secondary school?

- What does future readiness mean in the context of the everyday English classroom?
- How do ideas related to future readiness influence curriculum and instruction?
- How will any of it resonate with adolescents, if at all?

Much like the idea of future readiness, these questions may seem a little abstract—for now. Of course, abstractions don't work in schools. Educators and students need concrete plans to engage with curriculum and instruction so they can focus on learning and so that learning can be measured to set goals for ongoing work. This book brings clarity to those questions and makes future-ready English classrooms attainable and exciting for educators and students. For now, the good news is that it's not all new and abstract when it comes to identifying *why* students attend school.

MAINTAINING CORE VALUES

In their work for the Center on Education Policy at George Washington University, Nancy Kober and Diane Stark Rentner (2020) note that throughout the 19th century, the common school movement encouraged creating public schools for multiple purposes. In the 1830s, Horace Mann, a Massachusetts legislator and secretary of that state's board of education, was an early advocate for the creation of public schools. He emphasized that a public investment in education would benefit the United States by transforming young people into literate, moral, and productive citizens, no different from what the 21st century system strives for. Schools would teach reading, writing, arithmetic, history, geography, grammar, and rhetoric, along with a concentration on moral instruction to instill civic virtues. Advocates idealized education as a way of preparing students for citizenship and work and as a means for people to achieve happiness and fulfillment (Kober & Rentner, 2020).

The systems in our 21st century schools share similar values and purpose as the original pursuit of public education. Literacy, character, and citizenship are part of the fabric of the school experience. Promoting cohesion across social classes and improving social outcomes (Kober & Rentner, 2020) remain, along with academic achievement in multiple disciplines. These goals have emerged in educational discourse as reference points for learner agency. *Agency*, according to the Organisation for Economic Co-operation and Development (2018), implies a sense of responsibility to participate in the world and, in doing so, influence people, events, and circumstances for the better. Though the language we employ to capture these values may continue to change, the ideas behind them are foundational to our work in the classroom.

Research confirms these established priorities. Meltem Odabaş and Carolina Aragão (2023) of Pew Research Center report that in a study of over a thousand school mission statements across the United States, statements "most commonly emphasize preparing students for their futures after graduation. . . . 80 percent of all mission statements mention this issue, which might include goals such as college and job readiness, developing lifelong learners and creating productive citizens." As mentioned, citizenship has been and continues to be a core value of the education system. Educators honor that value through curriculum dedicated toward civic readiness, explorations in various perspectives on societal issues within several disciplines, and social-emotional learning programs that target the development of skills necessary to positively contribute to one's communities.

College and job readiness and lifelong learning, the other components of future readiness within mission statements (Odabaş & Aragão, 2023), continue to evolve from the original goals of public education in the 19th century and, for 21st century educators, even year to year. Future readiness has the potential to be abstract or blurry, but there is well-documented research that details the skills necessary for young people to participate in the job market and in local and global communities (World Economic Forum, 2023a, 2023b). The concept of future readiness challenges educators to be nimble and willing to accept change as a constant in their work of preparing young people for what the world demands of them beyond high school.

COMMITTING TO CHANGE

Although there seems to be no official record of it, former U.S. secretary of education Richard Riley is often attributed as having said, "We are currently preparing students for jobs that don't yet exist . . . using technologies that haven't been invented . . . in order to solve problems we don't even know are problems yet" (McCain & Jukes, 2001, p. 80). The truth of these words is hard to deny. Since the turn of the century, studies related to this idea have tracked and documented how the exponential growth in technology has shaped the evolution of jobs and the economy. What follows are a few anecdotes from the research that capture patterns in the documentation.

- In a report from the World Economic Forum, writers Rachel Hallet and Rosamond Hutt (2016) assert that 65 percent of children entering primary school at the time of publication would ultimately end up working in job types that weren't in existence yet. They follow up by sharing jobs that did not exist ten years earlier, like an app developer, a social media manager, and a data analysis scientist.

- According to the 2023 *Future of Jobs Report*, 23 percent of jobs are expected to change by 2027, with sixty-nine million new jobs created and eighty-three million eliminated (World Economic Forum, 2023b). Artificial intelligence and machine learning specialists, data analysts and scientists, and big data specialists are occupations expected to drive job growth.

The preceding items make it plain that as we study evolution within the job market, jobs become obsolete because of new technologies, and new jobs emerge in response to innovations that have changed the course of how people live and operate. Even long-standing professions that remain necessary—educators, health care practitioners, law officials, equipment operators, trade workers (World Economic Forum, 2023a)—have new learning on the horizon. According to the World Economic Forum's (2023b) *Future of Jobs Report*, 44 percent of workers' core skills are expected to change in the next five years, and more immediately, 50 percent of all employees will need reskilling by 2025 as adoption of technology increases. These statistics are situated within the time of this book's publication but represent an ongoing pattern as to how desirable skill sets change.

Skills targeted toward future readiness are transferable to the changing landscape and become the very literacies people need to be productive in professional and social spaces. There is an acknowledgment within the professional world that content knowledge traditionally taught in secondary schools is no longer enough to be prepared. The World Economic Forum (2016) directly addresses this notion:

> Technological trends such as the Fourth Industrial Revolution will create many new cross-functional roles for which employees will need technical and social and analytical skills. Most existing education systems at all levels provide highly siloed training and continue a number of 20th century practices that are hindering progress on today's talent and labour market issues. Two such legacy issues burdening formal education systems worldwide are the dichotomy between Humanities and Sciences and applied and pure training, on the one hand, and the prestige premium attached to tertiary-certified forms of education—rather than the actual content of learning—on the other hand. Put bluntly, there is simply no good reason to indefinitely maintain either of these in today's world. (p. 32)

The *how* and the *why* of learning have emerged as more significant than the *what*. This presents us with ample opportunities as we look to reframe English course content with an eye toward relevance and engagement.

There is great value to much of what we teach in the secondary English classroom. We use shared literature to explore perspective, ponder themes that help make sense of life circumstances, and learn about the creative process. We teach students to think in the context of the human experience and share their ideas through, most often, discussion and writing. We don't have to eliminate traditional course content, but we do have to think differently about it. We should consider broadening the scope of the literacies that frame coursework and evaluate students' opportunities to develop independence and readiness for postsecondary experiences. Designing a curriculum focused on traditional English course content or shared canonical texts fixed within a scope and sequence may run the risk of learning becoming irrelevant to students in their postsecondary school experience.

Moving forward, we must consider questions related to the secondary English classroom.

- Is there a balance of classic and contemporary texts within curricular plans so that students gain diverse perspectives through literature?
- Where are opportunities for choice topics in reading, writing, and creating so that literacy competency development is the crux of the learning?
- Is the curriculum reflective of current issues and literacies within our society?

And we must consider broader questions that span disciplines.

- What can students not find the answer to by asking Siri, Google, or Alexa?
- What analysis or critical thinking point has artificial intelligence (AI) not mastered?
- In what areas will a student's thinking and writing be more compelling than any artificial intelligence bot?
- Is the student at the center of the learning, or is the curriculum?

Anchored by our core values, we can dig into these questions and move forward in our work, knowing that embracing change and prioritizing skills over content will make all the difference in preparing our students for their futures.

Goals for Reading This Book

Educators will come to this book with their own experiences and ideas about the secondary English classroom, about engaging students in literacy practices, and about the relationship between academic spaces and social and professional communities. I celebrate the diversity in perspectives!

I think English teachers and leaders are aware that life planning for students is different from what they themselves experienced in middle school and when getting ready to graduate from high school. While educators are aware of the differences, responding to students' changing life landscape may be unclear. Let's consider these practical questions.

- How can awareness of students' changing needs lead to a reframing of what is necessary to teach in schools?
- How can this awareness support teacher readiness to engage in practices different from past secondary English classroom experiences?
- What is the purpose of what we teach in the English classroom in the 21st century?
- What is the purpose of how we teach in the English classroom in the 21st century?

Throughout the book, I provide steps to a process that English educators can follow to engage in this work in their own classrooms and as teams to articulate curriculum and instruction across secondary grade levels. Consider each chapter as an element of a how-to process for designing learning experiences that prioritize future readiness in literacy development. The six following themes transcend chapters and ultimately emerge as steps to take.

1. **Acknowledge change:** I will address change through the revolving literacy framework. The premise of *revolving literacy* is built on the Greek philosopher Heraclitus's notion that the only constant in life is change. Change is hard for people, but change doesn't have to mean that something in education is necessarily *wrong*. Students experience the world as it is and will enter a world after high school that has many shades of gray. We don't know of all the jobs and pathways that will be necessary or available. We don't know what new advancements in technology will bring. What would be *wrong* is not to acknowledge that what it means to be literate is constantly evolving. Local and global communities demand ever-shifting skill sets of people in order to be productive and positive contributors to society.

2. **Reflect on personal understandings of what it means to be literate:** The meaning of literacy constantly evolves because it is a sociocultural practice. Literacies are born in response to the communities we participate in. Future-ready skills are part of literacy development for students and adults who are already established in the workplace and need to reskill. I explain the components of literacy development and considerations to keep in mind when designing learning experiences in secondary English classrooms. Alignment in understandings of literacy helps educators collaborate when reflecting on curriculum and instruction.

3. **Learn:** Learning new information is essential to being a literacy educator. The revolving literacy framework depends on literacy educators' commitment to ongoing learning and professional development. I share research about the top-ranked future-ready skills for productivity in the workplace and what they mean, information about the fastest-growing occupations, and how to engage in a cycle of learning so that curriculum reflects future readiness research.

4. **Audit curriculum:** You will learn about a revolving literacy unit framework. The framework invites educators to consider all components of literacy development in curriculum design. Subsequent chapters invite you to reflect on the content of your current curriculum and how you can integrate revolving literacy work. You may consider redesigning scope and sequences or specific units of study based on your learning. You may also consider creating new units of study based on the chapter contents.

5. **Reflect on instructional practices:** You will discover a revolving literacy lesson plan. The lesson plan invites you to consider how components of literacy development are intentionally integrated into and made apparent to students in specific lesson plans. You may be able to draw parallels between your current instructional practices and those outlined for designing lessons. You may also choose to try something new because of your reading. The resources needed are available to you in this book.

6. **Establish protocols for ongoing reflection:** You have many opportunities to reflect on the contents of this book in relation to the work you are currently doing or want to do. Reflection is an essential component to revolving literacy work since expectations for literacy development and future readiness are constantly changing.

Develop a personal reflection protocol to continue beyond this book. Collaborate with colleagues to engage in ongoing reflection about curriculum and instructional practices relative to revolving literacy work.

With these larger goals in mind, let's take a look at what you can expect to find in each chapter that follows, along with repeating book features.

Chapter Overview and Book Features

As suggested in the preceding section, this book is written as a how-to guide for prioritizing future-ready skills as part of literacy development within the secondary English classroom. All chapters include information and practical steps for educators to use in their curriculum development and reflection process.

- **Chapter 1** provides an overview of the meaning of literacy with a visual model. The visual model is designed to aid educators in reflecting on their understanding of how multifaceted literacy development is. I emphasize top-ranked future-ready skills as part of literacy development. Chapter 1 also defines the revolving literacy framework, which is the framework situating the remaining chapters.

- **Chapter 2** provides a step-by-step process for establishing new visions and new priorities for curriculum planning using the revolving literacy framework. Practical tools and reflection protocols will aid you in preparing for curriculum work that makes the vision a reality.

- **Chapter 3** unpacks the revolving literacy lesson plan. I explain each part of the lesson plan and provide resources for practical application to your current work. Samples of completed revolving literacy lesson plans are featured at the end of chapter 4 (writing), chapter 5 (research), and chapter 6 (reading).

- **Chapter 4** takes a deep dive into the writing process, addressing authentic purposes for writing. I outline, define, and explain the stages of the writing process. I also provide strategies for navigating parts of the writing process, making explicit connections between the writing process and literacy development, and the writing process and future-ready skill development. At the end of the chapter, you will find a sample revolving literacy unit framework and lesson plan for a writing unit.

- **Chapter 5** explores the research process. The chapter begins with examples of how people engage in the research process in personal, professional, and academic spaces. Throughout the chapter, I outline, define, and explain the stages of the research process, making explicit connections between the research process and literacy development, and the research process and future-ready skill development. At the end of the chapter, you will find a sample revolving literacy unit framework and lesson plan for a research unit.
- **Chapter 6** introduces three structures of secondary reading processes: (1) independent reading, (2) book clubs, and (3) shared reading. Each structure is on a continuum of providing students with choice and agency in reading. Exposure to various reading structures in secondary English classrooms makes for a comprehensive experience for students. I provide resources for reading reflections and make explicit connections between the reading structures and literacy development, and reading structures and future-ready skill development. At the end of the chapter, you will find a sample revolving literacy unit framework and lesson plan for a reading unit.

As you navigate the book, please keep in mind that the chapters are cumulative. The information in this introduction and chapter 1 provide context for the classroom work. Chapter 2 provides practical steps and tools to get started. Chapter 3 explores instructional practices through lesson planning. Chapters 4, 5, and 6 incorporate all that is shared in the introduction and chapters 1 through 3 in the context of the English course pillars of writing, research, and reading.

Throughout the book, you'll find a wealth of resources to aid you in your work. Notably, each chapter includes several Stop and Think sections. Within these sections, reflection questions guide your own process of responding to the information and suggested practices in the book. If you are reading this book independently, consider it your own reading response journal space. If you are reading this book with a team, I invite you to write your own responses to the questions and make time to discuss them among your team members. If you are using this book for professional development, the questions may help identify areas of strength in your current practices as well as areas for further exploration and development in your planning.

You will find tools, including planning organizers, unit frames, lesson plans, reflection protocols, student thinking organizers, tools for collecting data, and questions for discussion throughout the book. I developed these tools based on work I have done in my own classroom and with teams of secondary teachers. I invite you to use them for your own revolving literacy work and to modify them to suit the needs of your classroom or school context.

The artifacts I share in this book are products of the revolving literacy work I have done with students and teacher teams. I share artifacts from revolving literacy classrooms to bring the work to life. I invite you to use them for reference in your own planning.

On a final note, I'd like to thank you for reading and for joining me on this journey—I'm so glad you're here.

Now, let's get started!

CHAPTER 1

NEWFOUND LITERACIES IN FUTURE-READY SKILLS

During one of the early courses in my doctoral program for literacy studies, my professor said to the class, "Congratulations! You've decided to pursue a doctorate in literacy studies. Now, what the heck does that even mean?" The class chuckled, and each person timidly looked around the room because I think most of us were asking ourselves the same question. My professor went on to say, "You're all laughing, but really think about it! If someone walks up to you in a bar and asks what literacy studies means, what would you say?" And this is how our scholarly conversations about the meaning of literacy started: a fictional drink in hand and a whole lot to think about.

The reason why the question seems so ambiguous is because literacy is not stagnant. As researcher Kathy A. Mills (2015) notes, the social, economic, political, and technological factors that arise in historical moments set the stage for ways of thinking about and addressing literacy. The work we do in schools is affected because education systems orbit these factors in our local and global communities. Literacy expectations evolve as communities develop, society changes, and advances in knowledge and technologies occur. While research (DeSilver, 2014; Strauss, 2017; World Economic Forum, 2016, 2020, 2023a) implies the unknown about the future of jobs and the workplace, it simultaneously illuminates something very clear that literacy educators need to respond to: Specific skills beyond the traditional understandings of literacy are necessary to navigate the opaque nature of jobs and career paths.

Students develop literacies in the classroom. Students blend life experiences and explicit instruction in areas of literacy development in school to make meaning of content and their own understandings of the world around them. In this chapter, we will explore the multifaceted meaning of literacy, which includes future-ready skills. We will also unpack the revolving literacy framework, a tool we will use to bring clarity to designing future-ready literacy experiences in the secondary English classroom throughout the book.

Defining Literacy

Literacy is often associated with traditional domains of language like reading, writing, listening, and speaking. However, according to Elizabeth Baker and colleagues (2010) and researcher Len Unsworth (2008), literacy also involves making meaning through multiple modalities, such as video viewing and creation, designing digital materials, and studying how aspects of media like sound, color, and images work together to create meaning for the consumer. Moreover, educators Wyn Kelley and Henry Jenkins (2013) explain that literacy is also about learning how to read, think, write, critique, and create together in a participatory environment. In their position statement about literacy in a digital age, the National Council of Teachers of English (NCTE, 2019) explain that literacy is a collection of communicative and cultural practices shared among communities. As society and technology change, so does literacy. NCTE (2022) expands on 21st century literacies in a later position statement: "Literacy is expanding, and English language arts educators at all levels must help learners develop the knowledge, skills, and competencies needed for life in an increasingly digital and mediated world." Aspects of students' lives outside of school like culture, technology, economy, and community influence their identities and dictate the literacy skills and competencies necessary to participate in brick-and-mortar and digital spaces. Secondary education should prepare students to participate in communities beyond the school walls. Since those spheres constantly evolve, literacy education must as well.

Literacy is not stagnant because it is a personal and sociocultural practice. The work of linguist James Paul Gee (2010) and language educator Brian Street (2016) confirms that literacies develop in response to social constructs and demands as well as the cultural practices of the communities to which one belongs. For example, discourse emerges in response to social groups (Gee, 1999, 2010), and technology impacts the ways in which we gather and share information and meaning (Mills, 2015). Identity, language, multiple modalities of meaning-making, and social practices within communities all contribute to how we engage in literacy. Evolving our understandings of what literacy is empowers us to build on current practices to develop a contemporary set of literacy skills connected to future readiness. When designing learning experiences, consider all five components of literacy development.

1. **Language:** Educators Heather Rubin, Lisa Estrada, and Andrea Honigsfeld (2022) write that literacy includes domains of language like reading, writing, listening, speaking, viewing, and visually representing. Reading, listening, and viewing are *receptive* skills. Writing, speaking, and visually representing are *expressive* skills.

2. **Future-ready skills:** While this component of literacy development will shift more rapidly than the others, being literate encompasses the ability to practice skills like analytical thinking, active learning, complex problem solving, critical thinking, creativity, leadership, problem solving, flexibility, and resilience. Each skill manifests differently within various career paths, but the core abilities need to be intentionally developed in schools. Students and teachers work together to generate knowledge and meaning-making through skill development (Schlam Salman & Inbar-Lourie, 2023). Learning is not transactional. In the next section, we will explore information that supports educators in cultivating their own readiness to design literacy experiences that include future-ready skill development.

3. **Identity:** Literacies are formed in response to social and cultural experiences (Clinton, Jenkins, & McWilliams, 2013; Gee, 2010; Heath, 1983; Jenkins, 2009; Kelley & Jenkins, 2013; Street, 1997, 2003, 2016; Taylor, 1997). We develop literacies as we develop our sense of self in response to our environment.

4. **Community:** As mentioned at the outset of this section, literacy is a critical set of social skills that encompasses learning how to read, think, write, critique, and create together in a participatory environment (Kelley & Jenkins, 2013). Accordingly, effective literacy instruction honors a range of communities that students may belong and contribute to: the classroom, the school, the district, teams, clubs, family, friendships, religious organizations, town centers or organizations, recreational groups, and so on. These communities are part of a student's identity, and they are central to the meaning-making and learning processes. Soft skills are essential when engaged in community participation.

5. **Multimodal meaning-making:** Literacy involves meaning-making through multiple modalities like signs and symbols (Baker et al., 2010), and music, sound effects, and digital navigation (Unsworth, 2008). Researchers Mary Kalantzis, Bill Cope, and Anne Cloonan (2010) explain that "in multiliteracies pedagogy all forms of representation, including language, are regarded as dynamic processes of transformation rather than processes of reproduction" (p. 70). They add, "Students don't simply use what they have been given; they are fully makers and remakers of signs and transformers of meaning" (Kalantzis et al, 2010, p. 70). Multimodal meaning-making in literacy development is born from multiliteracies pedagogy; there are several ways in which students communicate, create, and demonstrate understandings and ideas. Technology is a great support to the multimodal aspects of literacy. In addition, print skills are still an important component to literacy development and meaning-making (Jenkins, 2009). Engaging with texts that vary in format and medium gives us new perspectives and insights. Being literate means making choices and using texts and tools in ways that match purpose (NCTE, 2019).

Figure 1.1 offers a visual of the five components of literacy development.

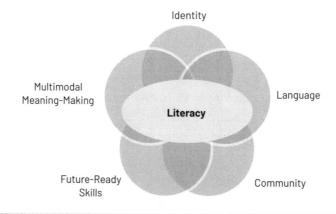

FIGURE 1.1: Components of literacy development.

When we give students opportunities to practice literacy skills and competencies in contexts that are of personal interest through choice in the classroom, literacy development becomes relevant to students. Since aspects of language domains, multimodal expression, identity, community spaces, and future-ready skills constantly evolve, literacy education must as well.

Write a response to a question of your choice.

- Which components of literacy development are highly cultivated within your current curriculum?
- Which components of literacy development have potential for growth within your current curriculum?
- Which components of literacy development did you not consider prior to reading this chapter? Has your thinking changed?

My reflection:

Visit *go.SolutionTree.com/literacy* for a free reproducible version of this reflection.

Digging Deeper Into Future-Ready Skills as Literacy

As I indicated in the book's introduction, literacy learning isn't about finding answers. Literacy learning is about discovering new ways to think, explore, collaborate, and generate meaning. This is shown in years of research conducted by the World Economic Forum about core skills for the workplace and reskilling to support the growth and development of education (DeSilver, 2014; Strauss, 2017; World Economic Forum, 2016, 2020, 2023a). The preface to the World Economic Forum's 2023 *Future of Jobs Report* states, "We hope that this report will contribute to an ambitious multistakeholder agenda to better prepare workers, businesses, governments, educators and civil society for the disruptions to come, and empower them to navigate these social, environmental and technological transitions" (Zahidi, 2023). Industry recognizes that there may be a disconnect between secondary school experiences and the skills needed for productivity in the workplace. It is useful for literacy educators to familiarize themselves with the research done in various companies to help frame learning experiences in the English classroom to bridge school and work life.

Literacy development encompasses highly ranked future-ready skills that are just as essential as development in the traditional domains of language. Table 1.1 (page 20)

TABLE 1.1: Core Skills for Workers in 2023 and Skills on the Rise for Workers From 2023 to 2027

Core Skills for Workers in 2023	Skills on the Rise From 2023 to 2027
1. Analytical thinking	1. Creative thinking
2. Critical thinking	2. Analytical thinking
3. Resilience and flexibility	3. Technological literacy
4. Motivation and self-awareness	4. Curiosity and lifelong learning
5. Curiosity and lifelong learning	5. Resilience and flexibility
6. Technological literacy	6. Systems thinking
7. Dependability and attention to detail	7. AI and big data
8. Empathy and active listening	8. Motivation and self-awareness
9. Leadership and social influence	9. Empathy and active listening
10. Quality control	10. Leadership and social influence

Source: World Economic Forum, 2023a, 2023b

compares core skills for workers in 2023 (World Economic Forum, 2023a) and skills on the rise for workers from 2023 to 2027 (World Economic Forum, 2023b). I share ten skills named in each report to be concise; there are additional future-ready skills listed in the sources that may be of interest when unit and lesson planning.

Critical thinking and problem solving top the list of skills that employers believe will grow in prominence, as these have been consistent since the first report in 2016 (World Economic Forum, 2020). These areas become the literacies in which students need to develop competency and versatility. The challenge is to consider how to give students opportunities to develop these skills in all content-area courses. We will explore this work in the context of English classes and how educators can measure success in these areas. We will think through this together throughout the book.

Consider the definitions of skills on the rise in the reproducible "Skills on the Rise for Workers From 2023 to 2027: What They Mean" (page 26) and work independently or with your team to define them within the context of your curriculum.

In the following section, I explain the importance of considering emotional intelligence when reflecting on future-ready skills. In later chapters, we will uncover the interconnection between job-ready skills and human relations and how we can create opportunities for students to develop their skill set in the English classroom.

THE INTERSECTION BETWEEN COGNITION AND HUMAN RELATIONS

If you are an English educator or work within the humanities, you probably just let out a sigh of relief. *Finally—some acknowledgment that human relations are important!* Trust me, I understand. The humanities remain in business.

The importance of skills related to emotional intelligence in the workplace is well supported in research.

Many of the skills highly regarded by growing occupations relate to cognition and management. These are often referred to as *hard skills*. The growing significance in "soft skills" as well is shown in an interview with *Rolling Stone* in 1994, where Steve Jobs, one of the great technological minds, said the following.

> Technology is nothing. What's important is that you have faith in people, that they're basically good and smart—and if you give them tools, they'll do wonderful things with them. Tools are just tools. They either work, or don't work. (Goodell, 2011)

As this quote indicates, Jobs believed in the intersection between human relations and technology.

Educators can also learn from Google. When Sergey Brin and Larry Page founded Google, they set out to hire employees with education in computer science from elite science universities. Project Oxygen and Project Aristotle were human resource research projects conducted within the Google organization to determine what makes an effective team. For example, psychological safety (comfortable emotional interactions and the ability for all voices to be heard and respected in a team meeting) emerged as most important in functional teams (Duhigg, 2016; Kolar, 2019).

Understanding Revolving Literacy

New literacies (New London Group, 1996; Street, 2003, 2016) is a concept that broadens the meaning of literacy from print-based work to include technologies and cultural practices. The sociocultural perspective of new literacies signifies that literacy changes as culture changes (Gee, 2010; Street, 2016). Literacy practices reflect the norms of society. New literacies suggest that conventional literacy education may not fully prepare students for modern working and social life (Gee, 2004; Lankshear & Knobel, 2007; Olthouse, 2013; Perry, 2012). Therefore, we must consider the multiliteracies and necessary future-ready skills that we know are needed in professional and social spaces when developing our English coursework.

The job market and social norms reflect society. Technology—social media, artificial intelligence, and increased data tracking—exemplifies how innovations in society impact jobs and transform the ways in which people identify with and communicate in social spaces. Identities and pathways beyond high school fluctuate depending on the needs and demands of society. These shifts in societal norms and demands call on literacy educators to respond to larger changes as we prepare students for postsecondary experiences. This is called *revolving literacy*.

I define the concept of *revolving literacy* as the relationship between what students experience outside of and beyond secondary education and the literacies they develop within the English classroom to prepare for those experiences. Students' learning experiences should be as though they are moving through a revolving door between school and outside of school. A student's experience should be fluid, with a clear relationship between school and out-of-school experiences. Students should be able to pass with ease in the circular motion that a revolving door offers. In contrast, hinge doors that typically push forward or pull back represent the limited transactional model of education. Hinge doors are binary. Revolving doors are perpetual.

Revolving literacy also encompasses the notion that literacy educators design curricula in response to the changing landscape of what it means to be literate, and that they do so to capture the fluidity of students' identities in response to society and professional demands. Like the meaning of literacy, curriculum is not fixed; it evolves. See figure 1.2 for a visual representation of this concept.

FIGURE 1.2: Revolving literacy as the relationship between school and students' lives outside of school.

Students thrive in their learning when what they do in school directly connects with what they need to be able to do outside of school. What we refer to as the *English* classroom should be regarded as a space where instruction in areas of *literacy studies* occur. The language educators use to talk about their work is important.

Reread the explanation of revolving literacy. What is the most important word in the explanation, and why?

Reread the explanation of revolving literacy. What is the most important phrase in the explanation, and why?

What about revolving literacy interests you?

*Visit **go.SolutionTree.com/literacy** for a free reproducible version of this reflection.*

Having laid out this concept we'll continue to build on, I'd like to take a moment to allay concerns you may have—and convey just how achievable it will be for educators to apply the framework, as it calls for consistency in a few broad areas of significance to English educators.

Since revolving literacy is a concept rooted in responsiveness to the identities of students and society, it may seem like there is a lack of coherence. If literacy instruction is always in a state of flux, then where is the continuity in what students learn? State standards and content instruction still remain. Revolving literacy calls for making room in curriculum and instruction for relevant skill development by incorporating student choice, articulating how future-ready skills are developed in English classes, and designing experiences that are diverse and relevant.

In schools, we appreciate consistency in expectations, practices, standards, and curriculum because so many people are working toward the same goal. Common language and reference points for the masses of educators who strive to row in the same direction when teaching young people are helpful. Revolving literacy requires consistency in the following areas.

- **A belief in and an embrace of the idea that English teachers are literacy educators:** As previously mentioned, not all curriculum and instructional practices need to change in response to revolving literacy. However, we may need to think about some of it differently. English teachers may make a commitment to consider the meanings of literacy and revolving literacy and use them as reference points to reflect on and audit curricular plans.

- **A commitment to learning:** The adults in a school community are the lead learners. Literacy educators need to remain as learners, just like the students in their classes. An open-mindedness to learn new information, opportunities, and advancements in local and global communities informs the learning experiences for students so new literacies fuel work in the classroom. Educators can work toward embracing the idea that the school experience will change over time in response to new learning.

- **Reflection and revision:** Constant and consistent reflection is needed among grade-level teams and curriculum teams. As literacy educators gain new knowledge, it is important to inventory practices and curriculum materials each year to ensure that they are relevant to current academic, economic, technological, and social spaces. It is also important to consider the various pathways that students may take throughout their lives outside of school so they can exercise contemporary literacy skills in different scenarios.

Summary

As we established in the introduction (page 1), students often learn in silos: silos of space like individual desks; silos of time like forty minutes per focus area; and silos of content like history, mathematics, and English language arts (ELA). The traditional content-driven curriculum may not be the best pathway for preparing students to participate in the often multifaceted and collaborative careers and communities during and after high school. Life after high school is rarely compartmentalized. College, career, and relationships require a myriad of academic and interpersonal competencies that work together like cogs in a wheel. Revolving literacy helps to capture the importance of relevance and engagement.

Revolving literacy acknowledges that literacy and learning are processes of evolution. Chapter 2 (page 29) provides tools and resources to help you think through this process.

What is your role in your school?

Consistency in revolving literacy	Where am I in my current thinking and practice?	Where is my team in its current thinking and practice?	Next steps
A belief in and an embrace of the idea that English teachers are literacy educators			
A commitment to learning			
Reflection and revision			

Visit *go.SolutionTree.com/literacy* for a free reproducible version of this reflection.

Skills on the Rise for Workers From 2023 to 2027: What They Mean

Consider the meaning of each future-ready skill and how it relates to your curriculum and coursework. Note that these will change over time.

Skill	Definition	What does this mean in the context of my curriculum and coursework?
Creative thinking	• The ability to formulate unique plans and solutions when presented with a task or problem • The ability to use one's unique perspective to offer ideas • The ability to generate new ideas when working within a team of various perspectives	
Analytical thinking	• The ability to categorize information based on observed patterns to interpret data, integrate new information, and make logical conclusions based on multiple factors • The ability to put effort into studying and understanding the way things work with the potential of developing new ideas or ways of accomplishing a task	
Technological literacy	• The ability to select digital tools to find and assess information for understanding and solving problems more effectively • The ability to create, understand, and improve a user's experience with technology; the ability to develop software, create applications, and design websites in user-friendly ways that meet the goals of the function	
Curiosity and lifelong learning	• The ability to pursue knowledge and skills throughout one's life • The ability to understand that education doesn't end with a degree or certificate, but continues as one grows and adapts to new challenges and demands in one's career	

Resilience and flexibility	• The ability to persevere through a challenging situation or task through careful planning and a willingness to accept failure as a means to keep trying • The ability to change the course of a project in response to new needs or circumstances • The ability to have strategies to manage challenging situations	
Systems thinking	• The ability to understand the relationships and connections between parts of a large project, problem, or organization • The ability to engage in analysis of parts for the greater good of the whole	
Artificial intelligence and big data	• The ability to use artificial intelligence with intention as a support to human cognition and not a replacement • The ability to use technology to understand the importance of data and how to turn data into insights and value	
Motivation and self-awareness	• The ability to initiate, guide, and continuously work toward a goal • The ability to understand how one's actions, thoughts, and behaviors align with expectations and influence others or work	

Skill	Definition	What does this mean in the context of my curriculum and coursework?
Empathy and active listening	• The ability to listen to understand another's perspective or feelings • The ability to listen—and not always with the intention to respond	
Leadership and social influence	• The ability to cultivate and deploy qualities like responsibility, dependability, and integrity to manage teams and projects in ways that result in what is best for the organization or cause • The ability to engage in the decision-making process through collaboration and goal setting • The ability to exert social influence by engaging with a following of others who trust in the influencer's abilities, interests, and perspectives • The ability to apply social influence to help organizations in decision making and managing online and physical spaces	

CHAPTER 2

TOOLS FOR DESIGNING NEW VISIONS AND NEW PRIORITIES

If literacy instruction is to consistently refresh itself (revolve) to pair with society and technology, then teachers must be agile when designing new practices and programs. According to researchers Frank Drzensky, Nikolai Egold, and Rolf van Dick (2012), as well as Alannah E. Rafferty, Nerina L. Jimmieson, and Achilles A. Armenakis (2013), successfully implementing new practices and programs requires individuals and organizational teams to possess sufficient readiness. Jonathan P. Scaccia and colleagues (2015) indicate that readiness includes the following traits.

- *Motivation* is a need or a desire that causes a person to act on something.
- *General capacity*, as psychology professor Abraham Wandersman and colleagues (2008) explain, includes factors that are helpful to any new initiative, such as leadership, professional relationships, and resources.
- *Innovation-specific capacity* includes factors that are helpful to the unique characteristics of the initiative, like knowledge of the subject matter, abilities, and related skills (Wandersman et al., 2008).

As we move into this chapter, I'd consider these items as well as your responses to the previous Stop and Think (page 25). Think about the three areas in which revolving literacy requires consistency: (1) a *belief* in and an *embrace* of the idea that English teachers are literacy educators, (2) the necessity of ongoing *learning* to keep English course content relevant to students, and (3) a commitment to *reflection* on and *revision* of curriculum and instruction. I hope that you reflect on your own motivation to do this work as you read on.

While the introduction (page 1) and chapter 1 (page 15) provided information to build knowledge of revolving literacy work, this chapter provides resources to guide initial discussion when making connections between the revolving literacy framework and your classroom or school context. Resources in this chapter are also useful for curricular planning.

In the pages that follow, we'll first look at the key components to planning when using the revolving literacy framework. In subsequent sections, I share steps for getting started with the work. These steps are designed to be carried out before you start lesson or curriculum planning. They help outline what you'll want to include when you start planning.

Readiness Reflection: Assess and evaluate your own readiness or the readiness of your team to engage in revolving literacy work. Use the evaluation to frame personal or team goals for planning and further reading in this book.

3 = I am ready! **2** = I am almost ready. **1** = I am not ready yet.

Readiness Factors	Myself	My Team
Motivation		
General capacity		
Innovation-specific capacity		
Notice the areas you rated a 3. How can those factors help your revolving literacy work and your experience reading the remaining chapters in this book?		
Notice the areas you rated a 2 or 1. Use the ratings to set goals for your own revolving literacy work. You may also set purposes for further reading in this book.		

Visit **go.SolutionTree.com/literacy** *for a free reproducible version of this reflection.*

Key Components to Planning When Using the Revolving Literacy Framework

The five elements of literacy development defined in chapter 1 (page 15) are the key components to consider when using the revolving literacy framework for lesson and curriculum design. These components are (1) language (English content as outlined by regional standards), (2) future-ready skills, (3) student identities, (4) community, and (5) multimodal meaning-making. Figure 2.1 indicates how to prioritize literacy components when developing learning experiences in the secondary English classroom.

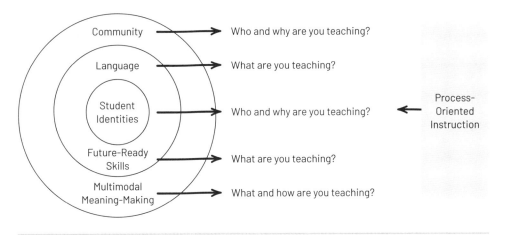

FIGURE 2.1: How to prioritize literacy components in the secondary English classroom.

As figure 2.1 shows, each component is accompanied by a straightforward question that impacts curriculum development.

- **Who and why** are you teaching? Root learning experiences in students' identities and the communities they belong to.
- **What** are you teaching? Prioritize developing future-ready skills as objectives for learning. Integrate ELA content into future-ready skill development.
- **How** are you teaching? Design experiences where students engage in an explicit process of learning over time.

The following explanations of each component will guide your thinking and discussions.

LANGUAGE

Language (English content outlined by regional standards) remains an important part of what students learn in the secondary English classroom. State and provincial standards vary. Content typically includes the development of skills related to reading, writing, listening, speaking, and creative thinking. Standards typically include reading and writing in various genres of text, studying their features, developing vocabulary, and practicing word study. I share a very broad description of English content because of the variation in what different states emphasize across the United States. I recommend knowing the English language arts standards of your region and including them in your revolving literacy planning. As I mentioned in the introduction (page 1), revolving literacy isn't about abandoning course content. Rather, revolving literacy invites literacy educators to consider shifting priorities in what we teach and how we teach it to align the English class experience with future readiness.

FUTURE-READY SKILLS

Future-ready skills are outlined by sources like the World Economic Forum's *Future of Jobs Report*, United States Census Bureau, and scholarship on new literacies (Gee, 2004; Lankshear & Knobel, 2007; Olthouse, 2013; Perry, 2012). Educators can also look to studies by professional organizations like Google's Project Oxygen and Project Aristotle to learn about emerging skills sets as outlined in chapter 1 (page 15).

STUDENT IDENTITIES

Student identities are at the core of literacy. The literacy practices that students come to school with are filtered through identity. Ultimately, identity is what drives students to make choices in relationships, learning, goals, and future planning. Being responsive to and inclusive of students' identities when designing literacy experiences helps to make learning relevant for students. In a groundbreaking essay on multicultural children's literature, educator and researcher Rudine Sims Bishop (1990) shares a metaphor to engage teachers and students in reflection on their reading experiences: Books are mirrors and windows. We can see our own lives and experiences mirrored in the larger human experience when reading becomes an act of self-affirmation (Bishop, 1990). Books are also windows that allow readers to become a part of the world the author has created. Through the window experience, readers learn to consider multiple perspectives and to engage in reflections rooted in empathy as they consider the feelings and actions of characters within literature.

Literacy instruction should provide students with reading experiences that are both mirrors and windows (Bishop, 1990). In addition to carefully selecting diverse texts for the whole group, providing choice in reading helps to accomplish this in the classroom. If literacy experiences are rooted in choice based on students' identities, the work is contextualized in ways that students can access. We will explore ways to manage choice in independent reading in chapter 6 (page 177).

COMMUNITY

Community contributes to identity but can be considered its own entity when designing curriculum. English educators may develop curricular experiences around students' communities. These can include academic communities in preparation for college, career communities where students learn trades, local communities that students want to participate in and give back to, and virtual communities like social media platforms and gaming groups. Literacy is participatory (Kelley & Jenkins, 2013); students need opportunities to engage in community spaces with the intention of learning to work with others. Leadership and social influence are among the top-ranked future-ready skills for career readiness (World Economic Forum, 2023a).

MULTIMODAL MEANING-MAKING

Multimodal meaning-making encourages students and teachers to work within several modalities for instruction and demonstrations of learning. New literacies (introduced in chapter 1, page 15) is a framework that incorporates media literacy skills with print skills. Students should explore various ways to create, design, and share meaning with intention.

PROCESS-ORIENTED INSTRUCTION

The revolving literacy framework for curriculum and instruction design transpires in the classroom within a process-oriented instructional model, as figure 2.1 (page 31) shows. Process-oriented instruction aims to teach strategies and content information in coherence. Students evolve in their thinking and demonstration of learning as they move through the learning process. As a result, they should be able to articulate why each part of the learning process is important to the overall outcome of the unit. This idea connects to the future-ready skill of systems thinking. It is important to make students aware of how and why systems are in place for learning and for projects. While the product of learning is significant, literacy educators may argue that the process of learning is more impactful.

A process for instruction exists at two levels: (1) a process for a singular lesson and (2) a process for how a unit of study unfolds. We will unpack a process-oriented approach to instruction in depth in chapter 3 (page 73). In summary, a reading, writing, creative thinking, and research process contains multiple spiraling phases of the work. Students need to learn multiple strategies during each phase of the work so they learn the process of learning. Lifelong learning is a top-ranked future-ready skill for career readiness (World Economic Forum, 2023a).

Once you and your team develop a shared understanding of the revolving literacy framework, you may start your planning! To do so, you will next find practical and actionable steps with accompanying resources to build both general and innovation-specific capacities in doing this work.

Step 1: Define the Language You Will Use for Your Curriculum Work

Think about the terms and ideas individuals and the team may need to clarify, define, and use in revolving literacy work. Are there shared understandings of terms like *identity*, *literacy*, *engagement*, *future readiness*, *relevance*, *text*, and *change*? Refer to chapter 1 (page 15) for explanations of key revolving literacy terms and future-ready skills.

You may use digital tools to gauge individuals' understandings of terms to determine which need clarification. Tools like Google Forms (www.forms.google.com), Google Docs (https://docs.google.com), AnswerGarden (https://answergarden.ch), and Menti (www.mentimeter.com) include polling features and online communication platforms for people to share their initial thoughts. Once determined, post your shared definitions in a space where all have access.

For example, when developing a curriculum with teachers using the revolving literacy framework, I worked with teams to create a set of shared understandings and agreements. Figure 2.2 depicts an agreement about *change*.

Agreements and Understandings
- Change doesn't mean anything is wrong
- End goal—what is it?
- Characteristics and "why" behind literature choices
- Shared experience across the grade level and where is the autonomy?
- Explore thematic frames for 9–12
- It's OK to say what you're thinking
- Treat every idea as a good one for at least fifteen seconds

---

FIGURE 2.2: Examples of agreements from a secondary English curriculum planning meeting.

This work led to identifying and defining the terms *change, texts, diverse,* and *identity* as follows.

- **Change** doesn't have to mean that something is wrong. Treat every idea as if it were a good one for fifteen seconds.
- **Texts** are tools for teaching students. We teach students, not texts.
- **Diversity** means giving students access to a variety of material in several areas: theme, topic, character, author, genre, language, format, publication date (classic and contemporary texts, historical and current news), and text structure.
- **Identity** includes the identities of the students and the identities of the curriculum decision makers. It is important to consider who is making curricular decisions for students so explicit and implicit biases are taken into account. Note that according to educators Donalyn Miller and Colby Sharp (2018), identity includes first languages, languages learned, race, ethnicity, national origin, religion, gender, culture, family structure, ability, interests, hobbies, and prior knowledge. Impactful community events like the COVID-19 pandemic and natural disasters also impact how one's identity forms.

Clear, shared language brings clarity to the process of revolving literacy curriculum work. It also assists with creating a vision and making it practical.

Stop and Think

Identify revolving literacy words and language that require definition.

Word	What I Think the Word Means	Team Definition

*Visit **go.SolutionTree.com/literacy** for a free reproducible version of this reflection.*

Step 2: Establish the Vision for Using the Revolving Literacy Framework

Whenever you begin a new project or decide to make a change in practice, it is important to establish the vision and the purpose of the work. Whether this is an independent or a team (grade-level, departmental) initiative, establishing the why for using the revolving literacy framework paves the way for shared understandings of the process and desired outcome of the work. It is especially important to have a shared vision within a team so you can plan toward the same goals. Thinking of the big picture from the start is helpful to district or school administrators because the vision should be shared among grade-level groups; the vision for literacy work in grade 11 should be similar to the vision in grade 9 and grade 7. Think of the system that students are part of and how to articulate literacy philosophy across the grades. It is also helpful for teachers to think of the big picture before unit or lesson planning because each portion of the curriculum should be tied to the vision. The vision guides the development of units and lessons.

There are several aspects of literacy development to include when designing a curricular vision for the secondary English classroom. The vision can vary using the revolving literacy framework. The revolving literacy framework outlines literacy aspects and is designed for educators to work within evolution and change. All classrooms and schools are different. Contexts are unique. Reflect on what your team values in teaching and learning and marry those values to the five elements of the revolving literacy framework: language, future-ready skills, identity, community, and multimodal meaning-making.

CREATE A VISION FOR REVOLVING LITERACY WORK

One-page planners are helpful when generating a vision for literacy work. They are similar to table place mats, which frame a space, situating the necessary items for dining. Each item has a purpose in facilitating the process of eating for the person sitting in that spot at the table: plates hold the food, cups hold the drink, forks pick up solid foods, knives cut or spread, spoons pick up liquid or soft food. We are going to create a place setting to facilitate discussions for establishing the vision for curriculum work where team members consider all components of literacy development. This helps teams with alignment. The place setting can also serve as a one-page outline for one unit of study. Starting on page 37, you will find questions you may use independently or with your team to discuss the vision for making revolving literacy relevant to your classroom or school context. You can also use these questions when designing individual units of study, as detailed in chapters 4 through 6 in the sample unit frameworks and lesson plans.

Figure 2.3 is a template for how a team might plan out a vision for a unit using the revolving literacy unit framework. It is similar to how one would set a dinner table: It contains all the components of literacy development to include in your work. There are several examples of completed revolving literacy unit frameworks in chapters 4, 5, and 6. Chapter 4 (page 87) contains a writing unit plan. Chapter 5 (page 127) contains a research unit plan. Chapter 6 (page 177) contains a reading unit plan.

Language	Future-Ready Skills	Identity
Community	Multimodal Meaning-Making	

FIGURE 2.3: A vision for a revolving literacy unit.

*Visit **go.SolutionTree.com/literacy** for a free reproducible version of this figure.*

The following section includes questions to guide you in developing instructional plans and goals for students. While all questions in each section are helpful for clarity, some are points of emphasis across a scope and sequence for the full school year. Note, too, that not all will come up in one unit of study. Having a vision includes short-term and long-term planning.

Students will develop language proficiency. Reflect on these questions.

- Reading
    + What are students reading during this unit?
    + Do students have choice in what they are reading?
    + How does what students are reading in this unit relate to what they have read in other units?
    + How does the reading work integrate future-ready skills? See chapter 1 (page 15) and chapter 6 (page 177).

- Writing
    + What are students writing during this unit?
    + Do students have choice in what they are writing?
    + Do students have sufficient time in all the stages of the writing process? See chapter 4 (page 87).
    + How does the writing work integrate future-ready skills? See chapters 1 and 4 (pages 15 and 87).
- Listening and Speaking
    + What opportunities are there for collaboration?
    + What opportunities are there for partner work?
    + How is peer feedback integrated into the unit?
    + Specific to listening, how will students demonstrate that they have taken actionable steps from listening to their teacher or peers?
    + Specific to speaking, how is accountable talk explicitly taught and practiced throughout the unit? How are students held accountable for using academic language associated with the content of the unit?
- Viewing
    + What are students watching during this unit?
    + What images and visual representations are students analyzing during this unit?
    + What are students learning about media consumption?
    + How is multimodality considered in receptive and expressive processes?
- Visually Representing
    + What opportunities do students have to demonstrate their understandings in multimodal ways?
    + How are students learning to read visual representations of information?
    + What are students learning about relationships between text-based and image-based reading?
    + When and where are students encouraged to use digital tools to create visual responses to literature and visual forms of information and analysis?

Learning experiences will be rooted in students' identities. See step 3 for ways to reflect on students' identities. Reflect on these questions.

- How are students' identities considered in the shared reading material?

- How are students' identities considered in creating opportunities for choice topics in writing?
- Where do students have opportunities to engage in personal reflection to make connections between their identities and course material?
- Do course materials give students opportunities to identify with those who are unfamiliar to them and explore empathy?

Develop connections to community engagement. Reflect on these questions.

- Are there opportunities for students to share their work within a community that they belong to?
- Does the work in the unit correspond to any form of community service?
- How does the work prepare students to participate in designated communities such as academic spaces (college), professional spaces (career), social spaces (relationships), and digital spaces (virtual communities)?
- Are there opportunities for students to share their work with one another to build classroom culture and community?

Provide choice multimodal avenues for meaning-making in receptive and expressive processes.

- What opportunities do students have to explore media to gather information?
- What opportunities do students have to write and create through a modality of their choice to demonstrate understanding of key concepts or in response to literature?
- How are print and digital texts paired to support students in meaning-making?
- What strategies are students learning to support navigating multimodal texts?

Prioritize future-ready skill development in curriculum and lesson design. Building future readiness is necessary content within the course.

- In what ways can the curriculum shift to make future-ready skills the objective within lesson design while exploring course content?
- Where might new lessons or units of study be needed to foster future-ready skill development?
- Where do students have opportunities to reflect on the future-ready skills they are learning before, during, and after a unit of study? Do students

have opportunities to reflect on how they can apply those skills to other areas of learning?

- How has assessment shifted to evaluate both students' growth and development in future-ready skills and their understanding of ELA content?

TURN YOUR VISION INTO A MISSION STATEMENT

With the vision in place, the next step is to develop a mission statement to capture the vision of your curriculum work and share it with stakeholders (administrators, teachers, students, and families). The mission statement serves as a tool to articulate the why of your curricular work. Mission statements can be shared among grade-level teams or whole departments. Figure 2.4 is a sample mission statement from revolving literacy planning.

We are committed to supporting all students as they develop as readers, writers, designers, creators, thinkers, and participants in academic, professional, and social spaces. While the definition of what it means to be literate consistently shifts in response to changes in societal norms and expectations, our core values remain:

- All students deserve a learning space where they are cared for and encouraged and feel safe.
- All students deserve to be part of a community that fosters kindness, leadership, collaboration, and growth.
- All students deserve opportunities to share their voices and perspectives through writing, design, and conversation while respecting those that are different from their own.
- All students deserve time to read, write, listen, speak, design, and create through various modalities in school.
- All students deserve to participate in literacy experiences that foster future-ready skill development to prepare them for the pathways beyond the school experience and the uncertainty of what the job market will entail when students enter it.
- All students deserve to read books of their choice and write about topics of their choice through guided and independent experiences.
- All students deserve access to high-interest, high-quality texts that serve as windows and mirrors (Rudine Sims Bishop, 1990) for their own lives and experiences to aid in self-discovery and developing empathy.
- All students deserve opportunities to write with intention for various purposes and to be coached through the writing process.
- All students deserve to develop print and digital competencies to participate in a variety of academic, professional, and social spaces.
- All students deserve access to a curriculum that is reflective of the world they live in, relevant to their interests and wonderings, and rooted in the New York State Next Generation English Language Arts standards.
- All students deserve literacy experiences that are equitable to maximize and actualize their potential.

Source: Long Beach Public Schols. Used with permission.

FIGURE 2.4: Sample literacy mission statement.

 Reread the sample mission statement and identify direct connections between the aspects of a revolving literacy vision and what the mission statement articulates.

Identify areas within the vision of revolving literacy that you would need to spend the most time discussing and thinking about in your initial discussions and planning.

Visit *go.SolutionTree.com/literacy* for a free reproducible version of this reflection.

Step 3: Create Student Profiles

Knowing your students is instrumental in revolving literacy work. What follows are ways to reflect on the identities of the students you teach so you can design curricular work relevant to students when preparing for social, academic, and professional pathways beyond high school.

QUESTION PROTOCOL

Generate questions to think about students' social, emotional, and academic attributes and habits in the classroom or school community. Here are examples of reflection questions for grade-level teams to consider when reflecting on who is in their classrooms.

- What do students think about?
- How do students make personal connections to their learning?
- What are our students' learning styles?
- What do students need to prepare for future grade-level work?
- What are the potential pathways for students in the future?
- What academic skills do students need to develop?
- What future-ready skills do students need the most support with?

- How do students learn to empathize with others?
- How do students learn to explore multiple perspectives?
- How do students communicate?

Evaluate your answers and then ask, "Are these ideas reflected in the current curriculum? In what areas does the curriculum address the student profile well? In what areas do we need to grow in making curriculum relevant to students?" Figure 2.5 is an example of a completed question protocol with a high school English ninth-grade-level team. See the reproducible "Student Identity Question Protocol" (page 64) for a template to use for your planning.

FIGURE 2.5: Completed question protocol with a grade 9 teacher team.

IDENTITY AUDIT

Consider the aspects of identity outlined in chapter 1 (page 15). People are a sum of their parts. What do students come to school with that influences their perspectives, the ways they approach their work, and the decisions they make? While fostering future-ready skills in school helps to prepare secondary students for pathways beyond high school, middle and high school are also places where students engage in self-reflection and self-discovery. Think about a student you know who entered middle school in grade 6 and how they changed by the time they entered grade 8. Or, think about a student who entered high school in grade 9 and how they transformed by the time they were getting ready to walk at graduation. Literacy experiences in the classroom can contribute to how students develop their identity and respond to it. Elements of an identity-safe classroom, such as respect for students' communities, cultures, and social knowledge, promote student achievement and attachments to school (Steele & Cohn-Vargas, 2013).

Reflect on aspects of students' identities within your class or school community to create a direction for your curriculum planning. For example, after looking across identity patterns of students in grade 7, my team noticed that friendships are an important part of how students develop their identities. Many students make new friends in middle school and part ways with friends from elementary school. Thus, my grade 7 team added a social issue book club unit of study with a focus on texts that featured navigating friendship relationships. You can follow up by asking students to share their identities with you (see the next section). Consider also reflecting on the identities of the decision makers (teachers, administrators) about curriculum. You can illuminate any implicit or explicit bias. You can also assess and evaluate how aware the adults are of the students' identities. Figure 2.6 is a chart to guide this work. See the reproducible "Identity Audit" (page 65) for a template to use for your planning.

Identity Components	Who are your students? Reflect on students' various identities. You may refer to your school report card for demographic information and what students share with you in their own reflections.
First Languages and Languages Learned	
Race	
Ethnicity	
National Origin	

FIGURE 2.6: Reflection space for an identity audit.

continued ▶

Identity Components	Who are your students? Reflect on students' various identities. You may refer to your school report card for demographic information and what students share with you in their own reflections.
Gender	
Culture and Communities	
Family Structure	
Ability and Disability	
Interests and Hobbies	
Prior Knowledge—What Does the Student Know a Lot About?	
Impactful Community Events	

Visit **go.SolutionTree.com/literacy** for a free reproducible version of this figure.

ME MAPS

Ask students to create a *Me Map*, which is an illustration of aspects of their identities. Invite them to revisit their Me Maps throughout the school year to reflect on how their identities shift as they grow. Also, engage students in discussion about the parts of who they are that don't change and the parts that do. Healthy discussions about change can help students as they mature.

Responses from students will vary. Some are comfortable sharing aspects of who they are, and some are less comfortable. My advice is to encourage students to share what they are comfortable with, what they are proud of, and what they want you as the teacher to know. You may also show students a variety of sample Me Maps. Ensure that students know that they can be selective in the topics they list. Some may feature a lot of hobbies and interests. Some may feature a lot of goals. Some may feature a lot of family traditions. Just like people are different, Me Maps can differ among the class.

Me Maps can serve as a tool for curriculum planning, as the following list indicates.

- Inventory what students share within their Me Map. Notice commonalities and differences between identities within one class and across classes. Consider the information when selecting course material. This is some of the most important data collecting you will do all school year.
- Encourage students to use these Me Maps as a tool to generate ideas for writing, research, and reading (see chapters 4, 5, and 6).
- Use Me Maps as a tool for establishing peer partnerships within the classroom. Students can engage in conversations about who they are, what is important to them, and personal goals. The relationship building will support the academic work they will do together. You may consider partnering students who share commonalities if you would like them to connect through a topic of study. You may also consider grouping students according to their differences so they can offer various perspectives. Me Maps may be helpful when reading a shared text or when students engage in book club discussions.
- Create a Me Map for yourself. Use it as a demonstration text to share with students as you model your own thinking process. Sharing parts of your identity with students aids in developing a classroom community.

Figure 2.7 is a way for students to think about various aspects of their identities and lists options of what they may choose to share. Invite students to choose the way they design their Me Maps—a web, with sticky notes, in a chart, a picture collage, and so on. Students may use print or digital tools. See figure 2.8 (page 46) for an example of a completed Me Map.

Who I Am	Where I Am From	Things I Do	Ways I Celebrate	My Goals and Aspirations
• Personality traits • Culture • Race • Ethnicity • Religion • Family structure • Likes and dislikes • Languages • Gender • Passions • Interests	• Neighborhood • Country • National origin • Landmarks in your area • Community • Region or town • Meaningful places near where you live • Community organizations	• Hobbies • Clubs • After-school activities • Job • Sports and fitness • TV and movies • Social media • Games • Books • Relationships	• Holidays • Traditions • Family celebrations • Foods • Song and dance • Accomplishments • Gatherings	• Job • Career • Short-term goals • Long-term goals • Dreams • Relationships • Personal goals

FIGURE 2.7: An outline for Me Map options.

Who I Am	Where I Am From	Things I Do	Ways I Celebrate	My Goals and Aspirations
• Introvert • American, Italian, and Colombian • Son to my mom and dad, brother to my two sisters, cousin to nine cousins • Speak English and Spanish • Football player • Fisherman • Camp counselor • Gamer	• Born in the United States • Live in Louisiana • Live in parish • Home of jazz music	• Play football (in school and home league) • Play video games • Hang out with friends • Volunteer at a youth sports camp • Chess club and Athletes Helping Athletes club • Camp counselor • Read on a Kindle	• Family tradition—annual fishing trip • Birthday celebrations—special cake • Football award—rookie of the year • Christmas Eve—eat fish • When I was little, my cousins and I used to bang pots and pans on New Year's Eve	• Be a star athlete on my football teams • Go to college—study engineering • Complete my school assignments on time • Keep my friendships after high school, make new friends in college • Be a good role model for my sisters

FIGURE 2.8: An example of a Me Map.

A reproducible "Me Map" is on page 66. See figure 2.9 for an example of a Me Map using sticky notes.

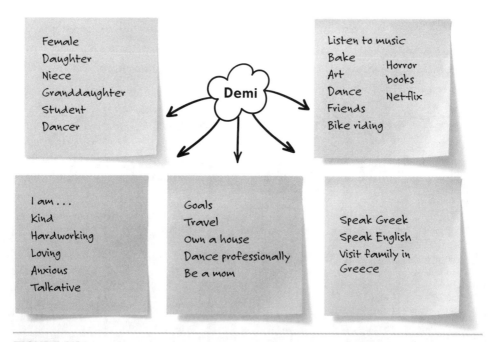

FIGURE 2.9: An example of a Me Map web using sticky notes.

Step 4: Establish *How* to Facilitate Learning

The revolving literacy framework considers not only what students learn but also how they learn. In chapter 3 (page 73), we dive into process-oriented instruction, which is part of planning for student learning within the revolving literacy framework. There is a wealth of research about how people learn best and the value of active learning strategies (Barron, 2006; Darling-Hammond, Flook, Cook-Harvey, Barron, & Osher, 2020; Hattie, 2009, 2012; Hattie & Gan, 2011; Wolpert-Gawron, 2017). In the following sections, we explore the high-leverage aspects pictured in figure 2.10 for teachers to specifically consider when establishing new visions and priorities in revolving literacy instruction.

Systematic and Explicit Instruction	Choice
Agency and Application	Ongoing Assessment, Evaluation, Feedback, and Reflection

FIGURE 2.10: Facilitating learning within the revolving literacy framework.

SYSTEMATIC AND EXPLICIT INSTRUCTION

It's important to articulate literacy instruction across a preK–12 continuum so goals and outcomes for learning align with where students are in their academic, social, and emotional development. Like many states' departments of education, the New York State Education Department (2024) issues a series of Science of Reading literacy briefs. Two of the principles of literacy instruction these briefs outline are (1) literacy instruction is *systemic and cumulative* and (2) literacy instruction is *explicit and direct*.

Systemic and cumulative means that teachers break the reading process into skills they introduce systematically and in a logical sequence (as in a scope and sequence or curriculum map). *Explicit and direct* means that instruction is clear, with teachers providing varied examples of what they're teaching. The way reading should be taught can serve as a model for incorporating future-ready skills into literacy instruction. For example, the ways in which students engage in analytical thinking and creative thinking are different in grades 7 and 10 (World Economic Forum, 2023a).

Finally, explicit modeling of and coaching in future-ready skills are necessary, much like how the reading process is taught. Students need experiences that bring future-ready skills to life—otherwise, the skills remain abstract, much like they may seem to educators (see the introduction). Educators should aim to provide well-scaffolded instruction and ongoing formative assessment that supports conceptual understanding, takes into account students' prior knowledge and experiences, and offers the right amount of challenge and support on relevant and engaging learning tasks (Darling-Hammond et al., 2020).

CHOICE

Providing students choice in what they learn and how they learn puts the student directly at the center of the learning experience. Student choice builds ownership in the learning, allows students to display their learning in ways they feel best represent their understandings, and enables true differentiation and personalization in learning (Wolpert-Gawron, 2017). Research shows that choice increases both engagement and motivation for tween (ten- to thirteen-year-old) and teenage (thirteen- to eighteen-year-old) students. Education researcher Robert J. Marzano shares, "When given choice by teachers, students perceive classroom activities as more important. Choice in the classroom has also been linked to increases in student effort, task performance, and subsequent learning" (cited in Wolpert-Gawron, 2018).

Literacy work is process oriented, where skills are the focus of instruction. Reading, writing, listening, speaking, viewing, and visually representing (Rubin et al., 2022) are not defined by specific content. Students can practice strategies to develop their language domains through various genres, content, and areas of interest. Interest-driven learning is particularly important for development because it requires self-regulating, defining and pursuing goals, and reflecting on how one is doing (Barron, 2006).

Choice is a natural root of literacy work, which allows future-ready skills to become areas of focus within the curriculum. In fact, skills like reasoning, flexibility, and using multiple learning strategies are among the most highly ranked future-ready skills (World Economic Forum, 2023a). Making choices within the secondary English classroom can foster developing future-ready skills. For example, author Alfie Kohn (2010) asserts that if we want students to take responsibility for their own behavior, we must first give them responsibility, and plenty of it: "Kids learn to make good decisions by making decisions, not by following directions" (p. 19). This is true in the classroom and in life beyond the school experience.

In chapters 4 and 5 (pages 87 and 127), we will explore ways to plan curricula that prioritize student choice.

AGENCY AND APPLICATION

In *How People Learn II: Learners, Contexts, and Cultures*, the National Academies of Sciences, Engineering, and Medicine (2018) includes fundamental principles of learning that are important for teaching. One principle is that students need to organize and use knowledge conceptually so they can facilitate its application. Teachers should structure material in a way that helps students fit it into a conceptual map that encourages application and transfer to new situations. This captures why the revolving literacy framework is important: Students need to learn skills that they can transfer to situations and tasks beyond high school. Students' abilities to transfer the skills are a measure of the depth of their learning. Consider the options students have to pursue: college, career, entrepreneurship, and community outreach. Secondary school is a time for students to develop literacies that can help them navigate pathways. Prioritizing future-ready skills in literacy instruction supports this notion.

ONGOING ASSESSMENT AND EVALUATION, FEEDBACK, AND REFLECTION

Teachers are partners to students in the learning process under the revolving literacy framework. The third principle of learning in the New York State Education Department (2024) Science of Reading literacy briefs is that literacy instruction is responsive and authentic to students' needs. Teachers have a responsibility to personalize learning pathways so students receive feedback for individual growth in aspects of revolving literacy work. Think back to our exploration of future-ready classrooms in the introduction. Teachers and students construct knowledge together. It is insufficient for teachers to give feedback about whether answers are right or wrong; instead, to facilitate learning, it is important to explicitly link feedback to goals and standards, and to provide students with strategies for improvement (Hattie & Gan, 2011).

Literacy work is rarely about being right or wrong; it is about inquiry, exploration, justification, reasoning for claims, meaning making, and connections. Teachers provide structures for students to approach this work through assessment and evaluation tools like rubrics, progressions, checklists, and conferences. Immediate opportunities to apply feedback are also important to the process. Research finds that this approach to feedback helps student develop their understanding of content and improve skills and learning strategies, as well as recognize personal relevance and meaningfulness in the work itself (Ames, 1992; Hattie & Gann, 2011).

Regular revision helps students develop a sense of confidence and competence as they see improvements in their work and a growth mindset that they can carry into other contexts (Darling-Hammond et al., 2020). This supports agency and application, as discussed in the previous section.

Finally, reflection is an essential component of students making sense of their learning and anticipating further applications of the skills they acquire. Revolving literacy prioritizes the development of future-ready skills. Reflection opportunities should focus on students' awareness and processing of the future-ready skills. Students can engage in self-assessment prior to a unit of study, trace their skill development throughout a unit of study, and self-assess and reflect at the end of a unit with a focus on transfer and application of learning. We will look at examples in chapters 4 through 6.

Step 5: Refocus *What* Is Taught

As I shared earlier, the revolving literacy framework does not suggest abandoning the traditional English course content, but it does emphasize that we may need to look differently at how we design our coursework. The emphasis in unit and daily objectives may shift. Remember: We teach students, not texts. The following sections offer strategies for refocusing instructional practices and curriculum design so literacy educators prioritize the *how* and *why* of learning while making decisions about *what* to teach.

RECONSIDER THE EMPHASIS ON SHARED CANONICAL TEXTS

Teaching strategies vary in designing English course curricula. For example, curriculum documents may feature a list of books organized by origin or time period across grade levels: Grade 9 reads classic American literature, grade 10 reads British literature, and grade 11 reads world literature. Another example is organizing books by theme across grade levels: Grades 7, 9, and 11 focus on identity, and grades 8, 10, and 12 focus on conflict resolution and decision making. Traditionally, most English coursework is designed around reading and writing about shared texts within these themes.

A *shared text* is a text that a class or group of people read together; all participants have a copy of the text in their hands so they can read along while listening to the text being read aloud. Shared texts in secondary English classrooms are primarily books that make up the literary canon. The literary canon consists of texts that have traditionally set a standard for high stylistic quality. The structure of the texts and stylistic choices that the authors made allow readers to engage in deep analysis, perspective development, and an opportunity to experience the time period the texts were written in. The texts reflect the controversies of their time periods and have had a long-term influence on society. Canonical texts are usually "household names," books that generations of people have read: *Romeo and Juliet* (Shakespeare, 1597), *The Great Gatsby* (Fitzgerald, 1925), *Of Mice and Men* (Steinbeck, 1937), *Animal Farm* (Orwell, 1945), and *Lord of the Flies* (Golding, 1954), to name just a few.

The revolving literacy framework includes integrating canonical texts into secondary English coursework but suggests that educators consider structuring literacy learning experiences that shift the emphasis on the canon. Here are six revolving literacy curriculum shifts.

1. Balance classic and contemporary texts as shared texts, book club texts, independent reading selections, and mentor texts for writing pieces.

2. Reduce the number of shared texts within the curriculum to make space for other literacy experiences within the secondary English classroom, like full writing process cycles (see chapter 4, page 87), research process experiences (see chapter 5, page 127), and independent reading and book clubs (see chapter 6, page 177).

3. Prioritize student choice by making time and space for independent reading (see chapter 6).

4. Prioritize student choice by including book club units of study within the curriculum (see chapter 6).

5. Plan to engage students in the full writing process at least four times during the year (see chapter 4). Students should write in a variety of genres, as outlined by regional standards. Consider how students engage in writing: Are they writing to complete a task or writing to discover ideas that are meaningful to them (Gallagher, 2022)? We will explore intentions for writing further in chapter 4.

6. Articulate a research progression across secondary grade levels so students are immersed in nonfiction texts and a process of uncovering information to support a claim that is meaningful to them (see chapter 5). Research should connect students with something they care about. Action research also provides opportunities for students to practice and reflect on future-ready skill development.

You may be thinking about one or more of the following questions.

- What about all the classic literature students should read before going to college?
- What about all the authors students should know about before leaving high school?

- Why not prioritize the canonical stories that capture the human experience that all readers can relate to? It doesn't matter when they were written.
- What about Shakespeare? All students need to read Shakespeare.
- What about the texts that I've built my curriculum on for years? The students like them.
- How am I supposed to teach when students are reading texts that I have never read or am not familiar with?
- How am I supposed to design instruction when all students are reading something different?
- How do I manage book clubs and independent reading? What if students don't actually read?
- How am I supposed to grade work that isn't written in response to a text that everyone has read?
- Isn't research already covered in science and social studies classes?
- What about the standardized tests I have to prepare students for? Scores matter.

I get it. I've been there. Take a minute to reflect on where you are in your thinking and what the student work in your classroom currently includes.

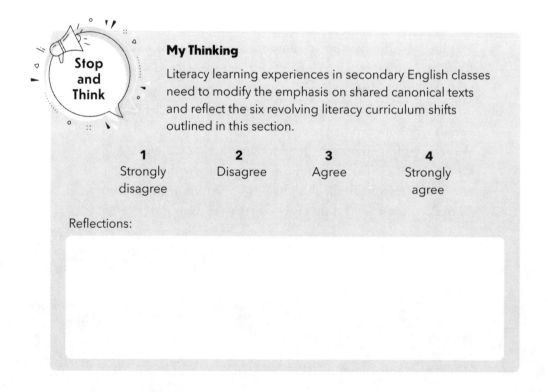

Stop and Think

My Thinking

Literacy learning experiences in secondary English classes need to modify the emphasis on shared canonical texts and reflect the six revolving literacy curriculum shifts outlined in this section.

1	2	3	4
Strongly disagree	Disagree	Agree	Strongly agree

Reflections:

My Classroom Coursework

The literacy learning experiences in my classroom or curriculum reflect the six revolving literacy curriculum shifts outlined above.

1	2	3	4
Strongly disagree	Disagree	Agree	Strongly agree

Reflections:

*Visit **go.SolutionTree.com/literacy** for a free reproducible version of this reflection.*

SHIFT FROM A SHARED TEXT-DRIVEN MODEL TO A STUDENT LITERACY-DRIVEN MODEL FOR PLANNING

Revising instructional approaches and how we structure literacy learning experiences for adolescents is not easy. I hope the chapters of this book share a compelling case for why the school experience should transform to be relevant to the world students are currently in. Figure 2.11 illustrates the shift when making choices about *what* to teach when planning with the revolving literacy framework.

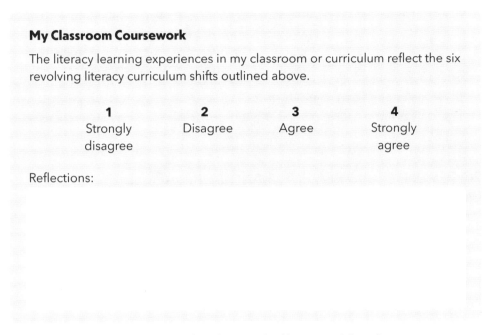

FIGURE 2.11: A shared text-driven curriculum model versus a student literacy-driven model.

Texts are tools for teaching a myriad of literacy skills and competencies that students should be able to apply to other academic work and personal areas of interest.

If we consider texts as tools for *how* we teach and not *what* we teach in the English classroom, then we open up pathways for a diversity in text selection to match the interests and identities of the students in the room. Students can also have choice in what they read and write about when curriculum isn't designed around shared texts. When future-ready and language skills become what teachers provide systematic and explicit instruction on, the texts that they use become secondary in decision making.

FOCUS ON FUTURE-READINESS AND LANGUAGE SKILLS DEVELOPMENT, WITH A TEXT ON THE SIDE

When determining what to teach, consider layering literacy work within the curriculum using standards, domains of language, and future-ready skills as the basis for teaching and learning. Once you determine those work areas, you then can plan the specific structures that support the literacy work. Consider the following questions as you plan.

- Will students develop the skills best in a book club or research club?
- Will students develop the skills best through a shared reading structure?
- Will students develop the skills best by reading text independently?
- Is a collaborative or independent experience best for this particular unit?

You can also plan for the specific products that match the learning outcomes. Consider these questions.

- Will students demonstrate learning best through a formal writing process and text?
- Will students demonstrate learning best through a multimedia creation?
- Are short, personal journal responses the best way for students to track their thinking and learning?
- Does a community outreach project support the learning outcomes?

These are all ideas to consider when you have a clear picture as to what standards, domains of language, and future-ready skills the unit emphasizes.

Figure 2.12 shows how to use the standards and domains of language—reading, writing, listening, speaking, viewing, and visually representing (Rubin et al., 2022)—as a base for the future-ready skills when planning.

FIGURE 2.12: Layering standards, domains of language, and future-ready skills when planning.

Regarding standards, refer to your state or regional standards for English language arts (see table 2.1 as a sample). Identify the skills, genres, and types of texts outlined for the domains of language. You may also note points of emphasis on curriculum and areas where there is room for growth to ensure you're addressing all standards within a particular grade or grade band.

The domains of language are part of English language arts standards and are foundational to how students acquire and practice future-ready skills. Multimodal meaning-making is included in the receptive (reading, listening, viewing) and expressive (writing, speaking, visually representing) forms of language development. Intentional instruction in modes of expression and integrating mixed media allow for a robust literacy experience for students.

Table 2.1 shows examples from the New York State Education Department (2017) Next Generation English Language Arts Anchor Standards. Notice the domains of language articulated throughout each language category (Reading, Writing, Speaking and Listening, and Language). Anchor standards refer to what should be taught in all grades, preK–12, with complexity and substandards varying by grade level.

TABLE 2.1: Examples of New York State English Language Arts Standards Organized by Language Domain

Reading	Writing	Speaking and Listening	Language
Read closely to determine what the text says both explicitly and implicitly and make logical inferences from it; cite specific textual evidence when writing or speaking to support conclusions drawn from the text.	Write arguments to support claims in an analysis of substantive topics or texts, using valid reasoning and relevant and sufficient evidence.	Prepare for and participate effectively in a range of conversations and collaborations with diverse partners; express ideas clearly and persuasively, and build on those of others.	Demonstrate command of the conventions of academic English grammar usage when writing or speaking.

continued ▶

Reading	Writing	Speaking and Listening	Language
Determine central ideas or themes of a text and analyze their development; summarize the key supporting details and ideas.	Write informative and explanatory texts to examine and convey complex ideas and information clearly and accurately through the effective selection, organization, and analysis of content.	Integrate and evaluate information presented in diverse media and formats (including visual, quantitative, and oral).	Demonstrate command of the conventions of academic English capitalization, punctuation, and spelling when writing.
Analyze how and why individuals, events, and ideas develop and interact over the course of a text.	Write narratives to understand an event or topic, using effective techniques, well-chosen details, and well-structured sequences.	Evaluate a speaker's point of view, reasoning, and use of evidence and rhetoric.	Apply knowledge of language to understand how language functions in different contexts, to make effective choices for meaning or style, and to comprehend more fully when reading or listening.
Interpret words and phrases as they are used in a text, including determining technical, connotative, and figurative meanings, and analyze how specific word choices shape meaning or tone.	Develop personal, cultural, textual, and thematic connections within and across genres through responses to texts and personal experiences.	Present information, findings, and supporting evidence so listeners can follow the line of reasoning. Ensure that the organization, development, and style are appropriate to task, purpose, and audience.	Determine or clarify the meaning of unknown and multiple-meaning words and phrases by using context clues, analyzing meaningful word parts, and consulting general and specialized reference materials, as appropriate.
Analyze the structure of texts, including how specific sentences, paragraphs, and larger portions of the text (such as a section, chapter, scene, or stanza) relate to each other and the whole.	Conduct short as well as more sustained research based on focused questions to demonstrate understanding of the subject under investigation.	Make strategic use of digital media and visual displays to express information and enhance understanding of presentations.	Demonstrate understanding of figurative language, word relationships, and nuances in word meanings.

Assess how point of view or purpose shapes the content and style of a text, drawing on a wide range of global and diverse texts.	Gather relevant information from multiple sources, assess the credibility and accuracy of each source, and integrate the information while avoiding plagiarism. Use technology, including the internet, to produce and publish writing and to interact and collaborate with others.	Adapt speech to a variety of contexts and communicative tasks, demonstrating command of academic English when indicated or appropriate.	Acquire and accurately use general academic and content-specific words and phrases sufficient for reading, writing, speaking, and listening; demonstrate independence in gathering and applying vocabulary knowledge when considering a word or phrase important to comprehension or expression.
Integrate and evaluate content presented in diverse media and formats, including across multiple texts.	Draw evidence from literary or informational texts to support analysis, reflection, and research.		
Delineate and evaluate the argument and specific claims in a text, including the validity of the reasoning as well as the relevance and sufficiency of the evidence.			
Analyze how two or more texts address similar themes or topics in order to build knowledge or to compare the approaches the authors take.			

Source: New York State Education Department, 2017.

Finally, future-ready skills will vary over time. This component of curriculum planning will require literacy educators to stay informed as to what the job market demands of people as they enter the workplace after high school. Literacy educators should remain flexible in their curriculum design and commit to change being a constant in their curricular evolution.

BE PURPOSEFUL ABOUT WHAT TO TEACH WHEN ARTICULATING CURRICULUM DEVELOPMENT ACROSS GRADE LEVELS

What is unique about English course content is that students work on similar language and thinking skills in all secondary grades, as exemplified by the New York State Education Department (2017) Anchor Standards for English Language Arts in table 2.1 (page 55). The following list indicates those similarities.

- In grades 7–12, students engage in character analysis.
- In grades 7–12, students engage in deciphering and crafting arguments.
- In grades 7–12, students engage in the research process and learn how to evaluate the validity of source material.
- In grades 7–12, students read to determine the central idea of a text and track how authors develop central ideas.

Genre study, author study, and variation in text type and complexity differentiate the work from year to year. Questions to consider include the following.

- How do we articulate curriculum from year to year to ensure a cohesive progression of skill development?
- How do we articulate the curriculum from year to year to ensure a cohesive progression with the reading experience (types of texts, types of reading experiences, themes)?
- How do we articulate the curriculum from year to year to ensure a cohesive progression in students' development as writers? Is there a different expectation for writers in grade 9 and writers in grade 11?
- How are the grade-level experiences different? Do students feel as though they are learning something new in each grade level? Do students feel that what they write and think about are the same from year to year?

Step 6: Designate Assessment as an Ongoing Component of the Learning Process

Secondary grades have a long association with using standardized testing as an indicator of student success and teacher performance. Students prepare for state-issued exams on subject-area curriculum for graduation credit. Many students also take national exams like the Scholastic Aptitude Test (SAT) and American College Test (ACT) as part of the college application process. Assessment is often synonymous with testing of knowledge and facts within disciplines, as well as competency in areas like reading, writing, vocabulary, and mathematical computation. In the revolving literacy framework, assessment is designed to support the growth and development of skills. Research supports that assessments that place value on growth rather than on scores create higher motivation, greater agency, higher levels of cognitive engagement, and stronger achievement gains (Blumenfeld, Puro, & Mergendoller, 1992; Stiggins & Chappuis, 2005).

In the following section, I share three key components for assessment under the revolving literacy framework: assessment, evaluation, and reflection. There is a shared responsibility among teachers and students in assessment and evaluation, with each addressing their roles and responsibilities.

THE THREE PARTS OF ASSESSMENT UNDER THE REVOLVING LITERACY FRAMEWORK

There are three parts to the assessment process under the revolving literacy framework.

1. **Assessment:** An *assessment* is the tool teachers and students use to gather information about students' understanding and proficiency in areas of literacy. Assessments include formal essays, research papers, creative projects, journal writing, speeches, verbal explanations in a conference, and multiple-choice questions. Tools like checklists, rubrics, progressions, and anecdotal notes help teachers and students capture information from assessments.

2. **Evaluation:** After gathering information from assessments, teachers and students evaluate, or determine the significance of, the information. Teachers and students look for patterns to determine areas in which the student demonstrates understanding or proficiency. They also look for patterns to determine areas in which there is room for growth. Naming the areas for growth helps to set goals for future work and learning.

3. **Reflection:** The reflection process is important for students and teachers.
    a. *Students*—A metacognitive approach to instruction can help students take control of their own learning using a set of personalized learning strategies, defining their own learning goals, and monitoring their progress in achieving them (Darling-Hammond et al., 2020). After evaluating their work, students can set personal goals for revision with what they are working on or for the next literacy experience. Goal setting should target the development of future-ready skills under the revolving literacy framework. Prioritizing student reflection on how they are acquiring and applying the skills can help with transferring the skills from the English classroom to other areas of learning within and beyond high school. Reflections can be written responses, shared verbally in a conference, tracked in a journal or chart, and so forth. Students should have choices in how

they want to track, monitor, and reflect on their learning (see the reproducible "Future-Ready Skill Student Reflection," page 67).

b. *Teachers*—By partnering with students in their reflection processes, teachers have opportunities to reflect on their instruction. By reviewing student work, participating in conference conversations, and reading or listening to students' reflections, teachers can identify areas of success. Teachers can note areas within the unit where the instruction was effective and the students showed interest. Teachers can also note areas within the unit where they can revise their approach to instruction or consider the relevance of materials based on feedback from students.

The revolving literacy framework celebrates assessment as part of the learning process. Formative assessments designed to advance students within their zones of proximal development will help students answer the question, Where am I now in my learning? This question creates a model for students to set goals based on reflection and scaffolding and for teachers to determine next steps for instruction (Darling-Hammond et al., 2020). Within this system, feedback from teachers and peers is always contextualized and responsive to the current needs of the student. Students should receive feedback during the learning process and not at the end of a unit or culmination of a writing piece (Darling-Hammond et al., 2020) so they can apply the feedback immediately.

By using a range of assessment strategies and tools—observations, portfolios, conferences, discussion maps, checklists, rubrics, progressions, and self-reflections—teachers develop a rich understanding of where students are in the learning process. They can then combine evidence of student learning with their own understanding of the literacy development process to plan and provide instruction to help students explicitly see how to improve (Stiggins and Chappuis, 2005). We will explore assessment strategies and tools further in chapters 4 through 6.

A CIRCULAR MODEL OF ASSESSMENT, EVALUATION, AND REFLECTION TO SUPPORT LITERACY LEARNING

Assessment, evaluation, and reflection in literacy development do not have an end point. A student doesn't move from point A to point B and stop their learning process. The assessment, evaluation, and reflection process is circular, not linear. By partnering with students in the process, you create conditions where assessment, evaluation, and reflection are part of how students learn and monitor their skill development. An ongoing assessment process does not suggest that students don't have to demonstrate learning in cumulative ways. Summative performance-based assessments are necessary and valuable. They provide opportunities for students to apply several skills and strategies that they have learned. Professors Linda Darling-Hammond and Frank Adamson (2014) suggest that performance assessments are tools for learning and give students a platform to demonstrate higher-order thinking, evaluation, reasoning, and deep understanding. These assessments directly support skill development in areas that are often noted in future-ready job skill reports, like complex problem solving, critical thinking, and analytical thinking (World Economic Forum, 2016, 2020, 2023a).

Figure 2.13 illustrates a visual model for the assessment, evaluation, and reflection process.

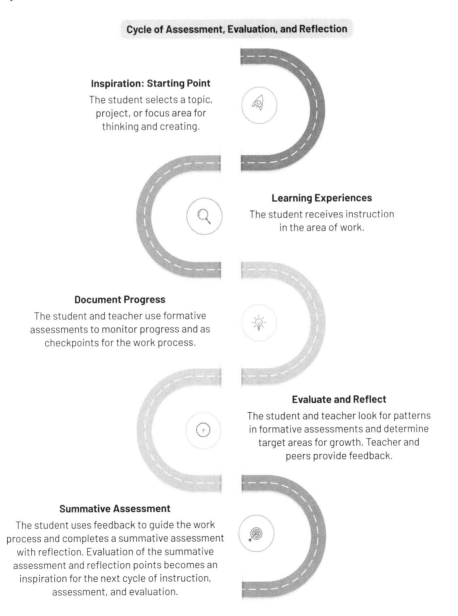

FIGURE. 2.13: A cyclical model of assessment, evaluation, and reflection.

Students should be able to transfer and continue developing skills and strategies from one unit to the next. Assessments that capture the goals of the curriculum build students' capacity to assess and guide their own learning and, through ownership of their own learning process, strengthen their interest and motivation (Darling-Hammond et al., 2020). Interest and motivation sustain the learning process.

WHAT ABOUT TESTING?

Traditional testing experiences are a reality for many adolescents. We still operate in an education system where numbers matter (an SAT score, an ACT score, a state-issued exam score) even though there is compelling research (some cited previously) that supports the value of formative assessments, performance-based assessments, feedback, and revision for learning. These numbers determine a student's graduation status. They also determine aspects of the college application process, like admission and scholarship grants. Some may say that if students participate in a robust, challenging, and authentic literacy curriculum, then they will do well on standardized exams. In my experience, I've found the following to be true.

- If students learn to read carefully with tools to analyze and think critically about text, they may do well on a standardized exam.
- If students learn to write comprehensively and develop a clear message across a text through organization, syntax, and craft, they may do well on a standardized exam.
- If students develop academic and domain-specific vocabulary through a high volume of reading, rich discussions, and exposure to content information, they may do well on a standardized exam.

However, students need to learn how to navigate and complete a standardized exam. They can certainly apply everything they have learned about reading and writing to the context of an exam, but they need instruction on the exam itself. Consider testing a genre of work. The *testing genre* consists of the following.

- Review of exam format
- Instruction on reading testing directions and requirements for individual parts
- Exposure to the evaluation tools (how points are accrued)
- Annotation strategies
- Review of language associated with exam questions
- Genre elements of reading passages
- Genre elements of writing tasks
- Instruction on approaching one-draft writing

Teaching how to take a standardized exam is clear because the structure of the exam does not change. Students can have exposure to exam-like tasks throughout their high school years, but the curriculum does not need to be designed around the structure of an exam. I recommend leaving the testing genre work to grade-level teachers the year students take exams. Designate a unit of study on the testing genre. If students focus on preparing for a standardized exam as the basis for their secondary literacy work, they lose the opportunity to discover authentic purpose for applying literacy competencies. The authentic elements of revolving literacy—language, future-ready skills, identity, community, and multimodal meaning-making—may get lost.

Summary

The steps outlined in this chapter can help you and your team design curriculum using the revolving literacy framework (see the reproducible "New Visions and New Priorities: Getting Started With the Revolving Literacy Framework," page 69). Use the tools throughout the chapter to reflect on each of the steps and determine whether they provide a path that meets the needs and interests of your team. While I present these steps in numerical order, I respect that all contexts are different, so you may modify the process in a way that suits your desired outcome. You may also review these steps and guiding questions within the context of the following reproducible planning tools. In the following chapters, you will discover practical resources for planning and curriculum implementation in the classroom for revolving literacy work.

Student Identity Question Protocol

Use this tool to reflect on students' identities and how this awareness may impact curriculum and instruction work.

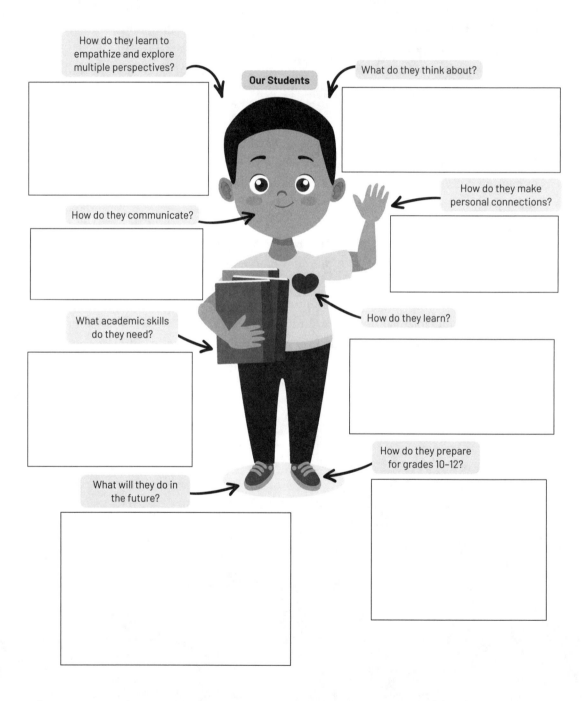

Revolving Literacy © 2025 Solution Tree Press • SolutionTree.com
Visit **go.SolutionTree.com/literacy** to download this free reproducible.

Identity Audit

Use this tool to reflect on the student population and how this awareness may impact curriculum and instruction work.

Identity Components	Who are your students? Reflect on students' various identities. You may refer to your school report card for demographic information and what students share with you in their own reflections.
First Languages and Languages Learned	
Race	
Ethnicity	
National Origin	
Gender	
Culture and Communities	
Family Structure	
Ability and Disability	
Interests and Hobbies	
Prior Knowledge—What Does the Student Know a Lot About?	
Impactful Community Events	

Me Map

Students may use this tool to reflect on aspects of their identity and how they impact the choices they make in curricular work in English class when given the opportunity. Students may add to this throughout the year and revisit it during several units of study.

Who I Am	Where I Am From	Things I Do	Ways I Celebrate	My Goals and Aspirations

Revolving Literacy © 2025 Solution Tree Press • SolutionTree.com
Visit **go.SolutionTree.com/literacy** to download this free reproducible.

Future-Ready Skill Student Reflection

Students may use this reflection tool throughout or at the end of a unit to consider how they developed future-ready skills as a result of their work.

Unit or project	
As a result of the process, I learned:	
What I enjoyed most about my work is:	
The most challenging part of my work was:	
What I may do differently next time is:	
Advice I'd offer to someone else doing this work is:	

Reflect on your future readiness as a result of this unit or project:

Future-Ready Skill	How I practiced this skill:	How I can apply my learning:
Creative thinking		
Analytical thinking		
Technological literacy		
Curiosity and lifelong learning		
Resilience and flexibility		
Systems thinking		
AI and big data		
Motivation and self-awareness		
Empathy and active listening		
Leadership and social influence		

New Visions and New Priorities: Getting Started With the Revolving Literacy Framework

Reflect on how the planning steps for engaging in revolving literacy curriculum work are applicable to your context.

Planning Steps	Guiding Questions	Notes and Next Steps
Define the language you will use for your curriculum work.	What language do you need to clarify or define to design your revolving literacy curriculum?	
	How will shared language benefit planning and articulating your curriculum design?	
Establish the vision for using the revolving literacy framework for student learning and teaching in the English classroom.	What parts of the revolving literacy vision are current strengths within your curriculum?	
	What parts of the revolving literacy vision are areas for development and growth within your curriculum? How do you plan to develop those areas?	
	What is important to you and your team to include in a literacy work mission statement? What kind of process will you engage in to develop your literacy work mission statement?	

Planning Steps	Guiding Questions	Notes and Next Steps
Create student profiles.	*Which identity protocols interest you for your curriculum planning process or in the classroom with students?*	
	How will prioritizing students' identities impact the way you and your team move forward with curriculum planning?	
Establish *how* you will facilitate learning.	*Which of the following areas of learning facilitation are current strengths within your curriculum?* • Systematic and explicit instruction • Choice • Agency and application • Ongoing assessment • Evaluation • Feedback • Reflection	
	Which of the following areas of learning facilitation are opportunities for development and growth? • Systematic and explicit instruction • Choice • Agency and application • Ongoing assessment • Evaluation • Feedback • Reflection	

Planning Steps	Guiding Questions	Notes and Next Steps
Refocus *what* you will teach.	*Discuss your reaction to this statement:* We teach students, not texts.	
	Discuss your thoughts about the two models of approaching reading in the classroom: the shared text–driven curriculum model *and* the student literacy–driven curriculum model.	
	Discuss the benefits of prioritizing future-ready skill development, standards, and domains of language in secondary literacy education.	
Designate assessment as an ongoing component of the learning process.	*How is this book's assessment model similar to and different from your existing model?*	
	Discuss your thoughts about testing as a genre.	

CHAPTER 3

HOW TO PLAN LESSONS USING THE REVOLVING LITERACY LESSON STRUCTURE

In chapter 2 (page 29), we reviewed, among other considerations for revolving literacy, *how* learning is facilitated in the framework: systematic and explicit instruction; student choice in what they read and write about, as well as how they demonstrate understanding; agency and application; and ongoing assessment, evaluation, feedback, and reflection. Teachers and students participate in this process together. Figure 3.1 (page 74) illustrates how teachers and students share construction of learning (Schlam Salman & Inbar-Lourie, 2023). Teachers are primarily responsible for planning approaches to instruction and assessment, while students are primarily responsible for making choices about their work and planning for application and transfer of skill development.

	Systematic and Explicit Instruction	Ongoing Assessment, Evaluation, Feedback, and Reflection
Teacher Planning		
	Choice	Agency and Application
Student Planning		

FIGURE 3.1: The co-construction of learning between teachers and students.

Darling-Hammond and colleagues (2020) assert that students learn more effectively if they do the following.

- Understand how they learn, as illustrated in the teacher planning portion of figure 3.1, with systematic and explicit instruction, ongoing assessment, evaluation, feedback, and reflection
- Develop ways to manage their own learning, as illustrated in the student planning portion of figure 3.1, with choice, agency, and application

In this chapter, we uncover how teaching and learning based on a process-oriented approach helps prioritize components of literacy development as focus areas for instruction. Process-oriented instruction preserves space for teacher planning and student planning (see figure 3.1). We examine literacy learning as a process through a lesson plan structure applicable to writing and design process instruction (chapter 4, page 87), research process instruction (chapter 5, page 127), and reading structures (chapter 6, page 177).

We will particularly examine the role of the teacher and the role of the student within the literacy lesson. Think of the lesson plan structure pictured in figure 3.2 as something you can implement daily so students know routines for learning within the classroom. The lesson structure is designed to support teachers in planning units of study that lay out a process for literacy work. The lesson structure also provides time for students to work independently at a pace conducive to their learning style. Not all students need to be in the same place in their work on any given day. The revolving literacy lesson structure allows for that.

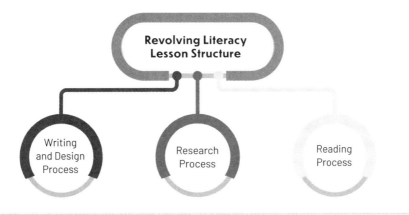

FIGURE 3.2: The revolving literacy lesson structure.

An Analogy for the Revolving Literacy Lesson

Do you remember how you learned to make a chest pass during your basketball unit in physical education class? It probably went something like this.

1. The teacher introduces what a chest pass is. The teacher may reference what you had been practicing in basketball and how the chest pass is an effective method of moving the ball down the court.
2. The teacher explicitly states that you will practice a chest pass during class to improve your overall game. The teacher may discuss the importance of practice when striving to improve any type of performance.
3. The teacher demonstrates what the chest pass looks like as well as the specific movement in the arms, hands, fingers, and feet to carry the pass through. The teacher explains when to use a chest pass.
4. After watching the demonstration, you practice making chest passes with a partner. The teacher observes while students practice. The teacher provides feedback to individuals. After a few minutes of practice time, the teacher may give general feedback notes based on patterns she noticed while observing partners' practice. She encourages you to apply those notes when playing in a game.
5. Game time! The class divides into groups to play a basketball game. The teacher asks you to focus on the chest pass during play time and apply what you learned about arm, hand, finger, and feet movement to make a successful chest pass.

6. With a few minutes left during the class period, the teacher asks you to reflect on how the techniques of a chest pass helped your overall gameplay and ways that you could improve during the following days of the basketball unit.
7. The next day, the teacher reviews the use of a chest pass and introduces a new type of pass, the bounce pass. The class follows the same structure for another pass to improve their basketball skills.

The learning experience I described from a physical education class can be applied to any performance-based scenario: a dancer learning steps to a routine, a musician learning notes to a song, a chef learning to cook a new dish, an actor learning a technique for expression during a scene, a football team learning a play for a two-point conversion. In a performance-based scenario, the learner is at the center of the learning experience, working toward independence. Independence is necessary in the arts and athletics because the learner is eventually the one to perform, not the teacher or the coach. Teachers and coaches are guides on the side (Couros & Novak, 2019). They design processes of learning for performers to participate in so they can acquire skills to be successful in their respective fields. Teachers need to be coaches in the secondary English classroom—coaches who prepare students to apply literacy skills independently in various situations in school and beyond.

The Lesson Structure

Following a similar routine each day helps teachers when planning lessons. It also helps students know what to expect in their English class. A predictable structure builds readiness in students; they know how the teacher will facilitate the learning and how they, as students, can actively engage in their learning. Teachers and students depend on one another for a supportive and productive classroom environment. The lesson structure is one routine that students can depend on. There are five parts to the revolving literacy lesson structure.

1. Context and relevance
2. Intention
3. Explicit instruction
4. Guided or independent practice
5. Daily closure

Before diving into an explanation of each part, let's match them up to the descriptors of the chest pass in a basketball lesson sequence, as table 3.1 shows.

CHAPTER 3: How to Plan Lessons Using the Revolving Literacy Lesson Structure

TABLE 3.1: Comparing Performance-Based and Revolving Literacy Lesson Structures

Physical Education Class: Performance-Based Lesson Structure	English Class: Revolving Literacy Lesson Structure
The teacher introduces what a chest pass is. The teacher explicitly states that you will practice a chest pass during class to improve your overall basketball skills.	• Context • Intention • Relevance
The teacher teaches how to do a chest pass by demonstrating what the chest pass looks like as well as the specific movement in the arms, hands, fingers, and feet to carry the pass through. The teacher explains when to use a chest pass.	• Explicit Instruction • Guided Practice
The teacher asks you to focus on the chest pass during play time and apply what you learned about arm, hand, finger, and feet movement to make a successful chest pass.	• Guided or Independent Practice
With a few minutes left in the class period, the teacher asks you to reflect on how the techniques of a chest pass helped your overall gameplay and ways that you could improve during the following days of the basketball unit.	• Daily Closure

Table 3.2 provides explanations about each part of the revolving literacy lesson structure. Prior to beginning instruction, there is typically the need for transition and lesson setup in secondary classrooms. Secondary teachers know that they need to allocate a few minutes of each period for bell-to-bell transitions and housekeeping items like taking attendance and making announcements. Teachers and students may also arrange the learning space and gather materials during this time. After all this, the lesson begins.

TABLE 3.2: The Revolving Literacy Lesson Structure

Lesson Component	Explanation
Context and Relevance	• Share the focus and objective of the lesson with students. Invite students to read a focus statement that shares the objective of the lesson. • Explain why today's lesson is important to the unit of study. • Explain how the focus-area skills can help students in situations beyond the English classroom. Be sure that a future-ready skill is the focus of instruction or paired with English content outlined by standards. • Assure students that they will have the opportunity to evaluate their learning during the period.
Intention	• Restate the focus and objective of the lesson. • Explain to the students how they will be involved in learning today.

continued ▶

Lesson Component	Explanation
Explicit Instruction	- Explicitly teach by modeling a process that you want students to engage in when working collaboratively or independently. Be sure that you act as the learner in front of students by doing what you invite them to practice during the class period. The bulleted list on page 79 provides practices for explicit instruction.

Guided or Independent Practice	- This part of the lesson takes up the most time during the English class because it is when students are actively involved in applying what they learned in the explicit instruction portion of the lesson. Teachers and students work together during this time so students receive the feedback and responsive instruction they may need. This work time is also the space where students make choices about their work and manage their productivity.
	- During this time, students may do the following.
	  + Apply and practice what they learned during the explicit instruction portion of the lesson.
	  + Participate in an individual or a group conference with the teacher.
	  + Participate in a peer conference with a partner.
	  + Work in a style conducive to the lesson or unit goals—independently, in a partnership, or in a group.
	- During this time, teachers may do the following.
	  + Host a conference with a student or group of students to share feedback.
	  + Teach a small group of students in response to their instructional needs (reteach, reinforce, scaffold material, introduce a strategy, provide tools, and so on).
	  + Assess and evaluate student progress by observing, conferring, and recording anecdotal notes.

Daily Closure	- There are several ways to bring closure to a lesson that help to anticipate future work. The teacher may do the following.
	  + Design a reflection protocol routine where students write a journal reflection about the future-ready and language skills they are developing during the unit of study and how those skills can support their work in other areas of life.
	  + Invite students to share something they are proud of with the class.
	  + Invite students to share something they want to develop more with the class.
	  + Invite students to share something they discovered during their work.

Daily Closure	• Share patterns they notice in students' work, providing both a class compliment and an area for growth.
	• Students may do the following.
	  + Share their progress with a partner. Partners give advice or feedback to each other.
	  + Make a work plan for the next day based on their progress from the current day.
	  + Submit an artifact of work as a formative assessment.

Explicit instruction is a crucial part of the lesson. Students need explicit instruction to develop literacy practices. It helps them approach their work with clarity so they can move toward independence. The following is a list of instructional practices to consider when designing lesson plans. As you plan, think about which method of instruction would best suit the focus of the lesson. Plan with intention.

- **Think-Aloud:** Model how to think about and reflect on the unit work. You may model strategies for thinking when engaged in analysis, complex problem solving, and critical thinking by posing questions aloud or synthesizing information. You may provide reflection questions for students to consider making personalized work plans. The think-aloud should match the objective of the lesson.

- **Demonstration:** If you are teaching students how to use a new tool, show them how to use it. If you are teaching students how to be a leader in conversations, show them how to do so. If you are teaching students a strategy for generating ideas for research, show them how to utilize the strategy on the board or in a notebook under a document camera. To put it simply, whatever you would like students to do, you must do it first so they can watch and develop a frame of reference for success.

- **Use of a Mentor Text:** A *mentor text* is a published text or image used as an exemplar to learn from. You may use a mentor text to show students a technique or craft move in writing so they can try it in their own writing. You may also show a mentor text to exemplify how images and text support each other to convey a powerful message. Be intentional with the mentor texts you choose; be sure that the technique you want students to try in their own work is visible and obvious. Coach students through discussion to share noticings from a mentor text so they understand that they are studying it as a tool for developing their own work.

- **Use of a Demonstration Text:** A *demonstration text* is a text that the teacher writes alongside the students. For example, if engaged in an argument-writing unit, the teacher writes an argument of their own and uses it as a tool to demonstrate strategies. Students can watch the teacher write in real time and think aloud during the writing process. The teacher talks about the decisions they make as a writer. The writing process comes to life in front of the students' eyes. Teachers often share with me that they are uncomfortable writing in front of students in real time for fear that they may have writer's block. I understand and not to worry! Part of your plan may be to write your demonstration text ahead of time. You may consider using artificial intelligence as a writing partner for ideas. When you are teaching, have a copy of your writing on the side and then you can copy from it while typing on the screen or writing in a notebook under a document camera. The purpose is for students to see the writing process unfold in front of them.

- **Show and Explain:** There are some instances where it is helpful for teachers to show students a sample product of what they are working on or working toward. Together, they describe how the example can help the learning process and maybe some things to avoid in the process. This is not considered a demonstration.
- **Shared Experience:** A shared experience is when teachers and students generate something together that can help students with the independent or collaborative work they will do for most of the class period. For example, if students are generating ideas for topics to explore in memoir writing, perhaps the teacher and students utilize a strategy together to generate ideas in a shared space that students can use for reference. A shared experience is effective when the teacher wants to teach how participating in a learning community benefits the process students are engaged in (much like in a professional space).
- **Media With Active Engagement:** Media (news clip, documentary clip, scene from a play, advertisement, social media video, and so forth) may be used for instructional purposes. When viewing media, build in strategic points for active engagement among students. Set a focus for viewing and develop ways for students to engage in analysis and conversation within a partnership or group. Select media with a purpose.

The Lesson Schedule

Time feels limited in secondary schools. As I mentioned in the introduction (page 1), the current structure for most secondary education still has students attending forty-minute classes throughout the day. By the time students attend to their work plan for the day during the guided or independent practice part of the lesson, it's almost time for the bell to ring. While the time we dedicate to portions of lessons varies, having a range of minutes for each lesson part helps keep teachers and students focused throughout the period. Anticipated time frames also help in the planning process to ensure that students spend time actively in their learning. Avoid passivity when working with adolescents.

Figure 3.3 illustrates a suggested schedule for each part of the revolving literacy lesson. Consider this as a guide and know that it can change with intention. Do your students need a full period of writing time with peer and teacher conferences for feedback? If so, shorten your explicit instruction. Is there something that will take extended time to explicitly teach and demonstrate? If so, shorten the guided or independent practice, but be sure to provide more active work time the next day.

2–3 minutes	2–3 minutes	1–2 minutes	10–15 minutes	18–25 minutes	5–6 minutes	
Transition and Setup →	Context for the Lesson →	Set the Intention →	Explicit Instruction →	Guided or Independent Practice →	Daily Closure →	Next Day's Work

FIGURE 3.3: Revolving literacy lesson schedule.

The Lesson Plan

A lesson plan is a way for teachers to show their thinking prior to facilitating a learning experience with students. The best lesson plans set an intention for learning but allow space for teachers and students to respond to needs and inquiries. A common fear that preservice and established teachers share with me is that a lesson goes in a different direction than indicated on a lesson plan. This fear is often heightened when it is time for a formal observation from an administrator. Teachers may think that lesson plans need to go exactly as planned for them to be successful. My advice is to be clear in a lesson's focus area, but remember that effective teaching is marked by a teacher's ability to respond to student needs. This is why the guided and independent practice portion of the lesson is imperative; it provides built-in space for teachers to coach students on where they are in their individual learning processes.

The reproducible "Revolving Literacy Lesson Plan Thinking Map" (page 83) is a template to guide your planning of a revolving literacy lesson. The lesson plan includes the lesson components outlined previously as well as a thinking space to make connections to components of literacy development (language, future-ready skills, identity, community, and multimodal meaning-making). This is a template for one lesson; it is important to note that not all components of literacy development will be focal points for instruction in a singular lesson plan. This is OK. Teachers should carefully articulate lessons throughout a unit of study so all components are present within the entire unit and across units when designing a scope and sequence for curriculum. Consider using the "Revolving Literacy Lesson Plan Thinking Map" reproducible for your daily plans and for formal observations.

Summary

Chapters 4, 5, and 6 (pages 87, 127, and 177, respectively) include examples of lesson plans for writing, research, and reading work to apply the revolving literacy lesson plan. You can also use the lesson plan as a tool to reflect on what and how you are currently teaching. Practice the exercise described in the next Stop and Think section to identify your next steps in revolving literacy work.

Think about a lesson that you recently taught. Write about the unit of study the lesson is a part of and what the objective of the lesson is.

Write a lesson plan for the lesson you recently taught using the "Revolving Literacy Lesson Plan Thinking Map" reproducible.

After writing the lesson plan, identify areas that have clear connections to the components of the lesson plan.

After writing the lesson plan, identify areas to revise so the lesson aligns with revolving literacy instruction.

*Visit **go.SolutionTree.com/literacy** for a free reproducible version of this reflection.*

Revolving Literacy Lesson Plan Thinking Map

Use this reproducible to plan lessons. It contains all the aspects of revolving literacy to help you think through your lesson design.

Lesson Plan Thinking Map		
Connections for Learning		
Context: Why is today's lesson important to the work in the current unit of study?		
Relevance: How does this lesson connect to future-ready skills, students' lives outside of school, or skills they may use in other areas of learning?		
Connections for Literacy Instruction		
Language: Which domains of language are targeted in instruction and application of learning?	**Future-Ready Skills:** What future-ready skills are students developing?	**Identity:** How can students personally connect to this lesson?
Community: How are students participating in a community of learners within the classroom? How is their work contributing to a larger community outside of the classroom? How is community influencing the work at hand?		**Multimodal Meaning-Making:** What modalities are students making meaning *from*? What modalities are students using to make meaning and demonstrate understanding?

Revolving Literacy © 2025 Solution Tree Press • SolutionTree.com
Visit **go.SolutionTree.com/literacy** to download this free reproducible.

Intention	
Objective (an intention for teachers): What is the goal for students to accomplish by the end of the lesson?	
Focus Statement (an intention for students): Ask students to state their objective in the first person as a way to take ownership of their learning.	
Standards: What standards does the lesson address?	
Explicit Instruction	
Tools and Texts: What resources and instructional materials are needed for this lesson? What is the teacher using to teach? What are students using or working with?	
Whole-Class Instruction: Describe the lesson. What instructional strategy or strategies will you use? Why did you select that instructional technique? How does it help accomplish the goal of the lesson?	Check the methods used in this lesson: ☐ Think-aloud ☐ Demonstration ☐ Use of a mentor text ☐ Use of a demonstration text ☐ Show and explain ☐ Shared experience ☐ Media with active engagement **Describe the lesson:**

Guided or Independent Practice: Describe what students are doing after the whole-class instruction. Share your conference or small-group instruction plan.	Describe what students are doing after whole-class instruction. What scaffolds and supports are in place for students who are in need?
	Share your conference or small-group instruction plan. What scaffolds, strategies, or tools will you use to support students you meet with? What is the purpose of meeting with these students?

Reflection and Next Steps

Daily Closure: How will you close the lesson to help future teacher or student planning? See table 3.2 (page 77) for closure options.	
After the Lesson: Evaluate the level of student engagement and the student work.	Based on your observations, name areas where the lesson was successful and where students were successful.
	Based on your observations, what is needed in future instruction?
	Based on your observations, did students connect with the context and relevance of the lesson? Were they aware of how their work was part of a process to develop the named future-ready skill?

CHAPTER 4
TEACHING WRITERS IN THE REVOLVING LITERACY CLASSROOM

When I was an English teacher, I used to include an invitation on all my writing assessment tools (rubrics, checklists, and the like) that I gave to students when sharing grades on writing pieces. The invitation was, "Want to improve your writing? Not satisfied with the grade you earned? Let's work on it. Come to extra help to revise your writing!" And, yes, if students revised their writing after submitting, they earned points back.

My thought, and what I would explain to my students, is that a writer is rarely ever done. And some students just need more practice time and more coaching from a teacher than what is allotted in the typical forty-minute secondary English class period. With this opportunity, I would have the occasional question from students: "So, I don't have to try the first time I hand in my writing? I can just make it up at extra help?" My students learned quickly—that wasn't the point of my invitation to revise.

Writing is a process. I wasn't concerned with the 0–100 grade range. I wasn't concerned with allowing extra time. I wanted my students to participate in a process of writing and a process of learning. In a presentation at the 2022 New York State English Council conference, literacy education expert Kelly Gallagher shares his research on contextualizing the importance of various writing process opportunities for high school students. Gallagher (2022) urges educators to consider moving away from prescribed, highly structured writing tasks and encouraged them to move toward teaching students strategies for navigating the writing process. We can't always predict what students will write about, but we know that we can teach them how to approach their writing. The following list provides examples of college writing invitations that Gallagher (2022) collected to demonstrate why writing process instruction is so important.

- **Plymouth State University:** Identify an idea or challenge in the world (such as mass incarceration or global warming) covered in a class reading. In a one-thousand-word essay, shape your thinking in response to the author's words.
- **North Carolina State University:** Choose a movie trailer and analyze it in a six to eight-page essay.
- **University of South Carolina:** Select a scene from a play we read and describe how you would stage it. Explain how your staging supports what the playwright is trying to accomplish.
- **Emerson College:** Write about the intersection of these three subjects: (1) identity, (2) family, and (3) place.

This research inspired me to reflect on the writing invitations I share with my own college students, who are preservice teachers. For example, here are two invitations.

- **Week 1:** Share your thinking about assessment and evaluation.
- **Week 14:** Go back to your original position paper from week 1. Take one idea from that paper and revise it based on your learning from this semester.

I also started collecting writing invitations or requirements that surfaced in non-academic spaces.

- Write a letter to a mortgage broker explaining that you don't own the home that your name is listed under.
- Write an email to a company explaining that you can't access your online account.
- Write a speech to recite at a fiftieth wedding anniversary celebration.
- Leave a comment.
- Write a review.

Whether writing for academic or personal purposes, there are ways for writers to approach their writing with intent and agency. Thinking through decisions about writing happens throughout a writing process. In this chapter, we explore the relationship between the writing process—answering the questions of why, what, and how students write—and the connection between writing and future-ready skills within the revolving literacy framework. We also review what student writing looks in an era of generative AI.

Questions About Student Writing

It is important to reflect on how we approach writing in schools. As I shared in the introduction (page 1), questions are a currency and can lead to new thinking. Let's explore the following questions about writing in secondary English classrooms together.

WHY DO STUDENTS WRITE?

In his presentation at the 2022 New York State English Council conference, Gallagher challenges English educators to ask themselves, "What kind of writing do students mostly do in high school English class—writing to complete tasks or writing to discover ideas?" Gallagher (2022) defines *writing to complete tasks* as answering the teacher's questions, filling out reading logs, writing literary analysis essays, and responding to a lesson objective or a teacher's idea. Gallagher (2022) defines *writing to discover ideas* as opportunities for students to do quick writes in notebooks, write fiction, write creative nonfiction, write spoken-word poetry, prepare TED Talks, and design projects. I share similar questions to the one Gallagher (2022) posed in his presentation:

> Do students mostly write to complete tasks, or do they write to discover ideas related to personal inquiries in English class?
> Who sets the intent for writing—the teacher or the student?

It is important to balance students' writing opportunities across a secondary school experience and a school year. Be intentional about when and why students write for a formal academic purpose and when they write for an authentic, personal purpose. This can be challenging. We are often preparing students for formal writing tasks prescribed by standardized exams and college applications. As I shared in the What About Testing? section of chapter 2 (page 62), there are strategies to teach students to prepare for one-draft writing on an exam. There are six traits of writing: (1) ideas, (2) organization, (3) voice, (4) word choice, (5) sentence fluency, and (6) conventions and layout (Anderson, 2005). If students have a solid foundation in how to convey meaning in writing through the six traits, they can apply what they learn to the structure and purpose of a particular writing task. Don't let standardized tests and prescribed tasks dominate the writing lives of students in high school. Create balance. Formalized tasks are part of the writing experience; they aren't why we write.

WHAT DO STUDENTS WRITE?

Once when I was working on revolving literacy work with a team of high school English teachers, the question of what students write in English class emerged organically as we were reflecting on the curriculum's relevance. It was clear and obvious that there was consistency in the type of writing students completed while in grades 9–12: literary analysis and argument essays with designated questions. There were also formulas to approach each genre. Students wrote to complete tasks. The team members quickly realized that they were spending time and energy on these two tasks because they appear on the statewide standardized exam that students take right before their senior year of high school. This realization led us to the question, *What kind of writing do you do in real life?* as figure 4.1 shows.

FIGURE 4.1: A question about writing that emerged during a team reflection.

From this prompt, we proceeded to identify the authentic writing opportunities and requirements that adolescents and adults encounter, shown in the following list.

- Text exchanges
- Emails
- Résumés
- Social media posts
- Blogs
- Listicles
- Formal letters
- Critiques, reviews
- College application questions (narrative bursts)

The list served as a tool for revising the curriculum to include more instruction in areas of authentic writing. For example, the first writing unit in English class during senior year became an authentic writing unit. Students learned to write professional emails, résumés, and formal letters. They wrote in real contexts or simulated contexts based on their interests and goals. For example, if a student was a server at a local restaurant, they practiced writing a professional email to their boss requesting time off. If a student was applying to a special program at their potential college, they practiced writing a formal letter about their interest in the program to include with an application.

You may be nodding your head in agreement that the types of writing in the bulleted list are what people write in real life. You also may be wondering where to find the time to include authentic writing opportunities within the curriculum when formal academic writing instruction is needed for standardized exams, required coursework, and preparation for college and participation in academic communities. I encourage you to balance the writing opportunities in your planning within the grade level as well as across grade levels. If students write in ways that connect to their prior knowledge, experiences, and personal interests, they may internalize what they learn about how to write well and transfer those skills to other contexts, including those required by standards. A bridge between students' experiences and school content draws on the familiar to make new ideas or content visible and explicit (Lee, 2007).

What follows are examples of alignment in writing across grades as well as ways to merge authentic writing with academic responsibilities within grade-level work.

- Students may write a **research paper** in grades 7–12 because the skill development for a research process is vast and wide. Topics vary. Products vary. As students mature, their research becomes more sophisticated.
- Students may practice **literary analysis** writing in grades 8–12 because their perspectives on themselves and the world grow as they mature. The ways in which readers analyze text in grade 8 are different from the ways in which they analyze text in grade 11. Approaches to instruction and analysis techniques can be distinguished.
- **Social media posting** can be formally embedded into the curriculum in grades 8–12 since social media is how many adolescents socialize, communicate, and engage in reading. In some places in the curriculum, social media posting can be tied to fictional characters to invite readers to reimagine their reading as a form of retelling. For example, what would John Proctor's TikTok account include?
- Formal instruction in **email writing** may appear in the curriculum in grades 8 and 9, with a brief review in the following grades.
- **Fan fiction** writing may appear in the curriculum in grade 7 and grade 10 to encourage students to approach reading and writing with creativity and active imaginations in middle and high school. Incorporating a fan fiction writing experience in middle school and again in high school contributes to the balance of students' writing progression across grades.
- **Reviews and critiques** of restaurants, movies, books, concerts, and so on may be the way students construct arguments in grade 10 as they

learn how to develop compelling claims supported by reliable evidence and reasoning.

- **Social commentary** may be the way students construct arguments in grades 11 and 12 as they learn how to develop compelling claims supported by reliable evidence and reasoning.
- Prioritize formal instruction in **résumé writing and formal letter writing** in grades 11 and 12 to prepare students to apply for college and careers.

You may also be wondering where to find the time to prioritize writing instruction when reading traditionally holds the most real estate in secondary English classes. Writing is often dependent on reading in the secondary English curriculum. In the shared text-driven curriculum model (see chapter 2, page 29), students typically read a shared text and write extended essays about the text—the theme, character development, and claims supported by research. This makes sense. Traditional secondary English classes celebrate literature and invite readers to share their insights and analysis through writing. The revolving literacy framework includes literary analysis but suggests that writing opportunities span beyond response to shared literature. A meta-analysis by writing instruction expert Steve Graham and colleagues (2018) finds that literacy instruction that balances reading and writing by teaching the subjects together, with no subject dominating more than 60 percent of instructional time, significantly improves students' reading comprehension.

There should be a balance in emphasis on reading and writing with opportunities for intentional listening, speaking, and design through multiple modalities. You may spend three to four weeks within a unit where the instructional intent is explicit teaching in reading (digital or print texts) with writing as a way to process and reflect on ideas. Then, you may spend three to four weeks on a unit where the instructional intent is explicit teaching in writing or design with reading as a support to the writing or design process. Reading and writing can be related thematically, or they can exist on their own. What we spend our instructional time on signals what we value in teaching and learning.

When planning instruction under each component of literacy development—language, future-ready skills, identity, community, and multimodal meaning-making—you pave the way to develop authentic writing opportunities for students. Each component prioritizes students as the center of decision making. As you reflect on why students write and the writing opportunities within the curriculum, use the questions in table 4.1 to stay committed to the core principles of literacy instruction. These questions will help prioritize students, relevance, and engagement in your planning.

TABLE 4.1: Connecting Writing Opportunities to Components of Literacy Development

Component of Literacy Development	Writing Opportunity
Language	• Where in the curriculum will teachers prioritize writing instruction as the unit focus work? • Where in the curriculum will students spend time in each stage of the writing process to produce an extensive writing piece? Where in the curriculum will writing be less formal and used as a vehicle for response, meaning making, and reflection? • Where in the curriculum does it benefit the reading process for students to write briefly and consistently in response to reading? • Where in the curriculum does it benefit the reading process for students to write formally and extendedly in response to reading? • Where in the curriculum can a writing unit of study exist independently of a shared fiction or nonfiction text (the writing doesn't depend on the reading)?
Identity	• How will teachers include a narrative writing or a personal essay in the scope and sequence? • How can students incorporate aspects of their identities into genres of writing other than narrative and personal essay? • When will students have opportunities to choose their own topics for writing? How can students use identity reflections (for example, a Me Map) as tools for generating writing ideas? • How can teachers strategically plan for students to incorporate personal choice into formal academic writing?
Future-Ready Skills	• What are the connections between future-ready skills and stages of the writing process? • How can teachers pair future-ready skills and writing strategies so that students begin to make connections between writing in English class and writing beyond English class? • Where are there opportunities for students to reflect on how they develop transferable skills through working through the stages of the writing process?
Community	• Where in the curriculum are students learning to write for the communities they belong to (social media posts, blogs, critiques and reviews, texts, emails, academic writing, and so on)? • Where in the curriculum can students have an opportunity to write for a larger community audience (their class, their school, a community member, a community organization, an online association, and so on)?

continued ▶

Component of Literacy Development	Writing Opportunity
Community	• Where in the curriculum are writers learning that sharing a comprehensive written message can impact a specific cause within a community? • How does the classroom culture make students feel like they belong to a community of writers within their classroom?
Multimodal Meaning-Making	• Where in the curriculum does literacy instruction focus on how media sources (texts, websites, books, movies, and so on) influence the way readers and consumers make meaning? • Where in the curriculum is media literacy prioritized? • Where are there opportunities for students to demonstrate understanding or share meaning through multimodal creation? • How is writing paired with other modalities for literacy work?

Do students in your classes mostly write to complete tasks, or do they write to discover ideas related to personal inquiries?

Who mostly sets the intent for writing in your current class or curriculum—the teacher or the student?

Identify an area or areas of literacy instruction that you could further cultivate in writing instruction. Use the questions in table 4.1 (page 93) to guide your reflections.

Identify areas within your existing curriculum where you can incorporate student choice in writing topics to establish relevance.

*Visit **go.SolutionTree.com/literacy** for a free reproducible version of this reflection.*

HOW DO STUDENTS WRITE?

It's important and practical to teach studentss writing techniques within various genres and for different purposes. But if we focus more on *how* we teach students to approach their writing rather than *what* they are writing, we are better preparing them to attend to a myriad of writing tasks, whether personal or prescribed. The writing process is consistent. What we are faced with writing about in school and life is not.

The way we teach students to write is tied to our philosophy on writing instruction. Do your research and experience guide you to embrace the purpose of writing as generating a product or completing a task? Or do you embrace writing as engaging in a process of knowing (McCrimmon, 1984) and discovering (Gallagher, 2022) ideas? The process itself guides writers in their discovery. Another way to frame this question is, Do we write for product or process?

Describe your philosophy for writing instruction.
- What is the purpose of writing?
- How should writing instruction be delivered?
- What are the essential elements of writing instruction that teach students how to write comprehensively and with intention?

*Visit **go.SolutionTree.com/literacy** for a free reproducible version of this reflection.*

Writing is often regarded as a process that has sequential steps. While there is a direction for engaging in the writing process, it is composed of stages, not steps. Steps imply that writing needs to be linear. There are some genres and tasks that call for a linear approach, but if we embrace writing as a way to discover ideas that weren't present before starting to write, we need to allow space for writers to engage in different strategies while in the stages of process. Various approaches during each stage open up pathways for new perspectives on ideas. Donald M. Murray is a prolific writer and thinker about teaching writing. Murray (1982) organizes the writing process into the following three stages.

1. **Prevision:** This stage incorporates all the work the writer does prior to writing the first draft.
2. **Vision:** This stage involves writing the first draft. The writer organizes ideas into a discovery draft (Murray, 1982) where writers figure out their messages.
3. **Revision:** This stage is where writers spend the most time. During this stage, they shape their content to communicate the message they want to convey to the reader.

The structure for the writing process in a secondary English classroom is based on Murray's (1982) framework. When planning revolving literacy work, it is helpful to subscribe to a consistent writing process so students can predict how the process will go. They can internalize the stages of writing and transfer their understanding of the process into other contexts of writing. Also, committing to instructing within the writing process allows for literacy educators to make changes to the curriculum to ensure writing opportunities are relevant for students as time passes. The process remains the same, but the content may change. Again, it's not necessarily *what* we teach students to write that is most impactful but *how* they approach writing it that leaves a lasting impression on writers.

Figure 4.2 illustrates the writing process within the revolving literacy framework. The sizes of the shapes in the figure indicate how much time to spend in each stage. The larger circles indicate areas in which more instructional and practice time are typically needed. See the reproducible "Explanations of Each Stage of the Revolving Literacy Writing Process" (page 112), which explains each step of the revolving literacy writing process.

CHAPTER 4: Teaching Writers in the Revolving Literacy Classroom

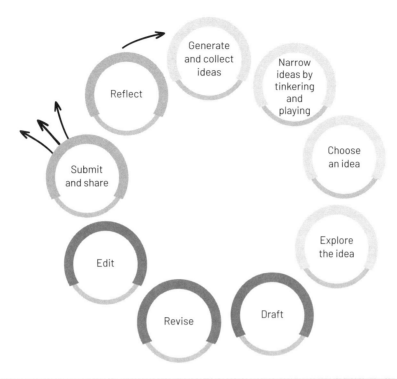

FIGURE 4.2: The writing process within the revolving literacy framework.

Reread the stages of the writing process and review how they are illustrated in figure 4.2. In what stages do students typically need the most support? Why do you think this?

In what stages of the writing process are you most confident when delivering instruction?

continued ▶

> In what stages of the writing process would you benefit from professional development? Write a few goals for your own professional learning.

Visit **go.SolutionTree.com/literacy** for a free reproducible version of this reflection.

The Connection Between Writing and Future-Ready Skills

Working through the writing process offers students opportunities to practice future-ready skills and develop competencies that span beyond just the writing process. Writing takes time to develop. Writers exercise various skills throughout the different stages of the process. Writers make intentional choices to develop their product so that meaning is clear to the reader. They engage in the process of metacognition, or thinking about one's own thinking (Georghiades, 2004). Asking students to reflect on how they develop their writing and the skills they apply to the process can help with future application of knowledge. The process of metacognition allows for more strategic learning and deeper conceptual understanding of content (Darling-Hammond et al., 2020).

What it means to be future-ready may change every few years as industries evolve and the job market remains responsive to economic and societal demands. As I shared in chapter 1 (page 15), revolving literacy teachers have a commitment to learning, tinkering, and change. The scope of the curriculum will shift as the meaning of future readiness evolves.

I use the skills on the rise from 2023–2027 listed in the World Economic Forum's (2023a) *Future of Jobs Report* as a resource for future-ready skills to consider in literacy lesson planning. Certain genres may lend themselves to a different distribution of future-ready skills. Resilience and flexibility, lifelong learning strategies, systems thinking, and motivation and self-awareness are situated in all the stages of the writing process because students develop these skills through engaging in the process as a whole. Teachers may keep students tuned in to these skills as they work through each stage of the writing process and invite them to include how they developed those skills throughout the process in their end-of-unit reflection.

You may choose not to emphasize every skill within your plan for a writing unit of study. Select the future-ready skills that are most appropriate for the type of writing students are engaged in and include those skills in your lesson planning and what you invite students to reflect on. Using the language of future-ready skills should be part of how students learn to speak about and reflect on their work. Naming the future-ready skills, explaining how they connect to English course content, and discussing how students can apply them in other contexts become part of the discourse in your classroom.

Figure 4.3 illustrates when future-ready skills are most prominent in stages of the writing process. Use this figure to plan lessons that not only target writing instruction but also encourage student reflection on their development of future-ready skills throughout the writing process. You may emphasize both writing and future-ready skill development in your explicit instruction. Note that *resilience*, *flexibility*, *lifelong learning strategies*, *systems thinking*, and *motivation and self-awareness* are in the middle of the cycle because students exercise those skills through each stage of the revolving literacy writing process and as they develop as writers. See the reproducible "The Connection Between Stages of the Writing Process and Future-Ready Skills" (page 119).

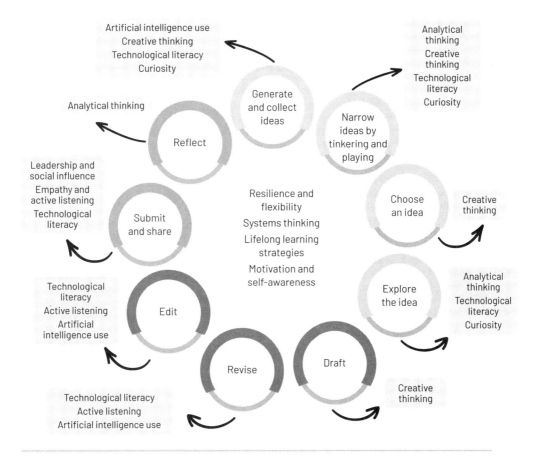

FIGURE 4.3: The connection between the revolving literacy writing process and future-ready skills.

Writing in the Era of Artificial Intelligence

The generative AI tool ChatGPT (https://openai.com/chatgpt) caused quite a stir in the field of education when it became popular in November 2022. For some English teachers, it seemed as though our lives as we knew them were over, but some were excited about the capabilities of the new platform. A common denominator among educators was curiosity. Initial questions may have been similar to these.

- How will artificial intelligence impact my role and responsibilities as a teacher?
- How will I encourage my students to write if a chatbot will write for them?
- How do I address plagiarism?
- What if teachers are no longer relevant?

Questions are good. Questions can lead to new learning, new thinking, and innovative practices. Changes with artificial intelligence happen so quickly. The rapid changes make it challenging for educators to develop deep pedagogical beliefs that guide curriculum development and instruction. The emergence of chatbots as writing tools is a symptom of a larger issue knocking on education's door and, thus, is the impetus for the revolving literacy framework: The world is changing. Technology advances. Advancements influence literacy practices and how we access and share content. Literacy educators need to be ready to adjust to technological and societal changes so the secondary school experience stays relevant for students. While it may be worrisome, and in some cases daunting, to consistently respond to how technology impacts our role as writing teachers, it is necessary for students.

I suggest approaching generative AI's place in the writing process with an open mind. Keep asking questions. Talk to your students about it. Don't pretend that it doesn't exist. Acknowledging the capabilities of artificial intelligence with students lets them know that you are aware and that you're thinking critically about it. Consider it a tool that adolescents need to learn how to use responsibly and effectively. I remember when I received an iPad cart for my classroom; then, a few years later, all my students had one-to-one devices. And then Google Classroom became the way classrooms were managed. These are all shifts that forced me to respond as a literacy educator so my students acquired digital literacy competencies and future-ready skills for the time. It is the same with AI.

Consider discussing the questions listed in figure 4.4 within your grade-level team, department, or collegial circle to plan for writing instruction in the era of artificial intelligence.

Question about artificial intelligence	Consideration	What does this mean in the context of my work or my team's work?
What does it mean to be a critical user of artificial intelligence?	Users should be highly aware that output from chatbots like Chat GPT is artificially generated. Users should know that information isn't always accurate and may not be generated in a way that communicates the intended meaning. How do we embrace this new era of critical thinking in teachable moments? Are there opportunities to reflect on how our curriculum addresses fact checking, evaluating sources, and synthesizing information?	
What language skills are imperative to students' literacy development when using artificial intelligence in the classroom?	If artificial intelligence can think through an assignment for a student, we may consider reflecting on the levels of thinking most assignments in courses ask students to engage in. Students should be invited to think creatively and critically when they feel they have a stake in what is being taught and assigned. If students have a personal investment in what they are working on, they may be less inclined to rely on AI for completion.	
What kind of writing are we asking students to do?	ChatGPT can actually be a tool to improve writing. There are endless possibilities to use it for lessons in structure, craft, conventions, and elaboration. But it's a writing partner, not a substitute for the writer, and students need to learn this. Additionally, educators may consider reflecting on what they ask students to write about. Is every student required to write about how a theme emerges in *Macbeth*? Imagine how many accounts of that question are stored in cyberspace. If we challenge students to write about authentic ideas relevant to them, there may be less of a chance that artificial intelligence will give them the answer.	

Source: Radice, 2024.

FIGURE 4.4: Questions and considerations about artificial intelligence.

continued ▶

Question about artificial intelligence	Consideration	What does this mean in the context of my work or my team's work?
How does artificial intelligence widen access to writing support?	The concept of students getting help with writing is not new. While all students have access to their teachers during the school day, only some have access to additional support from adults at home. Familiar questions include How can I say this? Can you read this and tell me what I need to fix? What else should I add? While conversation about writing can be helpful, artificial intelligence may offer a digital conversation to those who don't have adults available for support.	
What instruction do we have in place that addresses critical reading, fact checking, and analysis of reliable and valid sources of information? How might we need to change curriculum or instruction to address these skills in the world of artificial intelligence?	These are not new skills, but we need to address them within the context of artificial intelligence. Perhaps curriculum teams could be formed by grade level or department to audit curricular areas where it may be appropriate to integrate explicit teaching of artificial intelligence tools and the skills needed to use them ethically, responsibly, and creatively.	
How can we vary approaches to assessment so there isn't overuse or an overreliance on artificial intelligence?	There are many ways to gauge students' understanding of content and curricular themes. Presentations, debates, physical designs, visual representations, demonstrations, teacher-student conferences, and peer conferences are all ways to evaluate student learning and progress.	
How can artificial intelligence help teachers differentiate learning material and support various student needs?	Teachers undoubtedly need to have a strong foundation in instructional strategies that promote student learning. They also must understand why differentiated instruction is necessary in classrooms. Teachers develop their skill set through preservice coursework, reading, observing other teachers, engaging in professional development, and reflecting on their own teaching experiences. There are no substitutes for this type of work, and prior experiences can inform teachers' use of artificial intelligence tools for planning.	

How can artificial intelligence help teachers differentiate learning material and support various student needs?	Teachers also need to know their students' needs and the types of support that may benefit them before approaching artificial intelligence use. Artificial intelligence tools can generate scaffolded questions, vary the text complexity of reading material, develop prompts for generating ideas, translate text into different languages, and produce models similar to the assignment students may work on. Artificial intelligence can be a digital teaching assistant so teachers can focus on the instruction and confer with students in real time to move their learning forward.	
What privacy and security measures should we consider when using artificial intelligence tools in school?	It is important that your technology team is involved in planning for using artificial intelligence in school. There are education laws dedicated to data privacy. Teams will want to know the security level and compliance measures with education laws of artificial intelligence platforms the school is interested in using. While the content generated by platforms like ChatGPT is inherently artificial, this new technology is very much real. Involving multiple stakeholders in conversations about artificial intelligence helps generate responsible plans for use and think creatively about the next steps for implementation.	

*Visit **go.SolutionTree.com/literacy** for a free reproducible version of this figure.*

Writing in the Revolving Literacy Framework

In this section, you will find a sample writing unit of study framework planning sheet and a sample lesson plan. I also feature a narrative nonfiction writing unit that incorporates argument-writing techniques.

UNIT OF STUDY FRAMEWORK

The purpose of the unit of study framework is to help secondary literacy educators ensure that they incorporate all components of literacy development into the unit of study. As I described in chapter 2, use the framework template like a place setting on a dinner table. It holds each of the pieces needed for a revolving literacy-focused unit: language, future-ready skills, identity, community, and multimodal meaning-making. It does not include specific lesson plans. Figure 4.5 (page 104) presents a sample unit of study plan for studying the power of influencers.

Unit Summary: Social media has given ordinary people an opportunity to build their own brand through stimulating content and engagement. According to the Digital Marketing Institute (2024), as social media has become more integrated into our lives, influencer marketing has exploded. It's important for teens to be alert to the influencer industry as they scroll their social media platforms. Influencers don't just sell products—they also brand ideas and ideologies. Young people must be cautious of influencers. Teens are viewers and consumers. They must observe with a clear definition of what it means to be an influencer and what type of people they want to follow. This is a writing unit that invites writers to reflect on their moral compass and their personal beliefs in relation to the popularized term of *influencer* and what it really means to lead and influence.

Each year, *Time* magazine puts out an issue called "*Time* 100: The Most Influential People." Students will write a narrative nonfiction feature article similar to the articles in *Time*. Writers will develop an explanation of what it means to be an influencer. Then, using argument writing structure and techniques, writers will make a case as to why an individual—either a personal or cultural choice—should be considered an influencer. Through the development of the argument, writers will share information about their selected individual.

The purpose of this unit is for students to reflect on what it means to have a positive influence on community, society, or industry. Students will make determinations about what it means to be influential and be invited to evaluate their connections to influencers on social media. Are the people we follow examples of how we should lead? Students will also work through the writing process to craft a narrative nonfiction feature article about a person of their choice. They will employ argument writing and narrative writing techniques to present a strong case for why their person of choice should be considered an influencer in their respective field.	By the end of the unit, students will work through the writing process to craft a narrative nonfiction article about a person of their choice. Students will create a representation of their argument in a modality of their choice (for example, a brief documentary video, a recorded interview, a presentation, or a digital poster).

Language	**Future-Ready Skills**	**Identity**
• Students will write a feature article. • Students may gather information by discussing, interviewing, reading, watching videos, listening to podcasts, and so forth.	• Lifelong learning strategies • Analytical thinking • Leadership and social influence • Technological literacy • Resilience and flexibility • Artificial intelligence use	• Students choose an influencer to study and evaluate from their personal life, social media, or industry. • Students reflect on their own ideas of what it means to be an influencer and write based on that meaning. • Students share their own relationship to the person they choose to write about relative to leadership and being a follower.

Community	**Multimodal Meaning-Making**
• Students may choose a writing topic from a community they belong to. • Students will post their article on a class website. The website will be modeled after the digital *Time* publication. • Students will have a writing partner throughout the writing process.	• Students will create a representation of their argument in a modality of their choice (for example, a brief documentary video, a recorded interview, a presentation, or a digital poster). • Students may gather information by discussing, interviewing, reading, watching videos, listening to podcasts, and so forth.

FIGURE 4.5: The power of the influencer unit of study framework.

LESSON PLAN

Figure 4.6 depicts a lesson plan for a writing unit on the power of an influencer. This lesson occurs during the *generating and collecting ideas* stage of the writing process. It is not necessarily the first lesson in the unit. The lesson plan serves as an example of how to plan a writing lesson within the revolving literacy framework lesson plan.

Lesson Plan Thinking Map		
Connections for Learning		
Context: Why is today's lesson important to the work in the current unit of study?	This lesson supports students in generating and collecting ideas for writing, of which there are many ways. One way is to create charts or mind maps. As the thinking grows within the chart or mind map, a writing topic eventually emerges. Writers think during this process about what they connect to most. The lesson invites students to make personal and cultural connections in the beginning of the writing process to support engagement and enthusiasm.	
Relevance: How does this lesson connect to future-ready skills, students' lives outside of school, or skills they may use in other areas of learning?	**Future-Ready Skills:** • Lifelong learning strategies: Create a two-toned chart to represent different approaches to thinking about a central idea (students can also use this strategy for generating and planning ideas in other disciplines). • Leadership and social influence: While students are not exercising leadership or social influence in this particular lesson, they are considering these qualities in others and providing reasoning as to why one would be deemed a leader or influencer. **Connections:** • Students generate ideas about influencers after discussing the influencers they follow or see on social media during previous lessons. • The lesson invites students to make personal and cultural connections to the idea of an influencer.	
Connections for Literacy Instruction		
Language: Which domains of language are targeted in instruction and application of learning?	**Future-Ready Skills:** What future-ready skills are students developing?	**Identity:** How can students personally connect to this lesson?
Informal writing supports students generating ideas.	**Lifelong-Learning Strategy:** Create a two-toned chart to represent different approaches to thinking about a central idea (students can also use this strategy for generating and planning ideas in other disciplines.)	In this lesson, students list influencers in their personal lives with anecdotes. They also list influencers from the broader culture and society who they are interested in with anecdotes.

FIGURE 4.6: The power of the influencer lesson plan thinking map.

continued ▶

Connections for Literacy Instruction		
	Leadership and Social Influence: While students are not exercising leadership or social influence in this particular lesson, they are considering these qualities in others and providing reasoning as to why one would be deemed a leader or influencer.	
Community: How are students participating in a community of learners within the classroom? How is their work contributing to a larger community outside of the classroom? How is community influencing the work at hand?	**Multimodal Meaning-Making:** What modalities are students making meaning *from*? What modalities are students using to make meaning and demonstrate understanding?	
Students share their initial ideas with their writing partners, with some time left in the class period to add to their charts based on what they learned about their partner's list.	Students are creating a two-toned chart for idea organization. Some students may reference video or images for ideas.	

Intention	
Objective (an intention for teachers): What is the goal for students to accomplish by the end of the lesson?	Students will learn that writers have many ways of generating and collecting ideas for writing. One way is to create charts or mind maps. As the thinking grows within the chart or mind map, a writing topic eventually emerges. Writers think during this process about what they connect to most. Students will generate ideas for their feature article about an influencer. Students will list influencers in their personal lives with information they can recall about those people. Students will list influencers from culture, social media, or industry with information they can recall about those people.
Focus Statement (an intention for students): Ask students to state their objective in the first person as a way to take ownership of their learning.	I will generate ideas for my influencer feature article creating a chart. I will attach public and personal figures to my definition of an influencer and list what I know about these people from my personal experiences, prior reading, and brief internet searches. Creating a chart helps document and organize initial ideas.
Standards: What standards does the lesson address?	[Insert your state's standards here.]

Explicit Instruction	
Tools and Texts: What resources and instructional materials are needed for this lesson? What is the teacher using to teach? What are students using or working with?	Students need a writer's notebook or digital file for writing.
Whole-Class Instruction: Describe the lesson. What instructional strategy or strategies will you use? Why did you select that instructional technique? How does it help accomplish the goal of the lesson?	Check or highlight the methods used in this lesson: ☑ Think-aloud ☑ Demonstration ☐ Use of a mentor text ☐ Use of a demonstration text ☐ Show and explain ☐ Shared experience ☐ Media with active engagement

Whole-Class Instruction: Describe the lesson. What instructional strategy or strategies will you use? Why did you select that instructional technique? How does it help accomplish the goal of the lesson?	**Describe the lesson:** The teacher will explain that creating a chart and using digital color tools help document and organize initial ideas for writing. The teacher will think aloud about what it means to be an influencer and list people from their personal life who could be considered an influencer. The teacher informs the class about one or two examples while listing what they know about the person relative to them being influencers. The teacher will repeat this process for influencers of culture, society, and industry.
	My definition of influencer:
		Influencers in my personal life	What do I know about this person?	Influencers of culture and society	What do I know about this person?
	|---|---|---|---
	Students may use the internet as a tool
	The teacher will invite the students to create the chart like the one used for demonstration. The teacher invites students to engage in similar thinking protocols to the ones demonstrated.
Guided or Independent Practice: Describe what students are doing after whole-class instruction. Share your conference or small-group instruction plan.	**Describe what students are doing after whole-class instruction. What scaffolds and supports are in place for students who are in need?** Students will add ideas to their influencer chart. Students may consult videos, images, or articles for reference. After five minutes, the teacher will invite students to turn and talk with their writing partner to share about one person in each of their charts. This is to support students in getting started with generating ideas. After each partner shares, students will return to their writing.
	Share your conference or small-group instruction plan. What scaffolds, strategies, or tools will you use to support students you meet with? What is the purpose for meeting with these students? **Small-group plan:** The teacher will meet with student A, student B, and student C to support them in their thinking about influencers from culture, society, or industry. In prior writing units, students demonstrated the need for support in generating ideas and self-starting. The teacher will use passions to guide students in their thinking. On a small whiteboard, the teacher will model with the passion of sports and think aloud, "Who in the sports industry is an influencer? What do I know about them?" The teacher will invite students to co-create this list and encourage them to follow a similar process when working on their own chart.
Reflection and Next Steps	
Daily Closure: How will you close the lesson to help future teacher or student planning? See table 3.2 (page 77) for closure options.	With eight to ten minutes left in the class period, students will turn and talk with their writing partner again to share additional ideas. Students should listen with the intention of gaining an idea from their partner to add to their chart. The teacher will invite students to add to their charts based on something that their partner shared.

continued ▶

Reflection and Next Steps	
After the Lesson: Evaluate the level of student engagement and the student work.	**Based on your observations, name areas where the lesson was successful and where students were successful.** Students were able to create their own charts for generated ideas. Some students modified the chart shown in the explicit instruction portion to represent their own ways of thinking. All students were able to identify people of influence. Personal and cultural influencers varied among students.
	Based on your observations, what is needed in future instruction? I will share another strategy for generating ideas for writing. Although all students were able to participate in this lesson, new ideas for writing may surface with another tool for generating ideas.
	Based on your observations, did students connect with the context and relevance of the lesson? Were they aware of how their work was part of a process to develop the named future-ready skill? Students understood that this lesson was one way to generate ideas for writing. Part of future learning will be to raise awareness that there are multiple ways of generating ideas and are often personal to the writer. This is something to continue to work on—slowing down the process. I asked students to think about a long-term project they are working on in their personal lives or in another academic area and how they are generating ideas for that project. I invited students to try one of the strategies from this unit and to report back.

Summary

We explored several aspects of writing instruction in this chapter.

- Why do students write?
- What do students write?
- Connections between literacy instruction and writing opportunities
- How do students write?
- Writing and future-ready skills
- Writing in the era of artificial intelligence

While we study each of these individually to develop deep understanding, it is helpful to think about your approach to planning and executing writing instruction as a sum of these parts. Your values and beliefs within each aspect influence your values and beliefs about the others. Consider using the chart in the following Stop and Think to engage in your own metacognition about writing instruction, just as we explored the power of inviting students to think about their thinking throughout the writing process.

At First . . .
Share your thoughts about the topic prior to reading this chapter.

And Now . . .
Share how this chapter has influenced your thinking.

Next Steps
What actions will you or your team take in response to reading this chapter?

Why do students write? Who sets the intention?

At First . . .	And Now . . .	Next Steps

What do students write? Do the writing opportunities students have in coursework prioritize real-life application?

At First . . .	And Now . . .	Next Steps

What is the relationship between literacy (language, future-ready skills, identity, community, and multimodal meaning-making) and writing opportunities for students?

At First . . .	And Now . . .	Next Steps

continued ▶

> How do students write? When and how are students working through the full writing process during the school year?

At First . . .	And Now . . .	Next Steps

> What is the relationship between writing instruction and future-ready skill development? How does the writing process help to foster future-ready skills?

At First . . .	And Now . . .	Next Steps

> What is the relationship between writing instruction and artificial intelligence? How might literacy educators think differently about aspects of the writing process relative to artificial intelligence?

At First . . .	And Now . . .	Next Steps

*Visit **go.SolutionTree.com/literacy** for a free reproducible version of this reflection.*

After connecting with your own reflections, consider using figure 4.7 to plan opportunities for students to work through the writing process throughout a school year within a grade level.

Grade Level:			School Year:	
	Genre	Genre	Genre	Genre
What **standards** are addressed?				
What **future-ready skills** are explicitly taught?				
How are students encouraged to make **identity** connections through writing?				
How are students encouraged to make **community** connections through writing?				
What opportunities do students have to make meaning through **multiple modalities**?				

FIGURE 4.7: Revolving literacy writing opportunities planning tool.

*Visit **go.SolutionTree.com/literacy** for a free reproducible version of this figure.*

You may also use the reproducibles "Revolving Literacy Writing Articulation Planning Tool for Grades 7–12" (page 123), "Revolving Literacy Writing Articulation Planning Tool for Grades 7–9" (page 125) and "Revolving Literacy Writing Articulation Planning Tool for Grades 9–12" (page 126) to plan the opportunities for students to work through the writing process throughout a school year across grade levels to aid in articulation conversations. Those reproducibles can help to ensure all genres are accounted for and balance the writing opportunities a student has across their secondary English experience.

Explanations of Each Stage of the Revolving Literacy Writing Process

This reproducible outlines and explains the stages of the writing process with methodologies for navigating each writing stage with students. Use this as a guide for intentional and efficient planning and as a reference tool while working through the writing process stages.

Generate and Collect Ideas
What happens during this stage?
• Writers identify potential topics or ideas to study and write about within the genre. • Writers collect ideas from interest inventories, reading, mind maps, heart maps, and so forth. • Writers may create thinking webs and concept maps, make lists, sketch or draw ideas, or design charts. • Writers share ideas with a writing partner to help ideas unfold. The teacher should model various strategies to think about potential writing topics.
Where does the work happen?
• A writer's notebook • A digital file used for generating and collecting ideas
How long does it take?
• Writers should spend two to four class periods generating and collecting ideas. Each day, the teacher reveals a different strategy for writers to practice generating ideas for writing. By prolonging the start of the process, the teacher shows students that there are multiple ways to arrive at a topic or idea for writing.
How does the work happen?
• Where do ideas come from? Invite students to consider where ideas come from for writing and creating. Teach students to develop a relationship with their thinking. Ideas come from personal experiences, interests, media, social media, reading, and conversations. Invite students to connect to where they get ideas from and sketch them out on paper. • Write seed stories. Invite students to visit their Me Map (see chapter 2, page 29), interest inventory, or other writing they have done in English class or other classes to identify potential topics of interest for writing. Students should choose to write seed stories (anecdotes) about a few of the ideas on their map or inventory that are related to the genre in which they are writing. Seed stories contain just a few sentences. They help writers initiate thinking about a particular topic or area of interest. • Use images to spark thinking. Invite students to scroll through pictures on their phones to draw connections between potential personal topics and the genre they are writing. The teacher may also show a series of images or media clips representing various areas of study to aid students in generating ideas of interest related to the genre.

Narrow Ideas by Tinkering and Playing

What happens during this stage?

Writers identify two to three topics from their work that they are interested in writing about during the generating and collecting ideas stage. They spend time thinking more about these ideas in the context of the genre or assignment they are engaged in.

Where does the work happen?

- A writer's notebook
- A digital file used for generating, collecting, and tinkering with ideas

How long does it take?

Writers should spend two to three days narrowing down ideas. Each day, the teacher reveals a different strategy for writers to practice becoming more familiar with topics so they can make an informed choice for writing.

How does the work happen?

- **Read to learn more:** Invite students to read about potential writing topics. They should design a note-taking tool to record interesting or compelling information about potential topics. Learning more can help in the decision-making process of choosing a writing topic.
- **Write to learn more:** Writers often express interest in topics, but when they sit down to write, it is not something they are passionate about exploring further through writing. Invite students to write "long" about the two to three topics they are considering without any structure. They should see where their writing takes them and let the ideas unfold on the page. Assure students that the writing is meant to be exploratory, not formal.
- **Try it out by creating outlines:** Invite students to create an outline for each topic to plan the structure for each potential writing piece. Seeing the writing mapped out may help writers decide which topic they want to explore further.

Choose an Idea

What happens during this stage?

Writers look over their prevision work and select a topic for writing.

Where does the work happen?

The space where the prevision work was done.

How long does it take?

Writers should spend one class session or part of a class session selecting an idea. Teachers may invite writers to submit a reflection about the process of selecting a topic to write about. A reflection provides an opportunity for students to connect to the skills they developed while generating ideas and future-ready skills that they could carry into other areas of work.

How does the work happen?

- **Choose with intention:** Teachers may model thinking that shows intentionality when selecting a project to work on. Teachers may model self-reflection questions like the following.
  + Which topic is most important for me to spend time writing about?
  + Which topic do I connect with most?

- + Which topic am I most interested in?
- + Which topic will hold my attention?
- + Which topic has the potential to offer me something new to think about?
- **Stop and think:** Students pause to look back on the work they've completed thus far in the writing process. They identify which strategies were helpful to them in generating and narrowing ideas and reflect on how they ultimately made their choice about a writing topic. Students also make explicit connections to the future-ready skills that have been noted in the lessons prior to this point in the process.

Explore the Idea

What happens during this stage?

Writers collect information about their topics. Information may come from credible sources, such as research journals, images, interviews, articles, books, and well-vetted other media, including social media. The genre will dictate how writers dive deeper into a topic.

Where does the work happen?

- A writer's notebook
- A digital file that contains writing from the prevision work

How long does it take?

The genre may dictate how long writers work in the exploratory stage. Nonfiction work may require time (several days) for writers to read through sources, gather information while note taking, and so forth. Creative fiction writing may require time (several days) for writers to develop plotlines, character profiles, and the like. Narrative or personal essay writing may require less time to gather information and more time to create outlines, thinking maps, or personal organizers.

How does the work happen?

- **Give one, get one:** Teachers give students one version of a graphic organizer to help with note taking and collecting information. Students then develop their own version of a graphic organizer that fits their style of thinking and note-taking organization. This allows for personalization of work style in this part of the writing process.
- **Track information through a timeline:** Students create a timeline of events as they gather information about their writing topic. This may be taught as a form of note taking.
- **Partner talk to find out more:** Students share the information they collect with a partner during discussion. The partner poses questions in response to invite the writer to consider various perspectives or notice when they need a piece of information to craft a comprehensive message.

Draft

What happens during this stage?

- Writers write to figure out what their message is and how to articulate it clearly and cohesively.
- Writers use planning tools created during the prevision stage.
- Writers may write with structure and organization in mind but know that they will return to the structure and organization of the piece during the revision stage.

Where does the work happen?
- A digital file
- A modality similar to the final product (for example, a presentation tool or digital design tool).
How long does it take?
Writers spend several days drafting. Teachers host writing conferences to support students as they draft.
How does the work happen?
- **Write more, think less:** Of course, students need to think while drafting, but writers prioritize volume and ideas when initially drafting. Set a timer and encourage students to write with minimal interruptions to get all their ideas on the page or screen.
- **Write in chunks:** Students use the planning tools they created to determine the parts or sections of their writing. Students plan to write in chunks to make the process manageable and avoid getting overwhelmed by writing volume.

Revise

What happens during this stage?
- Writers study their drafts with focus areas to bring clarity to meaning: ideas, organization, voice, word choice, and sentence fluency.
- Writers change aspects of the writing, add ideas, remove ideas, restructure ideas, evaluate vocabulary and word choice, adjust the tone of the writing, and so on.
- Writers develop resilience and flexibility as part of the process.
Where does the work happen?
The draft of the writing
How long does it take?
Writers spend about four to five class periods in the revision stage. During the explicit instruction portions of the lessons, the teacher models a series of revision strategies that students try out in their writing.
How does the work happen?
- **RADaR:** Students use the following RADaR acronym to remember all parts of the revision process.
+ **R**eplace words that are not specific, don't evoke the right tone or message, or are repetitive. Replace sentences that are unclear, too complex, or passive.
+ **A**dd new information, descriptions, explanations, transitions, and connections between ideas.
+ **D**elete unrelated ideas, unnecessary words, ideas that repeat too much, and ideas that don't support your overall message.
+ **R**eorder words, sentences, or paragraphs for clarity.
- **Peer revision:** Students work with their writing partner to revise written work. Partners learn how to provide feedback for revision and language to push their partner's thinking. Partners may use a digital comment tool to share comments on each other's writing.

Edit

What happens during this stage?

- Writers study their drafts with focus areas to bring clarity to meaning in conventions and layout.
- Writers check for appropriate grammar, capitalization, punctuation, syntax, spelling, references, and citations.

Where does the work happen?

The draft of the writing

How long does it take?

Writers spend about one to two class periods in the editing stage. During the explicit instruction portion of the lessons, the teacher models a series of editing strategies that students try out in their writing. The teacher may also clarify proper conventions in writing.

How does the work happen?

- **Use a checklist:** Provide students with a checklist of items for editing. Students can use the checklist while writing or after writing.
- **Read, reread, and read again:** Writing tends to look different each time you look at it. Students plan to read their writing three different times on three different days for the purpose of editing. They should make corrections each time they read with fresh eyes.
- **Peer editing:** Students work with their writing partner to edit written work. Partners may use checklists or tools provided by the teacher for guidance. Partners have a conversation about necessary edits.

Submit and Share

What happens during this stage?

- Writers officially submit their work to the teacher.
- Writers share their work with writing partners.
- Writers share their work in a whole-class celebration.
- Writers share their work with a community outside of the classroom.

Where does the work happen?

- Writers may submit and share within the classroom or with a community outside of the classroom.
- Teachers may consider using an online management system like Google Classroom for online submissions.

How long does it take?

The amount of time will be determined by the way in which the teacher decides to bring closure to the unit of study.

How does the work happen?

The following are ways to share and celebrate.

- **Socratic seminar:** A student initiates a Socratic seminar about their topic of study. The student may use key ideas or findings in their writing to facilitate conversation and gauge others' ideas in response to their own.

- **Museum gallery walk:** Students share an artifact of their writing in a print or digital museum gallery. Students write a museum card to describe what they are sharing.
- **Website:** Students post their writing on a shared class website. Platforms like Google Sites allow for multiple contributors to work on a site simultaneously. The teacher may also manage the site.
- **Share within the school:** When appropriate and with permission from school leaders, students share their writing in school spaces. For example, reviews of a school musical may appear on a digital scroll in an auditorium or library area. A student may also submit their writing to a school newspaper or literary publication. A student may also submit writing related to a school issue to a school leader.
- **Share within a community space:** When appropriate and with permission from school leaders, students share their writing in community spaces. Students may submit writing to a local community newspaper. Students may also submit their writing to community organizations with a particular cause.
- **Partner share:** Students share key ideas and passages from their writing with a partner. Partners follow a feedback protocol during and after listening. Students may use the following feedback sentence starters.
  + An interesting idea you shared is . . .
  + Something that's got me curious is . . .
  + A question I have is . . .
  + I appreciate the way you . . .

Reflect

What happens during this stage?

- Writers reflect on the progress and development of their writing from working through all the stages of the writing process.
- Writers also reflect on their growth as a writer by identifying the skills for writing and productivity they learned. They should make explicit connections to applications of those skills in academic, professional, and personal areas of work.

Where does the work happen?

A personal reflection space (notebook or digital file)

How long does it take?

Writers may spend one to two class periods developing a reflection. Teachers may choose to incorporate this into at-home work.

How does the work happen?

The following are examples of reflection prompts.

- An aspect of my identity that is connected to this writing piece is . . .
- My personal connection helped me to develop my writing by . . .
- Making choices about my writing helped my process by . . .
- A challenging choice I had to make while writing was . . .
- The way I chose to present or share my writing was important to the overall meaning because . . .

- *I developed [insert future-ready skill here] by...*
- *An aspect of [insert future-ready skill here] I need more practice in is _____ because...*
- *Through this writing process, I learned _____. I can use this in other areas of learning by...*
- *I developed [insert future-ready skill here] through this writing process. This will help me in the future because...*
- *The future-ready skills I learned throughout this process are _____. I can use these skills in other classes when... I can use these skills at work when... I can use these skills outside of school when...*

The Connection Between Stages of the Writing Process and Future-Ready Skills

This reproducible explains how each stage of the writing process connects to future-ready skills. it describes how students foster future-ready skills within each stage, making this reproducible a useful guide for developing lesson plans and reflection tools for students.

Generate and Collect Ideas

- **Creative thinking:** Writers begin the process of choosing a topic to write about. Writers begin the process of determining the purpose and audience for writing. They start the creative process.
- **Technological literacy:** Writers use technology (digital tools and the internet) to explore ideas for topic selection.
- **Curiosity:** Writers generate ideas for writing that they want to know more about or want to explore.
- **Artificial intelligence use:** Writers may query artificial intelligence as a starting point for ideas to consider. AI can be a writing partner.
- **Resilience and flexibility:** Generating and collecting ideas may be challenging for some writers. Writers need patience to try multiple strategies to arrive at a topic that has meaning and significance. Writers are flexible in their approaches.
- **Systems thinking:** Writers are working within a system—the system of writing. Writers are at the beginning of a multifaceted process and will begin to think about how the first stage relates to the stages that follow.
- **Lifelong learning strategies:** Writers use a series of strategies for and approaches to generating and collecting ideas that they could apply to other contexts when starting a project.
- **Motivation and self-awareness:** Writers are in a state of negotiation with themselves throughout the writing process. Writing takes time. Writing takes patience and the will to approach writing through different lenses and strategies.

Narrow Ideas by Tinkering and Playing

- **Analytical thinking:** Writers engage in analysis when considering topics and ideas. Writers select topics that are meaningful and appropriate for the task or genre. Writers may consider information from reading source material during the generating and collecting ideas stage.
- **Creative thinking:** Writers continue the process of choosing a topic to write about. Writers consider authenticity and the potential of offering new ideas relative to the task, genre, or purpose for writing.
- **Technological literacy:** Writers use technology (digital tools and the internet) to learn more about potential writing topics.
- **Curiosity:** Writers' curiosity is high at this stage. Writers are closer to choosing a topic and are learning more about potential options.

- **Resilience and flexibility:** Writers remain flexible in their thinking as they narrow down ideas from initial brainstorming. Writers also remain patient as they engage in thinking protocols for selecting a writing topic.
- **Systems thinking:** Writers are working within a system—the system of writing. Writers are at the beginning of a multifaceted process and will begin to think about how this stage is leading them to focus on their writing.
- **Lifelong learning strategies:** Writers develop ways to narrow ideas. They may read, create charts, or design thinking maps to organize information.
- **Motivation and self-awareness:** Writers stay motivated to tinker and play with a few ideas before choosing one. They may become aware that they want to select an idea right away instead of slowing down during this stage.

Choose an Idea

- **Creative thinking:** Writers select a topic that they are passionate about and can offer new thinking to the task, genre, or purpose for writing.
- **Resilience and flexibility:** Writers may choose a topic that they didn't originally consider. Writers consider topics for various reasons.
- **Systems thinking:** Writers realize that they needed to think through the first two stages of the writing process to be confident in this stage. They learn that this stage is pivotal in the process.
- **Lifelong learning strategies:** Writers participate in a decision-making process for selecting a writing topic.
- **Motivation and self-awareness:** Writers develop a new interest as they select a topic. This stage serves as fuel for exploring the idea and drafting.

Explore the Idea

- **Analytical thinking:** Writers read and discuss information about their topics. Writers make determinations about the significance of source material and new learning about their topics.
- **Technological literacy:** Writers use the internet, research databases, and digital tools to access information for writing.
- **Curiosity:** Writers approach this stage with newfound questions and interests now that they have a focus for writing. Their curiosity is often what leads them through this stage.
- **Resilience, flexibility, reasoning, and problem solving:** Writers may be challenged by collecting information and thinking about a topic for writing. Writers may experience writer's block. Writers may not initially find source material that is relevant. Writers develop plans for overcoming such obstacles.
- **Systems thinking:** Writers make a connection between exploring an idea and drafting. The work they do in this stage supports them in developing their draft with content.
- **Lifelong learning strategies:** Writers develop tools for collecting ideas and information. Writers learn how to navigate source material. Writers develop personal work plans.
- **Motivation and self-awareness:** Writers may reflect on their motivation level. Are they excited about writing? Are they fatigued by the preparatory work? They can develop an awareness of their work productivity and how they feel throughout the process.

Draft

- **Creative thinking:** Writers share their messages in authentic ways. Writers structure their writing in ways that are creative and authentic to the purpose of writing. Writers share their own voice and insights.
- **Resilience, flexibility, motivation, and self-awareness:** Writers may experience writer's block. Writers may be challenged by how to articulate ideas. Writers may need to develop stamina. Writers develop strategies to navigate such obstacles during the drafting process.
- **Systems thinking:** Writers learn that this stage marks a turning point in their writing. It is the first time that they are compiling ideas in a cohesive way as they develop their message throughout.
- **Lifelong learning strategies:** Writers develop personal plans for drafting. Writers use planning tools created during previous stages of the writing process to aid in the drafting process.

Revise and Edit

- **Technological literacy and artificial intelligence use:** Writers may use artificial intelligence to gain feedback, ideas for revision, and suggestions for editing. AI can be a writing partner.
- **Active listening:** Writers may receive feedback from the teacher or peers during writing conferences. Writers need to listen with intent so they can further develop their writing using the feedback.
- **Resilience, flexibility, lifelong learning strategies, motivation, and self-awareness:** Writers exercise patience in revisiting their writing multiple times to restructure it, add to it, and change it. Writers use multiple strategies for revision depending on the genre. Writers try out different techniques and make decisions about their writing to ensure that they are clearly communicating meaning and messaging.
- **Systems thinking:** Writers are keen to know how the earlier stages of the writing process created a foundation for them to now approach their writing with craft and technique.

Submit and Share

- **Leadership and social influence:** Writers may offer a solution or new idea relative to a personal issue or community concern. This depends on the genre for writing. Writers present their writing to other writers or community members to share personal thoughts and new thinking.
- **Technological literacy:** Writers may compose digitally. Writers may submit and share their work via a digital classroom management tool. Writers may use a digital tool to write and create.
- **Empathy and active listening:** Writers participate in their writing community. They listen as other people share their work. They connect with their writing partners. They empathize with ideas that other writers convey through their writing.
- **Resilience, flexibility, motivation, and self-awareness:** Writers may make decisions about how to share their writing in a way that makes their messaging powerful. Writers may be challenged by sharing their writing with a larger community.
- **Systems thinking:** Writers develop an understanding of the relationship between all stages of the writing process and their contribution to developing a cohesive, meaningful piece of writing.
- **Lifelong learning strategies:** See earlier notes in other skill areas within this stage.

Reflect
- **Analytical thinking:** Writers consider what they have learned and how they learned throughout the writing process. Writers decide what was most impactful about their experience. Writers reflect on the challenges they faced throughout the writing process and how they overcame challenges. Writers determine the skills they learned that they can transfer to other academic and personal spaces.
- **Resilience, flexibility, motivation, and self-awareness:** Writers consider this skill area in their reflection. See earlier notes.
- **Lifelong learning strategies and systems thinking:** Writers learn that reflection is part of any learning process. Writers reflect on the strategies they learned throughout the writing process that helped them to internalize the skills they practiced.

Revolving Literacy Writing Articulation Planning Tool for Grades 7–12

Use this as a tool when articulating writing experiences across grades 7–12. The questions included are intended to guide planning.

Revolving Literacy Components	Grade 7	Grade 8	Grade 9	Grade 10	Grade 11	Grade 12
What **genres of writing** are included in the scope and sequence?						
What **standards** are addressed?						
What **future-ready skills** are explicitly taught?						

page 1 of 2

Revolving Literacy Components	Grade 7	Grade 8	Grade 9	Grade 10	Grade 11	Grade 12
How are students encouraged to make **identity** connections through writing?						
How are students encouraged to make **community** connections through writing?						
What opportunities do students have to make meaning through **multiple modalities**?						

Revolving Literacy Writing Articulation Planning Tool for Grades 7–9

Use this as a tool when articulating writing experiences across grades 7–9. The questions included are intended to guide planning.

Revolving Literacy Components	Grade 7	Grade 8	Grade 9
What **genres of writing** are included in the scope and sequence?			
What **standards** are addressed?			
What **future-ready skills** are explicitly taught?			
How are students encouraged to make **identity** connections through writing?			
How are students encouraged to make **community** connections through writing?			
What opportunities do students have to make meaning through **multiple modalities**?			

Revolving Literacy © 2025 Solution Tree Press • SolutionTree.com
Visit **go.SolutionTree.com/literacy** to download this free reproducible.

Revolving Literacy Writing Articulation Planning Tool for Grades 9–12

Use this as a tool when articulating writing experiences across grades 9–12. The questions included are intended to guide planning.

Revolving Literacy Components	Grade 9	Grade 10	Grade 11	Grade 12
What **genres of writing** are included in the scope and sequence?				
What **standards** are addressed?				
What **future-ready skills** are explicitly taught?				
How are students encouraged to make **identity** connections through writing?				
How are students encouraged to make **community** connections through writing?				
What opportunities do students have to make meaning through **multiple modalities**?				

Revolving Literacy © 2025 Solution Tree Press • SolutionTree.com
Visit **go.SolutionTree.com/literacy** to download this free reproducible.

CHAPTER 5

TEACHING RESEARCHERS IN THE REVOLVING LITERACY CLASSROOM

When I was a middle-level English teacher, my students spent the last quarter of the school year engaged in research. How I approached research evolved over time. I adjusted my planning each year as I learned more about the process, the ways in which students experienced the stages of research, and the skills that the research process required. One factor that remained constant in my approach to teaching research was student choice. Whether the unit was designed around a research question or research topic, my students selected what they wanted to study and how they wanted to write about it.

When I was a new teacher, I met with my supervisor, the English curriculum director, twice a month to discuss planning, instruction, and my reflections on teaching and learning. These conversations were integral to my growth as a literacy educator. During my first-year teaching research, I met with my supervisor, glowing with excitement, to tell him about the vast topics my students had chosen to research: the state of Louisiana, Michael Jordan, the Great Barrier Reef, the evolution of Mickey Mouse, Great Danes, Jim Carrey, Greek mythology, manatees, and . . . makeup. Yes, makeup. One of my students, Fiona, wanted to do a research project on the application of cosmetics.

When I got to Fiona's topic, my supervisor stopped me and said, "Do you really think the student will be able to do in-depth research about makeup? What do you think about guiding her to choose something more academic?" I paused with frustration and fear. I was frustrated because I'd had a research conference with Fiona that week, and we discussed a comprehensive outline to her process with appropriate source material for her reading. Fiona explained to me that her aunt was a cosmetologist, and she, too, might one day want to apply makeup to actors on television sets. Makeup was part of Fiona's identity. It was a connection to her family. It was an art that she was interested in pursuing, and she chose to learn more about this personal endeavor in my class! What more could a literacy educator want?

Despite this, I was also fearful. I thought, "Should I go against what I philosophically believe (and what research says) about engaging students in learning because my supervisor suggested it? Will I be in danger of losing my job because I disagree with the powers that be? Does learning always have to be very academic in school for it to matter?" I decided to remain professional and explained why it would be best for Fiona to continue researching makeup. I gave reasons supported by research and was able to speak to my own anecdotal notes about my process in coaching Fiona. I also told my supervisor that in addition to a formal research paper as a unit product, I offered Fiona the opportunity to do my makeup at the end of our research unit so she could apply all that she learned about technique, color, and design as a result of her research. My supervisor trusted my rationale.

Fiona did exactly that. When we finished our research work, Fiona attended an extra help session after school to do my makeup. Fiona's classmates were intrigued by this opportunity and joined the extra help session to watch her. Not only did this makeup endeavor connect to Fiona's family community, but her passion for learning also captured the attention of peers. This learning event initiated community building within our class. While Fiona was applying the makeup, she was able to tell me and her classmates why she was making the choices she was making. She made claims about the relationships between my skin tone and the shape of my facial features in relation to the colors and techniques she was choosing. She was able to provide reasoning for her choices and explain what she learned through reading and watching demonstration videos during the research process. This is an experience I will never forget and one that impacted my trajectory as an educator.

I often tell this story. Years later, a high school English teacher approached me and informed me that she was Fiona's college essay adviser. Fiona had included the makeup story in her college essay about people and experiences that allowed her to find her identities and passions. She wrote about how she had the opportunity to study something she was passionate about in her English class and how she would never forget being able to apply makeup to her teacher. I wasn't the only one impacted by the power of student choice and authenticity in learning.

I share this story here because it's one to keep in mind as we move through this chapter on the research process in secondary English classrooms. Fiona's experience is one type of research endeavor. The process this chapter describes can support various purposes for research with different outcomes. As I shared in chapter 3 (page 73), the revolving literacy framework is designed for process instruction. Committing to teaching a process (writing, research, reading) allows teachers to adjust content and desired outcomes to ensure curriculum stays relevant to students' interests and the skills they need for postsecondary pathways.

The National Academies of Sciences, Engineering, and Medicine's 2018 report on how people learn indicates that teachers should support conceptual understanding, engagement, and motivation by designing relevant, problem-oriented tasks that combine explicit instruction on key ideas with well-designed inquiry opportunities that use multiple modalities for learning. Throughout this chapter, we explore how students' engagement in research requires explicit instruction in skill areas that transcend multiple disciplines and contexts. We also explore how the five components of literacy development—language, future-ready skills, identity, community, and multimodal meaning-making—fuel the research process in secondary English classrooms. Student-generated inquiry makes the work relevant to students and potentially the communities they belong to.

Research and Its Relevance

In chapter 4 (page 87), we explored the revolving literacy writing process. Although the process is complex, teachers prepare students for success by prioritizing the five components of literacy development within the process. Teachers also prepare students by implementing productive, research-supported strategies like explicit instruction (Darling-Hammond et al., 2020), designing meaningful work that builds on students' prior knowledge and experiences (Cantor, Osher, Berg, Steyer, & Rose, 2018), and engaging students in rich tasks that help them achieve conceptual understanding and transferable knowledge and skills (Cantor et al., 2018). The process is the learning.

Another process that is imperative to developing authentic literacy practices and future readiness is research. According to the *Oxford English Dictionary*, *research* is the systematic investigation into and study of materials and sources to establish facts and reach new conclusions (Research, 2024). In the secondary English classroom, research instruction involves coaching students to engage in a systematic process of discovering answers, new meanings, and more questions. One of the goals is to establish a process with students so they can apply what they learn in other disciplines and have authentic research experiences. In postsecondary school, careers, and personal endeavors, research is often an independent task. We want to prepare students to be strategic, thoughtful, and systematic in their independence.

The research process is integrated into academic, professional, and social spaces. It may not follow the same sequence of process steps in all contexts, but research skills transcend context. Let's look at a few examples in table 5.1.

TABLE 5.1: Research in Academic, Professional, and Social Spaces

Research in Academic Spaces	Research in Professional Spaces	Research in Social Spaces
• Investigate an assigned topic or question connected to a unit within a discipline of study through a formal research paper or project presentation • Investigate a choice topic or question related to a discipline of study through a formal research paper or project presentation • Investigate a career path • Investigate a college path	• **Culinary:** Determine how mixing certain food ingredients may impact the outcome of a recipe • **Law:** Discover precedents that may impact the construction of a case • **Finance:** Study financial trends and how they may impact financial decisions in personal or corporate finance • **Social media influencer:** Evaluate how different social media platforms may impact viewership and what the influencer works to sell or share • **Home construction:** Investigate the cost and construction of materials for home projects to offer customers a fair price for materials and labor	• **Dining:** Choose a restaurant by reading reviews, social media postings, menus, location information, and dietary and allergy accommodations • **Travel:** Design an itinerary with activities, meals, and transportation • **Living space:** Make decisions about moving to a new location or moving into a new living space • **Transportation:** Make decisions about transportation (purchasing a car, using public transportation, and so on) • **Purchasing:** Investigate potential purchases by reading reviews, studying prices, and so on

Stop and Think

Identify spaces where you engage in the research process. You may consider sharing these examples with students during the context and relevance portions of lessons.

Academic spaces (current or past):

Professional spaces:

Personal spaces:

Visit **go.SolutionTree.com/literacy** *for a free reproducible version of this reflection.*

Stages of the Research Process

Conducting research involves exploring a research question or topic as well as participating in a research community. Scholars share research within their field through conversation, presentations, and citations of published work in academic spaces. Professionals share research with supervisors or research teams to advance a project. Individuals may share research with peers, friends, and family via conversation, social media, or other platforms in Social spaces. Belonging and contributing to a community is part of what defines the research process. Students can experience this in their English classrooms. Research teams enhance the work of individuals even when the product of a task or project is not designed to be collaborative. Developing a community of learners, or researchers, within the classroom helps teachers manage the classroom because students feel more connected and peers offer greater assistance and collaboration, gaining in competence and agency (Darling-Hammond et al., 2020).

The Consistency Management and Cooperative Discipline® model is a well-researched example of the effectiveness of a shared learning space between teachers and students (Brophy & Freiberg, 1999; Freiberg, Huzinec, & Templeton, 2009). This model builds shared responsibility for learning and classroom organization between teachers and students, similar to how Schlam Salman & Inbar-Lourie (2023) define future readiness. Together, teachers and students develop procedures, establish classroom work plans, make decisions about use of time, and engage in academic learning. Students become citizens of the classroom, assuming responsibility for how the learning space is run. In a set of evaluations from urban public schools using this approach, researchers found an increase in student and teacher attendance, a reduction in discipline referrals, and improvements in classroom climate, learning time, and long-term student achievement (Brophy & Freiberg, 1999; Freiberg et al., 2009). Shared decision making between teachers and students during the research process, or any process-oriented work, fosters future readiness in students (Schlam Salman & Inbar-Lourie, 2023). They may develop leadership skills, empathy, and active learning strategies in their roles as citizens of the classroom.

There may be nuances to the research process that are dependent on the discipline or purpose for research. For example, research in STEM areas like chemistry and physics have unique aspects and differ from studies in humanities like literary research and historical and social issue studies. There is, though, a general process to teaching students in English classes that can help guide them through their humanities coursework and that they can use as a framework in other research contexts. The following sections provide explanations of each of the nine stages of the research process: (1) establish a purpose, (2) generate ideas, (3) narrow ideas, (4) choose an idea and develop a research question, (5) gather information and evaluate source material, (6) develop a thesis statement, (7) provide claims and explanations, (8) share conclusions or findings, and (9) reflect. The following sections also include general approaches for coaching students in each stage. A reproducible tool, "Explanations of Each Stage of the Research Process" (page 163), provides an at-a-glance version of each stage.

ESTABLISH A PURPOSE

Researchers start by identifying the origin of or impetus for the research study. The study may be assigned and defined by a teacher, or ideas for the study may be student generated. This requires students to identify relevant issues within literature, society, or a disciplinary area and begin to think of those specific issues as broader constructs. The broad construct will help to eventually generate a research question. Researchers then perform the following actions.

- **Move from issue to topic:** Researchers create a T-chart. In one column, they list the specific issues in literature, society, or the disciplinary area that interests them. In the next column, they write the broader topic related to the issue.

- **Use questions to frame thinking:** The teacher shares a list of questions with students. Some of the questions should be fact based, some opinion based, and some exploratory. Students identify the types of questions in the list. Since their research will be framed around an exploratory question, students will have several ways to interpret, construct an argument for, and share perspectives based on findings.

GENERATE IDEAS

Researchers identify potential topics to study and pose questions about. They can collect ideas from interest inventories, reading, mind maps, or other sources. Researchers may create thinking webs and concept maps, make lists, sketch or draw ideas, or design charts. Researchers share ideas with a research team to help ideas unfold. The teacher should model various strategies to generate ideas for research. Researchers then perform the following actions.

- **Question dump:** After reviewing notes on moving from research issues to topics in the previous stage, researchers can select a few topics of interest and generate a list of questions for each topic. Researchers should write down questions quickly without spending too much time on each one. After, researchers can review all the questions they have about each topic, noticing patterns, themes, and the types of questions that come to mind.
- **Journal to surface ideas:** Researchers acknowledge and reflect on what they currently think about their potential research topics in a journal. They may acknowledge what they know and don't know. Students' ideas will grow using this strategy. Writing about potential topics in a journal helps surface where they currently are in their understanding. This will move the direction for inquiry. Guiding questions for journaling include the following.
  + What have I read about this topic? What historical information do I have on this topic?
  + What background information do I have about this topic?
  + Do I have personal experiences that connect to the importance of this topic?
  + What confuses me about this topic?
- Teachers may model a think-aloud and journaling to explicate discovering ideas.

NARROW IDEAS

During the generating ideas stage, researchers identify two to three topics or questions that they are interested in writing about. They spend time thinking more about these ideas in the context of researching a broad question about a topic or an assignment they are given. Researchers then perform the following actions.

- **Read to learn more:** The teacher invites students to read about potential research topics. Students should design a note-taking tool to record interesting or compelling information about potential topics. They may

also record questions and wonderings. Learning more can help in the decision-making process of choosing a research topic.
- **Team talk:** Students meet with a research partner or research group to share their initial findings about preliminary ideas. The goal of the conversation is to help students focus their work and develop new perspectives based on the questions others ask and the ideas they share.

CHOOSE AN IDEA AND DEVELOP A RESEARCH QUESTION

Researchers look over preliminary work—idea webs, issues and topics, questions, journal entries, reading notes—and choose an idea to study. They begin to craft a research question. If the research question was assigned or already generated, then students will not create their own question during this stage. Researchers then perform the following actions.

- **Craft questions:** Developing a research question can be challenging. Teachers may provide students with examples of research questions and coach students to choose language carefully so the purpose of the question is clear. Teachers and students may also consult an artificial intelligence tool to help craft a research question. Examples of sentence frames include the following.
  + What are the factors contributing to *[issue]* in *[specific setting]*?
  + What strategies can be implemented to improve *[specific outcome]* in *[field of work]*?
  + To what extent does *[trend, action]* impact *[population, setting]*?
  + How does *[historical event, development]* influence *[current situation]*?
- **Reflection:** Students reflect on their work during the beginning stages of research and discuss how they decided on their topic of study. Students may discuss what influenced their decision, what intrigues them, questions they are looking forward to exploring, and why they are interested in the topic. Reflections may be written or oral via a conversation or video submission.

GATHER INFORMATION AND EVALUATE SOURCE MATERIAL

Researchers spend time reading various sources of information connected to their topic. They develop systems for collecting notes and tracking sources for appropriate citations.

During this stage, formal instruction on navigating databases may be necessary. Lessons on internet navigation, fact checking, and evaluating website information for reliability may take place as well. If possible, partner with your school librarian during this stage.

Since students will spend several days reading, teachers may use this stage as an opportunity to reteach high-leverage reading skills during the explicit instruction portion of lessons. Key high-leverage reading skills necessary for research are summarizing, analyzing, synthesizing, thinking critically, and organizing information. Focused reading will help students develop a strong thesis statement with claims and evidence to support it. Researchers perform the following actions to gather information and evaluate source material.

- **Summarize to understand:** Students learn to identify parts of a text that reveal what the whole text is mostly about. They also learn to identify supporting details. Teachers may model this process through think-alouds and demonstration. Guiding questions include, What is this text mostly about? How does the text's structure help me develop meaning while reading? See the reproducible "Summarize to Understand" (page 165) to support this strategy.

- **Evaluate to make meaning:** Students will learn to assess source material and evaluate the value of their findings in relation to their research question. When reading, students must determine the purpose of a text and how it develops the research idea. Teachers may model this process through think-alouds and demonstration. Guiding questions include, How can I use this source to explain my research question? Does this source shape any new ideas related to my research question? See the reproducible "Evaluating Sources to Make Meaning" (page 166) to support this strategy.

- **Synthesize to share:** Researchers need to synthesize information to notice how source material connects and supports existing ideas or leads to new discoveries. Synthesis provides direction for a thesis statement and how researchers share their findings. Teachers may model this process through think-alouds and demonstration. A guiding framework for synthesis is, source A and source B say . . . So, I say. . . . Researchers look for commonalities and differences in the information found. See the reproducible "Synthesize to Share" (page 167) to support this strategy.

Ways to gather information will vary. In addition to reading source material, students may conduct action research by doing the following.

- Conducting interviews
- Creating focus groups
- Developing questionnaires or surveys
- Conducting observations
- Studying media sources

DEVELOP A THESIS STATEMENT

Researchers share a position or a complex idea that addresses the specific focus area of the research. Thesis statements appear at the beginning of a research paper or presentation and are supported by relevant facts and details. Researchers perform the following actions to craft their thesis statement.

- **Write it three times:** Although thesis statements are not long, they often require multiple revisions to ensure that word choice and sentence structure blend to convey a strong stance to the reader. With this strategy, students write their thesis statement three different ways. They may consult a thesaurus or artificial intelligence tools to play with language to compose a thesis that is most appropriate to the research focus.
- **I write, you write, I write:** Students work with their partner to craft a thesis statement. One partner creates and shares a digital document with the other partner. Both partners should have editing access to the document. In the document, students create a chart with the following statements.
    + I write . . .
    + You write . . .
    + I write . . .
    + Partner A
    + Partner B
- **Each partner writes their thesis statement in the first "I write" column:** Then each partner reads the other's thesis statement and writes it in a different way in the "You write" column. Partners look at the original thesis statement and their partner's version of the thesis statement and revises their thesis statement in the third "I write" column.

PROVIDE CLAIMS AND EXPLANATIONS

Researchers develop the idea in their thesis statement by providing multiple claims and explanations. They support their claims and explanations with information from relevant and reliable sources. Researchers participate in a research community by appropriately citing sources when they present their information.

Teachers may refer to the reproducible "Explanations of Each Stage of the Revolving Literacy Writing Process" in chapter 4 (page 112) to guide students through the writing process of a research paper. Since students will spend several days writing, teachers may also use this stage to teach high-leverage research writing skills including summarizing, paraphrasing, in-text citations, and development of analysis. Researchers then perform the following actions.

- **Use color tools to evaluate the researcher's voice presence:** The researcher's voice should be the most prominent. Information from source material supports what the research asserts. To check the "volume" of their voice, students highlight source material evidence in one color and their original ideas in another color. Students then evaluate which color fills most of the space.
- **Use strong transitions:** Using strong transitions signals a shift from the researcher's ideas to the source material evidence. Transitions include the following.
  + The author asserts . . .
  + This idea is supported in the article . . .
  + Bodies of research suggest . . .
  + An example is . . .

SHARE CONCLUSIONS OR FINDINGS

Researchers provide a concluding statement or section that explains the significance of the information they presented.

Through writing or multimodal presentations, researchers use digital media or visual displays to enhance the reader's understanding of their findings and engage the reader. Researchers perform the following actions.

- **Declare the relevance of the research:** Students state why the research topic is important in the conclusion and specify a target audience or community who would be interested in the topic.
- **Share research implications:** Students share how their findings can impact a group or space and suggest areas for future study. Sharing research implications is part of belonging to a research community.

REFLECT

Researchers reflect on the following aspects of their work.

- How they navigated the process
- What they learned from their research
- The implications of their research on their own identities or communities
- How they developed future-ready skills they can use in other research contexts

Examples of reflection prompts include the following.

- Making choices about my research helped my process by . . .
- A challenging choice I had to make during this process was . . .
- Something interesting I learned from my research is . . .
- My perspective has changed because . . .
- New questions I have as a result of my research are . . .
- An aspect of my identity that is connected to my research is . . .
- The community that my research is relevant to is . . .
- The way I chose to present or share my research is important to the overall meaning because . . .
- I developed [insert future-ready skill here] by . . .
- An aspect of [insert future-ready skill here] I need more practice in is _____ because . . .
- Through this research process, I learned _____. I can use this in other areas of learning by . . .
- I developed [insert future-ready skill here] through this writing process. This will help me in the future because . . .
- The future-ready skills I learned throughout this process are _____. I can use these skills in other classes when . . . or I can use these skills outside of school when . . .

The purpose of research may influence how teachers coach students. You may also review table 3.2 (page 77) to support your planning since there are aspects of the writing and research processes that support each other.

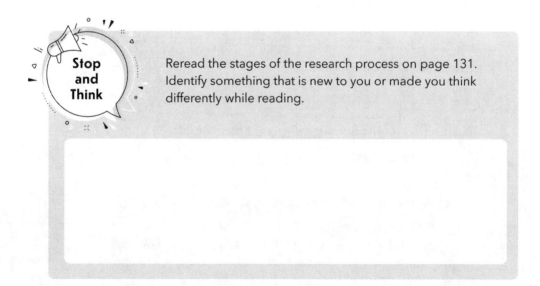

Stop and Think

Reread the stages of the research process on page 131. Identify something that is new to you or made you think differently while reading.

In what stages of research do students typically need the most support? Why do you think this?

In what stages of the research process are you most confident when delivering instruction?

In what stages of the research process would you benefit from professional development? Write a few goals for your own professional learning.

Visit **go.SolutionTree.com/literacy** *for a free reproducible version of this reflection.*

The Connection Between Teaching the Research Process and Literacy

Students participate in the research process several times throughout their secondary education years. While the purpose for research may vary in science, history, and English classes, the process of inquiry remains a common denominator across experiences. Inquiry provokes active learning and student agency through questioning, consideration of possibilities and alternatives, and applications of knowledge (Darling-Hammond et al., 2020). Including research study units in secondary English classes lets literacy educators design inquiry units of study using the revolving literacy framework, allowing students to personalize their learning and actively develop future-ready skills. All components of literacy development—language, future-ready skills, identity, community, and multimodal meaning-making—connect to the stages of the research process. The process-oriented instruction in areas of inquiry perpetuates transferable learning (Bransford, Brown, & Cocking, 2000) for students. Consider how the research process aligns with the following revolving literacy framework as you design your research process instruction and units of study.

LANGUAGE

The research process requires receptive language skills—listening, reading, and viewing—and expressive language skills—writing, speaking, and visually representing—as students gather information and share their findings. While language skills are fluid throughout the research process, it is important to design specific and explicit instruction in each of the language domain areas so students develop awareness in using language skills for specific purposes. What follows are suggested stages of the research process to prioritize instruction in language domains and questions to guide instruction. Also, see the reproducible "The Connection Between Literacy Development Components and the Research Process Checklist" (page 169).

RECEPTIVE LANGUAGE SKILLS (LISTENING, READING, AND VIEWING)

ESTABLISH A PURPOSE AND GENERATE IDEAS

- How does visual media consumption influence what students are interested in researching and studying? Literacy educators are aware that students' access to digital information and entertainment may influence what they are interested in studying.

NARROW IDEAS

- How does partner talk and the perspectives of partners influence the way researchers understand their own ideas for research?
- How can reading to learn more about potential topics help the researcher choose a focus area for research?

GATHER INFORMATION

- What listening strategies should researchers use when gathering research from sources such as social media posts, news broadcasts, and interviews? How do researchers capture the necessary information?

- How do high-leverage reading skills like summarizing, evaluating, analyzing, and synthesizing information help researchers gather information they need to support their thesis statements?
- What viewing strategies should researchers use when gathering research from sources such as social media posts, news broadcasts, and documentaries? How do researchers capture the necessary information? How does viewing impact a researcher's interests and understandings?

SHARE FINDINGS

- How does listening to or reading feedback from the research community impact the way researchers conceptualize their findings? How do the questions posed by the research community impact the next steps for research and learning?

PROVIDE CLAIMS AND EXPLANATIONS

- How does a researcher's reading process influence the ways in which they develop their own claims and explanations?

EXPRESSIVE LANGUAGE SKILLS (WRITING, SPEAKING, VISUALLY REPRESENTING)

GENERATE IDEAS

- How can doing quick jots and preliminary writing about ideas help researchers discover their interests?
- How does engaging in conversations with research partners and teams help researchers share and discover ideas?
- How do different ways of visually representing initial thoughts and brainstorming ideas help researchers develop a relationship with their thinking?

DEVELOP A RESEARCH QUESTION

- How can writing a series of research questions help researchers focus their research? Researchers may also verbally share a series of questions with a research partner to help craft their question.

DEVELOP A THESIS STATEMENT

- How can writing a series of thesis statements help researchers develop a research focus? Researchers may also verbally share different thesis statements with a research partner to get feedback.

PROVIDE CLAIMS AND EXPLANATION

- How can participating in stages of the writing process help researchers clearly articulate claims and evidence to support the thesis of the research?
- How can visually representing ideas using multiple modalities help researchers communicate ideas to their audience?

SHARE CONCLUSION OR FINDINGS

- How can participating in the stages of the writing process help researchers clearly articulate conclusions and findings?
- How can visually representing concluding ideas with multiple modalities help researchers communicate ideas to their audience?

REFLECT

- How can reflective writing or conversations with partners, teams, or the teacher support researchers' awareness of what they learned and goal development in future work?

EVIDENCE OF LITERACY LEARNING: WHAT TO LOOK FOR IN STUDENTS' PROCESS AND PRODUCT

- Students take notes during conversations with their research partners and their teachers. Students can use their notes to revise and add to initial thinking.
- Students develop a system for tracking information and responses while listening to source material (webs, charts, lists, and so on).
- Students reference information they learned from their reading when providing a rationale for choosing a research topic or developing claims and explanations.
- Students document their summaries, evaluations, analyses, and syntheses of information in a teacher-provided chart, note-taking organizer, or space.
- Students write down questions and reactions from the research community when sharing their findings. Students reference these responses in reflections.
- Students develop different ways of visually representing their thinking while generating ideas (charts, webs, mind maps, and so on).
- Students use writing to discover what they know and want to know more about when generating ideas for research. Students write quick jots about potential research topics.

- Students write a series of research questions that are similar but crafted in different ways to experiment with language, vocabulary, and syntax. Teachers may see notes from research partner conferences that aid in the revision process.
- Students write a series of thesis statements, crafted in different ways, to experiment with language, vocabulary, and syntax. Teachers may see notes from research partner conferences that aid in the revision process.
- Students write claims, explanations, and conclusions or findings with evidence of drafting, revisions, and edits. Evidence may be writing multiple drafts, reflecting during the writing process, utilizing different colored fonts to show revisions and edits, and so on.
- Students present research findings using multiple modalities in a presentation, video, documentary, infographic, poster, or other form.
- Students share a written reflection.
- Students prepare notes for a reflection conversation with a research partner or the teacher.

FUTURE-READY SKILLS

- Connect future-ready skills to stages of the research process. Introduce and reinforce the future-ready skills as you plan your lessons using the lesson plan outline in chapter 3 (page 73). See the following section, The Connection Between Teaching the Research Process and Future Readiness, for how to embed future-ready skills in the research process.

EVIDENCE OF LITERACY LEARNING: WHAT TO LOOK FOR IN STUDENTS' PROCESS AND PRODUCT

- Students demonstrate their understanding of their future-ready skills progress through the research process in reflection writing and conference conversations.
- Students identify the future-ready skills they are able to transfer to personal, social, and other academic spaces.

IDENTITY

- Engage students in reflection about the difference between personal interests and personal passions. Students should consider what they are interested in and what they are passionate about and contemplate what kind of topic will hold their attention while working through the research process.
- Design a research unit in which students make choices about the topic of the research.

- Design a research unit in which students develop their own research question so their work is rooted in self-generated inquiry.
- Design a choice board for students to use when deciding how to present their findings.
- Provide opportunities for students to share rationales as to why they are making certain choices throughout their process.
- Provide opportunities for formative and summative personal and academic reflection.

EVIDENCE OF LITERACY LEARNING: WHAT TO LOOK FOR IN STUDENTS' PROCESS AND PRODUCT

- Students choose their own topic for research.
- Students develop their own research question based on something they are interested in or want to learn more about.
- Students choose how they want to organize, present, and share their findings. This multimodal artifact can be in addition to a research writing piece.
- Students provide rationales in writing and conversation for the personal and academic choices related to their work.
- Students can articulate how their work connects to aspects of their identity.
- Students can reflect on their learning and how their learning will transfer into personal, academic, and social spaces.

COMMUNITY

- Design a research unit or series of research units across grade levels that connects to a community students belong to. For example, students may engage in an activism research unit where they choose an activism topic related to their local community (such as the benefits of sunscreen dispensers in local playgrounds) or an activism topic related to a community subgroup (such as the importance of diverse menus in restaurants for those with dietary restrictions).
- Design a research unit in which students create a research product to share within the community space connected to the research (for example, students create infographics for the high school counseling office after learning about the positive effects of peer mentorship on high school students).
- Design a research unit that invites students to make positive contributions to their school community after researching areas of need.

EVIDENCE OF LITERACY LEARNING: WHAT TO LOOK FOR IN STUDENTS' PROCESS AND PRODUCT

- Students make a connection between their research and a community they belong to or are connected to.
- Students share or plan to share their findings or their research product within the community connected to the research.

MULTIMODAL MEANING-MAKING

- Demonstrate various ways for students to visually represent their understandings, both as they generate and narrow ideas and when they're gathering information.
- Incorporate explicit instruction on how to read digital texts and navigate media sources for gathering information.
- Expose students to a variety of digital tools and platforms for creations.
- Design a unit of study in which students share their findings in various modalities in addition to a research writing piece.

EVIDENCE OF LITERACY LEARNING: WHAT TO LOOK FOR IN STUDENTS' PROCESS AND PRODUCT

- Students design various ways to share their thinking when generating and narrowing ideas and gathering information. Students may work with print or digital materials to create images, charts, webs, maps, and so on. They may use color tools to organize and categorize ideas.
- Students create a product based on their findings on a digital platform of their choice.

Identify an area of literacy instruction that interests you relative to the research process. Why does it interest you?

continued ▶

> Identify something that you learned or are thinking more about after reading the previous section, The Connection Between Teaching the Research Process and Literacy.
>
> Identify an area or areas of literacy instruction that you could further cultivate in how you teach or design research process instruction.

Visit **go.SolutionTree.com/literacy** *for a free reproducible version of this reflection.*

The Connection Between Teaching the Research Process and Future Readiness

In the previous sections, we identified and defined the nine stages of the research process.

1. Establish a purpose
2. Generate ideas
3. Narrow ideas
4. Choose an idea and develop a research question
5. Gather information and evaluate source material
6. Develop a thesis statement
7. Provide claims and explanations
8. Share conclusions or findings
9. Reflect

We also bridged the relationship between the research process and the revolving literacy framework. The section shines a light on the future-ready skill component of revolving literacy. The skills associated with each stage of the research process make teaching future-ready skills accessible for teachers. Research requires a unique skill set that aligns with designing future-ready thinking and work (Schlam Salman & Inbar-Lourie, 2023; World Economic Forum, 2016, 2020, 2023a) for students to engage in. The following list describes fifteen skills that students develop through the research process.

1. **Identify** problems, issues, or inquiries to explore
2. **Develop** focused questions for inquiry, exploration, and guided reading
3. **Gather** valid, reliable, and relevant sources of information
4. **Be alert** to false information and fabricated sources
5. **Analyze and evaluate** information
6. **Delineate and evaluate** an argument and specific claims
7. **Synthesize** information
8. **Introduce and organize** complex concepts the researcher developed from their findings
9. **Present** claims, findings, and supporting evidence clearly, concisely, and logically
10. **Avoid** plagiarism and **follow** a standard citation system
11. **Choose** a modality or platform to share research findings that will enhance the researcher's message or position
12. **Make strategic use** of digital media or visual displays in presentations to enhance understanding of findings, reasoning, and evidence, and to add elements of interest to engage the audience
13. **Present** research findings to a community through oral presentation, visual representation, or written word
14. **Participate** in a research community by **discussing and listening** to research plans, questions, reading, information, and findings with research partners or groups
15. **Reflect** on how the stages of research supported the outcome of the project and set goals for future work based on reflections

Table 5.2 (page 148) shows how research process skills can align with future readiness. When designing lessons within each stage of the research process, reference this chart to make explicit connections to future-ready skills within the context and relevance portions of the revolving literacy lesson plan (see chapter 3, page 73). You may also ensure that students reflect on the future-ready skills they practice in class throughout the research process. The metacognitive approach to research will aid students in transferring knowledge to other spaces and contexts (Darling-Hammond et al., 2020). As I shared in previous chapters, literacy educators may use table 5.2 (page 148) as an example of how to align research skills and future-ready skills in the future, since future-ready skills will change in response to job demands.

TABLE 5.2: Research and Future-Ready Skill Alignment

Stages of the Research Process	Future-Ready Skills (Projected for 2023–2027)	Research Process Skill
Establish a purpose	Creative thinking Leadership and social influence Curiosity	Researchers identify problems, issues, or inquiries to explore. Researchers choose what body of research they want to connect with and contribute to.
Generate ideas Narrow ideas Choose an idea and develop a research question Gather information and evaluate source material	Analytical thinking Creative thinking Curiosity Technological literacy Use of artificial intelligence	Researchers gather valid, reliable, and relevant sources of information. Researchers analyze and evaluate information. Researchers are alert to false information and fabricated sources.
Develop a thesis statement	Systems thinking	Researchers establish a position or direction for research based on initial explorations.
Provide claims and explanations	Analytical thinking Creative thinking	Researchers summarize and synthesize information. Researchers introduce and organize complex concepts of their own based on findings. Researchers avoid plagiarism and follow a standard form of citation. Researchers present claims and supporting evidence clearly, concisely, and logically.
Share conclusions or findings	Creative thinking Analysis Empathy and active listening	Researchers present findings clearly, concisely, and logically. Researchers present research findings to a community through oral presentation, visual representation, or written word. Researchers avoid plagiarism and follow a standard form of citation. Researchers choose a modality or platform to share research findings that will help enhance the researchers' message or position. Researchers make strategic use of digital media or visual displays in presentations to enhance understanding of findings, reasoning, and evidence, and to add elements of interest to engage the audience.
Reflect	Analysis	Researchers reflect on how the stages of research supported the outcome of the project and set goals for future work based on reflections. Researchers reflect on the skills they developed throughout all stages of the process and how to transfer skills to other academic and personal spaces. Encourage reflection in these areas: active learning and learning strategies; leadership and social influence; technology use; and resilience, stress tolerance, and flexibility.

| All stages of the research process | Lifelong learning strategies
Resilience and flexibility
Systems thinking
Motivation and self-awareness | Students learn the relationship between each stage of the research process, product, and how future-ready skills develop throughout. Lifelong learning strategies, resilience and flexibility, systems thinking, and motivation and self-awareness may be addressed at any stage and throughout the process. |

Curriculum Implications

Each section in this chapter is a layer to conceptualize how literacy instruction, process-oriented instruction (in research), and future-ready skill development are connected. The guiding principles of literacy instruction remain at the center. High-leverage skill sets connect to each stage of the process linked to future-ready skills. Figure 5.1 provides a visual for how the nine-stage research process connects with teaching future-ready skills. Use the visual as a tool for developing pedagogy, creating a vision for curriculum and instruction, designing units of study, and writing lesson plans. A goal for reading this chapter and this book is for literacy educators to develop a relationship with the revolving literacy framework and how it creates pathways for curriculum and instruction development that are relevant, engaging, and transferable for students.

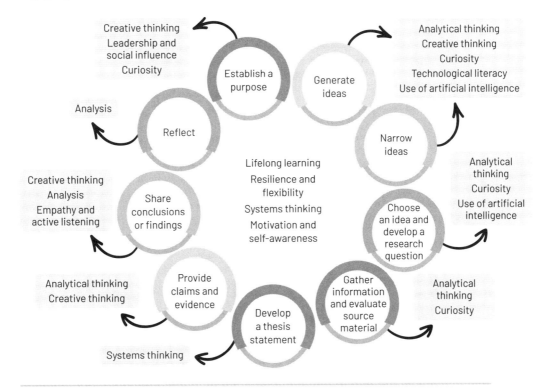

FIGURE 5.1: The connection between the research process and future-ready skills.

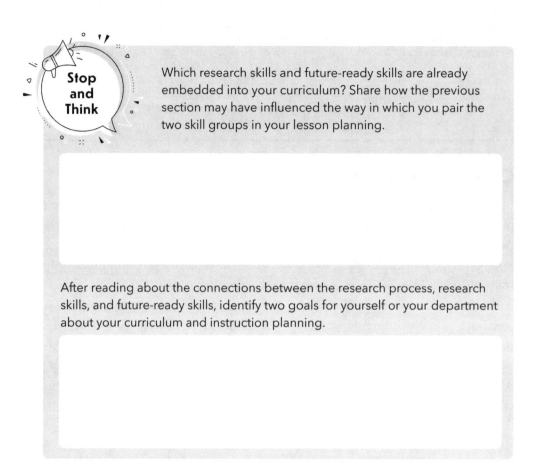

Stop and Think

Which research skills and future-ready skills are already embedded into your curriculum? Share how the previous section may have influenced the way in which you pair the two skill groups in your lesson planning.

After reading about the connections between the research process, research skills, and future-ready skills, identify two goals for yourself or your department about your curriculum and instruction planning.

Visit **go.SolutionTree.com/literacy** *for a free reproducible version of this reflection.*

When I became a preK–12 director of literacy, high school English teachers informed me that research had been phased out of the curriculum in grades 9–12. Only students in college-level courses while in high school engaged in research. This signaled that research was relevant only to those students who participated in academic spaces. As I discussed in the opening of this chapter, research is an authentic practice that people engage in for various professional and personal reasons. Not surprisingly, teachers were eager to have all students in all grades learn and practice research skills.

As with reading and writing experiences, literacy educators should consider the research students conduct within each grade level and within various disciplines to create a vertically articulated research experience. Vertical articulation is the careful consideration of what content and materials students experience in each of the grade-levels throughout their secondary experience. For example, there should be a relationship between curriculum in grade 9 and grade 10. Units should complement one another, and the rigor and expectations should change as students progress. Use regional standards as a guide for this work.

In English class, students may conduct research connected to fiction (literary) and nonfiction (informational or expository) reading. Since literary research most likely will not appear in other disciplines, consider prioritizing it in selected grade levels in English classes. Figure 5.2 shows an example of vertical articulation for research in English classes in grades 3 to 12. Also, see the "Revolving Literacy Research Articulation Planning" reproducibles (page 171, 173, and 175). The units listed are designed for the purpose of teaching the research process.

Grade 3	Grade 4	Grade 5	Grade 6	Grade 7
Country research	Weather events	Research-based argument (choice topic)	Activist research	Research-based argument (choice topic)
Advocacy research: Issues in the school community (choice topic)	**Advocacy research:** Issues in a personal or social community (choice topic)	**Advocacy research:** Issues in the local or global community (choice topic)		Interdisciplinary research study with social studies class on a shared theme (for example, conflicts and compromise)

Grade 8	Grade 9	Grade 10	Grade 11	Grade 12
Literary-based research: Investigate a question derived from a novel Interdisciplinary research study with social studies class on a shared topic (for example, World War II and the Holocaust)	Social issues research (choice topic)	**Literary-based research:** Investigate a question derived from reading short stories in a book club	**Literary-based research:** Investigate a question derived from reading novels in a social issue book club	Local community issue research study
			Social commentary opinion-writing	Literary-based research investigation

FIGURE 5.2: Vertical articulation of research units in grades 3–12.

Curriculum design is no easy task. The grade levels listed in figure 5.2 represent six different school buildings (four elementary schools, one middle school, and one high school) and about seventy-five different teachers. Articulation requires that a curriculum leader or team of curriculum leaders communicate with teachers of multiple grade levels about the work. It also requires a shared philosophy and shared vision for the work. Using the tools shared in this book related to revolving literacy components and alignment between process-oriented instruction and literacy development can help in the planning process. There are also guiding questions for vertical articulation when designing research units of study. Figure 5.3 (page 152) includes questions to use when discussing vertical alignment in designing research units of study across grades.

Vertical Articulation Discussion Questions	What do I think?	What does my team think?	Next Steps
How are the topics or focus areas for research determined in each grade? Are they varied? Do any focus areas repeat?			
In what grades does it benefit students to collaborate with content-area colleagues or connect to content-area learning within the grade level?			
How can we scaffold a research skill progression across grades? What skills should we prioritize in earlier grades? How do the skills elevate in complexity as students mature?			
Do the research topic and skill progression across grades align with how standards are articulated across grades?			
How can we scaffold a future-ready skill progression in research across grades? What skills should we prioritize in earlier grades? How do the skills elevate in complexity as students mature?			
Is there a shared tool to monitor progress during the research process across the grades for consistency in instruction and students' expectations?			

Is there a shared vision for reflection during and after the research process?			
Is there variation in the research products? When are students writing a research paper? When are students writing an annotated bibliography? When are students sharing a presentation? When do students have opportunities to create with digital tools and media?			
Is there variation in the origin for research? Is there a balance of research rooted in nonfiction text and research that stems from literary works?			
Is there professional time for literacy educators to meet and discuss student progress in research and reflect on curriculum and instruction?			

FIGURE 5.3: Research unit vertical alignment discussion questions.

*Visit **go.SolutionTree.com/literacy** for a free reproducible version of this figure.*

Research in the Revolving Literacy Framework

In this section, you will find a sample research unit of study framework planning sheet and a sample lesson plan for the unit of study. I feature a social issue research unit derived from literary experiences. In this unit, students participate in social issue book clubs. After reading, students choose a social issue that emerged in the reading to research and explore. While the social issue derives from fiction reading, the research component is composed of nonfiction reading on websites and databases.

UNIT OF STUDY FRAMEWORK

The purpose of the unit of study framework helps secondary literacy educators ensure that they incorporate all components of literacy development into the unit of study. As I described in chapter 2 (page 29), use the framework template like a place setting on a dinner table. It holds each of the pieces needed for a literacy-focused unit: language, future-ready skills, identity, community, and multimodal meaning-making. It does not include specific lesson plans. Figure 5.4 is a sample unit of study plan on exploring social issues through literature.

Unit Summary: This research unit may follow any experience where students have read fiction stories that surface social issues that are historical, systemic, newly realized, or a combination. Students will learn that literature often illuminates issues in society relative to certain populations or humanity as a whole. Students will learn that this is what makes literature so important: It reflects the human experience, and these reflections are often timeless. Literature acknowledges the struggles, triumphs, confusion, and perseverance of the human experience and can serve as a springboard for readers to make a decision about their own internalization of the issue at hand. What impact will the reading experience have on the reader's life experience? Can a text inspire readers to take action? When students engage in the research process and personal reflection, these questions can drive the work of the research. Readers read . . . now what?

Throughout this unit, students will engage in a research process to identify, explain, and share about a social issue to influence the hearts and minds of others. Students will write a research paper and design an infographic. Students will begin their process by identifying a research topic derived from the social issue and will eventually generate a thesis relative to the topic after gathering information. Students will read nonfiction texts related to the social issue they choose to explore. Students will explain and synthesize the information they are learning from reading sources relative to the social issue through an annotated bibliography. Students will identify how each source helps to uncover aspects of the research topic leading to a deeper understanding of the issue. From this work, students will then generate a research question. The last part of the unit requires students to use the information gathered in the annotated bibliography to write a research paper. Students will then create an infographic that addresses the thesis to share with a larger audience to generate interest in and awareness of the social issue. Students will consider aspects of design and intentional messaging through the creation and presentation of the infographic.

The purpose of this unit is to inspire students to draw connections between literature and the societal issues it can illuminate for groups of people. Students will select their area of study in response to reading. Students will engage in the research, writing, and creative processes.	**By the end of the unit,** students will work through the research process to write a research paper about a social issue. Students will also create an infographic to illustrate their findings about the issue they study. Students will reflect on their process via writing or speaking. **Option:** Students may formally present their research to the class in small research groups or to community members. **Modification:** The product of the research could be an infographic or any other multimodal expression. Students may write an introduction to the research and infographic along with a formal written reflection.

Language	Future-Ready Skills	Identity
• Students will read sources of information. • Students may gather information by engaging in discussion or interviews, viewing videos, listening to podcasts, and so on. • Students will write a research paper. • Students will design an infographic, visually representing their research findings. • Students will reflect on their process via writing or speaking. • Students may orally present their research to the class in small research groups or to community members.	• Analytical thinking • Lifelong learning strategies • Creative thinking • Leadership and social influence • Technological literacy • Use of artificial intelligence • Resilience and flexibility	• Students choose a topic that is interesting or meaningful to them from the book they chose to read in their social issue book club. • Students may or may not make personal connections to their research topic

Community		Multimodal Meaning-Making
• Students select a research topic in response to their experience in a book club. Reading and club discussions may influence the research topic they select. • Students may select a social issue to study that reflects a community they belong to. • Students will share their infographic with a person or group of people connected to the topic. For example, if a student creates an infographic about the benefits of student mentorship for college application, the student will share the infographic with the school counseling department. • Students will have a research partner throughout the research process.		• Students will write to make meaning through an annotated bibliography, note taking, research paper, and reflection. • Students will use a digital design tool to create an infographic with text, images, color schemes, graphics, and charts. The design of the infographic has an impact on how meaning is constructed and shared. • Students may gather information by engaging in discussion or interviews, reading, watching videos, listening to podcasts, and so on.

FIGURE 5.4 Readers read . . . now what? Social issues illuminated through literature.

LESSON PLAN

In figure 5.5 (page 156), I share a lesson plan for the "Readers Read . . . Now What? Social Issues Illuminated Through Literature" research unit in this section. This lesson occurs during the stage of the research process in which students develop their thesis statement. The lesson plan serves as an example of how to plan a research lesson within the revolving literacy framework lesson plan.

Lesson Plan Thinking Map		
Connections for Learning		
Context: Why is today's lesson important to the work in the current unit of study?	This lesson supports students in moving from a research topic to a thesis statement. Crafting a thesis statement is pivotal to the research process as it is the statement that researchers develop through their writing and presentation of findings. Through the thesis statement, the researcher establishes a focus for the work. The thesis statement presents as a "contract" the researcher provides to their readers—the researcher promises to address the ideas presented in the thesis and stay committed to those ideas.	
Relevance: How does this lesson connect to future-ready skills, students' lives outside of school, or skills they may use in other areas of learning?	**Future-Ready Skills:** Lifelong learning strategy—Create a chart to organize reflections from multiple text sources to develop a thesis statement. Organizing ideas will help to synthesize ideas. Analytical thinking—Students collect ideas from previous reading and analyze their relevance and effectiveness in the research topic of study. Students think critically about preliminary reading to formulate a thesis statement that conveys the researcher's position. **Connections:** Crafting a thesis statement is universal to the research process. Students may use the active learning strategy taught in this lesson to formulate thesis statements for research in other disciplines (history, mathematics, science). They may also use the active learning strategy in future literary or information research processes. In life, people frequently take positions on issues. While adults may not craft thesis statements every time they establish a position on a social issue, they do engage in similar thinking protocols as taught in this lesson. The lesson ultimately invites students to establish a position about a topic they are personally interested in studying. They establish their position through the thesis statement.	
Connections for Literacy Instruction		
Language: Which domains of language are targeted in instruction and application of learning?	**Future-Ready Skills:** What future-ready skills are students developing?	**Identity:** How can students personally connect to this lesson?
Reading sources of information Writing a thesis statement	**Lifelong Learning Strategy:** Create a chart to organize reflections from multiple text sources to develop a thesis statement. Organizing ideas will help to synthesize ideas.	The lesson ultimately invites students to establish a position about a topic they are personally interested in studying. They establish their position through the thesis statement.
	Analytical Thinking: Students collect ideas from previous reading and analyze their relevance and effectiveness in the research topic of study. Students think critically about preliminary reading to formulate a thesis statement that conveys the researcher's position.	

Community: How are students participating in a community of learners within the classroom? How is their work contributing to a larger community outside of the classroom? How is the community influencing the work at hand?	**Multimodal Meaning-Making:** What modalities are students making meaning *from*? What modalities are students using to make meaning and demonstrate understanding?
Students share their initial ideas with a research partner. Partner talk may support the revision process of the thesis to ensure its clarity and focus.	Students create a chart to organize ideas from reading to establish a thesis statement. Students may choose to write in a notebook or in a digital format.

Intention

Objective (an intention for teachers): What is the goal for students to accomplish by the end of the lesson?	Students will learn that a thesis statement establishes a position for a writer as they determine a focus and direction for the topic at hand. Students can think of a thesis statement as a contract the writer gives to the reader: The writer promises to address the ideas presented in the thesis and to stay committed to those ideas. The reader should know that there won't be any surprises. Therefore, students learn that a thesis must be broad and inclusive and address the overall message they will communicate. Students will create a chart to develop a thesis statement. They will recall important takeaways from their prior reading to establish the relationship between source material and their position. Students will write the first draft of a thesis statement.
Focus Statement (an intention for students): Ask students to state their objective in the first person as a way to take ownership of their learning.	*I will use what I learned through reading, evaluating, and reflecting on sources to write the first draft of my thesis statement. I will create a chart to help me develop a thesis statement. I will recall important information from my reading and analyze how that information helps me focus my research.*
Standards: What standards does the lesson address?	[Insert your state's standards here.]

Explicit Instruction

Tools and Texts: What resources and instructional materials are needed for this lesson? What is the teacher using to teach? What are students using or working with?	Students need a notebook or digital file for writing and source material (texts, notes from prior reading, viewing, or listening to source material). Teachers need a sample research topic, sample source material, and sample thesis statement chart.
Whole-Class Instruction: Describe the lesson. What instructional strategy or strategies will you use? Why did you select the instructional technique? How does it help accomplish the goal of the lesson?	Check or highlight the method(s) used in this lesson: ☑ Think-aloud ☑ Demonstration ☐ Use of a mentor text ☑ Use of a demonstration text ☐ Show and explain ☐ Shared experience ☐ Media with active engagement

FIGURE 5.5: Research lesson plan using the revolving literacy framework.

continued ▶

Explicit Instruction	
Whole-Class Instruction: Describe the lesson. What instructional strategy or strategies will you use? Why did you select the instructional technique? How does it help accomplish the goal of the lesson?	**Describe the lesson:** Teachers will coach students to generate a thesis statement by modeling how to think through developing a thesis. Teachers will show the relationship between the information in the sources and using that information to develop a thesis. Teachers will demonstrate how to write a thesis statement about a demonstration topic in front of the class. Teachers may use the chart that follows. | My takeaway from each of my sources	After reconnecting with my sources, I notice . . .	Thesis statement
---	---	---
Source 1:		
Source 2:		
Source 3:		
Source 4:			 The teacher will invite the students to create a version of the chart used in the demonstration. The teacher asks students to engage in thinking protocols similar to ones in the demonstration to generate a thesis statement.
Guided or Independent Practice: Describe what students are doing after the whole-class instruction. Share your conference or small-group instruction plan.	**Describe what students are doing after whole-class instruction. What scaffolds and supports are in place for students who are in need?** Students work through the process taught during explicit instruction. Students will have several opportunities to generate, develop, and revise their thesis statements. They will do this through peer partnerships and conferencing with the teacher. **Share your conference or small-group instruction plan. What scaffolds, strategies, or tools will you use to support students you meet with? What is the purpose for meeting with these students?** **Option 1:** As students are working, the teacher visits each student's previously established inquiry journal and provides feedback to support students in developing their thesis statements. This is not the first time the teacher has seen the inquiry journal. The teacher may work with small groups of students with similar feedback from inquiry journals. **Option 2:** The teacher designs a lesson for small-group instruction for students who have analyzed and synthesized their sources of information. The teacher coaches students to write three different versions of a thesis statement with techniques to vary language choice. The teacher works with students to use an artificial intelligence chatbot to peruse different versions of thesis statements students have written.

Reflection and Next Steps	
Daily Closure: How will you close the lesson to help future teacher or student planning? See table 3.2 (page 77) for closure options.	**Share and submit:** At the end of class, all students copy their thesis statements onto a shared document as a form of data collection for the teacher. The teacher should read all original drafts of thesis statements and make an instructional plan for the following day based on noticings. What needs to be developed?
After the Lesson: Evaluate the level of student engagement and the student work.	**Based on your observations, name areas where the lesson was successful and where students were successful.** The lesson challenged students to consider why and how reading valid and reliable sources of information can influence how a researcher develops a position on a topic. Students demonstrated understanding of a thesis statement. This is evident by the data collection tool used (Google Doc). Some students need to revisit their thesis statements to reevaluate the connection between reading and taking a position (details in the following row).
	Based on your observations, what is needed in future instruction? Two needs for follow-up instruction emerged. Group 1 (Troy, Louisa, Angelica, Christian, Anna, Fiona, Layla, John, Robert, Sofia, Lukas, Josh, Hilary) will work on making the language of their thesis statement more sophisticated. The connection between their initial source material and the thesis statement is clear. Group 2 (Jeff, Andy, Francine, Paul, Patrick, Christopher, Sarah, Jennifer) will work on revising their thesis statement to better connect with the initial reading takeaways to show an informed position.
	Based on your observations, did students connect with the context and relevance of the lesson? Were they aware of how their work was part of a process to develop the named future-ready skill? Students demonstrated understanding of a thesis statement and its importance in the research process as evidenced by the data collected. Revision is needed by all for different purposes. I asked students to share when they had to write thesis statements in other situations. Many shared about other disciplines.

Summary

This chapter began by illuminating the authentic aspects of research. People engage in research processes in academic, personal, and professional spaces for various reasons. Research is foundational in postsecondary experiences. In this chapter, we explored the relationship between the stages of the research process, components of literacy development, and future-ready skills. We also explored examples of how to articulate research across grade levels within English classes. It is important to be intentional in planning a research sequence within and across grade levels so students are exposed to a variety of research contexts. It is also important to be aware of what type of research students are conducting in content-area classes so the explicit teaching in English classes can both support research in other contexts and offer students something new.

At First . . .
Share your thoughts about the topic prior to reading this chapter.

And Now . . .
Share how this chapter has influenced your thinking.

Next Steps
What actions will you or your team take in response to reading this chapter?

What types of research do students engage in outside of school?

Why do students research in school, and who sets the intention?

At First . . .	And Now . . .	Next Steps

How do students make connections between school and personal research opportunities? Does coursework prioritize opportunities for real-life application?

At First . . .	And Now . . .	Next Steps

What is the relationship between literacy (language, future-ready skills, identity, community, and multimodal meaning-making) and research opportunities for students?

At First . . .	And Now . . .	Next Steps

When and how are students working through the full research process during the school year?

How are the products of research varied across grade levels?

At First . . .	And Now . . .	Next Steps

What is the relationship between research instruction and future-ready skill development? How does the research process foster future-ready skills?

At First . . .	And Now . . .	Next Steps

Visit **go.SolutionTree.com/literacy** *for a free reproducible version of this reflection.*

After connecting with your own reflections, consider using figure 5.6 (page 162) to reflect on the research experiences students have throughout their secondary English years. You may use this as a follow-up to reflections in the reproducible "The Connection Between Literacy Development Components and the Research Process Checklist" (page 169) to get started with your planning. It can help to balance the research opportunities a student has across their secondary English experience.

Research Opportunities School Year:				
	Grade:	Grade:	Grade:	Grade:
What **type of research** do students engage in (literary, informational, persuasive)?				
What **standards** are addressed?				
What **future-ready skills** are explicitly taught?				
What **research** skills are emphasized?				
How are students encouraged to make **identity** connections through research?				
How are students encouraged to make **community** connections through research?				
What is the **product** of research? How do students share their findings?				
What opportunities do students have to make meaning through **multiple modalities**?				

FIGURE 5.6: Revolving literacy research opportunities planning tool.

Explanations of Each Stage of the Research Process

Use this as a resource to review stages of the research process so they are all are covered in your planning. Consider using the strategies listed in your lesson planning and during small group instruction.

Stage of the Research Process	What Happens During This Stage	Strategies for Supporting Researchers
Establish a Purpose	Researchers identify the origin or impetus of the research. Students identify relevant issues within literature, society, or an area of discipline and begin to think of those specific issues as broader constructs.	Move from issue to topic. Use questioning to frame thinking.
Generate Ideas	Researchers identify potential topics to study and pose questions about.	Use a question dump. Use journaling to surface ideas.
Narrow Ideas	Researchers identify two to three topics or questions from their work during the generating ideas stage that they are interested in writing about. They spend time considering if and how they will pursue the ideas.	Read to learn more. Use team talk.
Choose an Idea and Develop a Research Question	Researchers look over preliminary work, choose an idea to study, and craft a research question. If the research question was assigned or already generated, then students will not create their own question during this stage.	Use crafting questions. Provide reflection prompts.
Gather Information and Evaluate Source Material	Researchers spend time reading various sources of information connected to their topics. They develop systems for collecting notes and tracking sources for appropriate citations.	Summarize to understand. Evaluate to make meaning. Synthesize to share.

page 1 of 2

Stage of the Research Process	What Happens During This Stage	Strategies for Supporting Researchers
Develop a Thesis Statement	Researchers share a position or a complex idea that addresses the specific focus area of the research. Thesis statements are supported by relevant facts and details.	Write it three times. I write, you write, I write.
Provide Claims and Explanations	Researchers develop the idea in their thesis statement by providing multiple claims and explanations. Claims and explanations are supported with information from relevant and reliable sources.	Use color tools to evaluate the researcher's voice presence. Use strong transitions.
Share Conclusions or Findings	Researchers provide a concluding statement or section that explains the significance of the information they presented.	Share the relevance of the research. Share research implications.
Reflect	Researchers reflect on various aspects of their work, including the research process, the significance of their findings, the impact of the learning, and future-ready skill development.	Provide reflection prompts.

Summarize to Understand

Students may use this tool to summarize source material during the research process to develop understanding about their topics.

Source:	What key words related to the topic repeat throughout the text?	
	What is this text mostly about?	
	How does the text structure help me develop meaning while reading?	
Source:	What key words related to the topic repeat throughout the text?	
	What is this text mostly about?	
	How does the text structure help me develop meaning while reading?	
Source:	What key words related to the topic repeat throughout the text?	
	What is this text mostly about?	
	How does the text structure help me develop meaning while reading?	

Evaluating Sources to Make Meaning

Students may use this tool to determine the connection between research source material and the research question.

Source:	How can I use this source to explain my research question?	
	Does this source shape any new ideas related to my research question?	
Source:	How can I use this source to explain my research question?	
	Does this source shape any new ideas related to my research question?	
Source:	How can I use this source to explain my research question?	
	Does this source shape any new ideas related to my research question?	
Source:	How can I use this source to explain my research question?	
	Does this source shape any new ideas related to my research question?	

Revolving Literacy © 2025 Solution Tree Press • SolutionTree.com
Visit **go.SolutionTree.com/literacy** to download this free reproducible.

Synthesize to Share

Students may use this tool to synthesize source material during the research process to process how ideas from source material influences their own thinking.

Synthesize to Share: Two Sources

Source **A** explains, describes, or argues:	Source **B** explains, describes, or argues:

So, I . . .

Synthesize to Share: Three Sources

Source **A** explains, describes, or argues:	Source **B** explains, describes, or argues:	Source **C** explains, describes, or argues:

So, I . . .

Synthesize to Share: Four Sources

Source **A** explains, describes, or argues:	Source **B** explains, describes, or argues:	Source **C** explains, describes, or argues:	Source **D** explains, describes, or argues:

So, I…

The Connection Between Literacy Development Components and the Research Process Checklist

Use this as a resource to make connections between literacy components and the research process. This resource explains how literacy is embedded within the research process.

Components of Literacy Development	Evidence of Literacy Learning: What to Look for in Students' Process and Product
Language	☐ Students take notes during conversations with their research partners and their teachers.
	☐ Students develop a system for tracking information and responses while processing source material.
	☐ Students reference information learned from reading when providing a rationale for choosing a research topic or developing claims and explanations.
	☐ Students document their summaries, evaluations, analyses, and syntheses of information in a chart, note-taking organizer, or space provided by the teacher.
	☐ Students write down questions and reactions from the research community when sharing their findings.
	☐ Students develop different ways to visually represent their thinking while they are generating ideas.
	☐ Students use writing to discover what they know and want to know more about when generating ideas for research.
	☐ Students write a series of research questions that are similar but crafted in different ways to experiment with language, vocabulary, and syntax.
	☐ Students write a series of thesis statements but crafted in different ways to experiment with language, vocabulary, and syntax.
	☐ Students write claims, explanations, and conclusions or findings with evidence of drafting, revisions, and edits.
	☐ Students present research findings using multiple modalities.
	☐ Students share a written reflection.
	☐ Students prepare notes for a reflection conversation.
Identity	☐ Students choose their own topic for research.
	☐ Students develop their own research question based on something they are interested in or want to learn more about.
	☐ Students choose how they want to organize, present, and share their findings. This multimodal artifact can be in addition to a research writing piece.

Identity	☐ Students provide rationales in writing and conversation for the personal and academic choices related to their work.
	☐ Students can articulate how their work connects to aspects of their identity.
	☐ Students can reflect on their learning and how it will transfer into personal, academic, and social spaces.
Community	☐ Students make a connection between their research and a community they belong to or are connected to.
	☐ Students share or plan to share their findings or their research product within the community the research is connected to.
Future-Ready Skills	☐ Students demonstrate their understanding of how they are developing future-ready skills through the research process in reflection writing and conference conversations.
	☐ Students identify the future-ready skills they can transfer to personal, social, and other academic spaces.
Multimodal Meaning-Making	☐ Students design various ways to share their thinking when generating and narrowing ideas and gathering information. Students may work with print or digital materials to create images, charts, webs, maps, and so on. They may use color tools to organize and categorize ideas.
	☐ Students create a product based on their findings on a digital platform of their choice.

Revolving Literacy Research Articulation Planning Tool for Grades 7–12

Use this as a tool when articulating research experiences across grades 7–12. The questions included are intended to guide planning.

Revolving Literacy Components	Grade 7	Grade 8	Grade 9	Grade 10	Grade 11	Grade 12
What **type of research** do students engage in (literary, informational, persuasive)?						
What **standards** are addressed?						
What **future-ready skills** are explicitly taught?						
What **research skills** are emphasized?						

Revolving Literacy Components	Grade 7	Grade 8	Grade 9	Grade 10	Grade 11	Grade 12
How are students encouraged to make **identity** connections through research?						
How are students encouraged to make **community** connections through research?						
What is the **product** of research? How do students share their findings?						
What opportunities do students have to make meaning through **multiple modalities**?						

Revolving Literacy Research Articulation Planning Tool for Grades 7–9

Use this as a tool when articulating research experiences across grades 7–9. The questions included are intended to guide planning.

Revolving Literacy Components	Grade 7	Grade 8	Grade 9
What **type of research** do students engage in (literary, informational, persuasive)?			
What **standards** are addressed?			
What **future-ready skills** are explicitly taught?			
What **research skills** are emphasized?			

Revolving Literacy Components	Grade 7	Grade 8	Grade 9
How are students encouraged to make **identity** connections through research?			
How are students encouraged to make **community** connections through research?			
What is the **product** of research? How do students share their findings?			
What opportunities do students have to make meaning through **multiple modalities**?			

Revolving Literacy Research Articulation Planning Tool for Grades 9–12

Use this as a tool when articulating research experiences across grades 9–12. The questions included are intended to guide planning.

Revolving Literacy Components	Grade 9	Grade 10	Grade 11	Grade 12
What **type of research** do students engage in (literary, informational, persuasive)?				
What **standards** are addressed?				
What **future-ready skills** are explicitly taught?				
What **research skills** are emphasized?				

Revolving Literacy Components	Grade 9	Grade 10	Grade 11	Grade 12
How are students encouraged to make **identity** connections through research?				
How are students encouraged to make **community** connections through research?				
What is the **product** of research? How do students share their findings?				
What opportunities do students have to make meaning through **multiple modalities**?				

CHAPTER 6
TEACHING READERS IN THE REVOLVING LITERACY CLASSROOM

Secondary literacy educators know that motivation and engagement are equal parts necessary and challenging when it comes to students and their reading in middle school and high school. I begin this chapter by immediately acknowledging that very real challenge. Secondary English teachers often share with me how they are navigating obstacles to motivation and engagement in reading. There is also compelling research that shows a decline in motivation to read among young people. In the United States, the number of nine-, thirteen-, and seventeen-year-olds who say they read for fun almost daily has dropped to the lowest levels since the mid-1980s (Schaeffer, 2021). Many tweens and teens lack an interest in and commitment to reading, both necessary for growth in their academic and personal reading identities (Schaeffer, 2021).

Reading hasn't become any less important; there are external factors that compete for space in adolescents' minds and personal time, like relationships, jobs, community involvement, volunteer work, family responsibilities, academic work, and technology and social media use (Rideout, Peebles, Mann, & Robb, 2022). Just because motivating and engaging students in reading have become increasingly challenging, secondary literacy educators don't have to be deterred or feel discouraged. It may force us to think differently about the ways we engage students in reading by building reading cultures and implementing different structures and systems of practice.

With this challenging environment in mind, I've organized this chapter a bit differently from what you may have gotten used to in chapters 3 through 5. Recall that in chapter 2 (page 29), we explored the shared text-driven curriculum model and student literacy-driven curriculum model. In this chapter, I share ways to design literacy experiences that prioritize student choice and engagement by varying curriculum reading structures. Each model serves a unique purpose in building a comprehensive approach to reading in secondary classrooms.

While explicit reading instruction can take place within various reading structures, this chapter is not about how to teach reading or aspects of reading proficiency. This chapter explores structures and systems for three models of reading within the secondary English classroom: (1) independent reading, (2) book clubs, and (3) shared text experiences, as figure 6.1 shows. It also emphasizes how different reading structures can impact engagement and active participation in reading.

Text-Driven Curriculum Model	Student Literacy-Driven Curriculum Model	
Shared Reading Experience	Book Clubs	Independent Reading

FIGURE 6.1: Reading curriculum models.

English Teachers Are Reading Teachers

This chapter is about how secondary English educators can position students to be active in their reading by implementing a variety of reading structures. This chapter also introduces ways to engage students in active reading by creating a classroom reading culture. Students should not be passive in their reading; readers need to read, think, reflect, and engage in conversation to support the meaning-making process, according to the foundational work of researcher Louise M. Rosenblatt (1978). The role of the secondary English teacher is evolving. Secondary English teachers are teachers of reading and all its parts.

It's important for English teachers to commit to reading instruction through explicit teaching of strategies to navigate reading skills like summarizing, analyzing, synthesizing, acquiring vocabulary, and thinking critically. In addition to prioritizing practicing skills and thinking protocols of proficient reading in instruction, it is important that secondary English classrooms have a culture of reading with systems and structures that foster an intrinsic motivation to read. The reading culture can encourage students to recognize the importance of reading and to read for pleasure or personal interest. Whether students develop a love, an appreciation, or a tolerance for reading, literacy educators strive to impart to students that reading is important and for students to discover their own purposes for reading.

Before writing this book, I had the opportunity to talk with middle and high school students about their reading experiences in school. I was interested in finding answers to the following questions.

- What motivates students' reading in their secondary school years?
- How do the conditions for reading in school influence students' perception of themselves as readers and motivate them to read outside of school for academic purposes and personal interest?
- How does the classroom reading culture influence students' expectations for success and personal belief systems about their reading identities?
- How can the environment in which students read and learn (Darling-Hammond et al., 2020) and develop their mindsets (Dweck, 2016; Yeager & Walton, 2011) influence reading volume and engagement?

Research into the relationship between motivation and learning and the relationship between reading volume and reading achievement guided my inquiry.

- According to educational psychologist Jacquelynne S. Eccles (2005), learning tasks are more valuable to students if they believe the learning is important, relevant to their lives, and connected to events they have experienced or care about.
- Students are more likely to value learning when intrinsic reasons for learning are emphasized and when processes and products of learning have an audience beyond the teacher (Ryan & Deci, 2000).
  + Research emphasizes the relationship between reading volume (Allington, 2014; Allington & McGill-Franzen, 2021), motivation (Guthrie & Wigfield, 2000; McBreen & Savage, 2020), and achievement.

Students shared with me their personal anecdotes about reading in middle and high school. The information I gathered helped me evaluate the culture of reading within classrooms as well as the influence structures and conditions for reading have on students in secondary English classes. What I found was both encouraging and invigorating. The patterns that emerged from what students shared indicate the following are important.

- Choice in reading through book clubs
- Choice in reading through independent reading
- Exposure to a variety of genres through shared texts, book clubs, and independent reading
- Participation in a reading community through partner discussions, book club discussions, whole-class discussions, and celebrating reading successes
- Personal connections to content and characters in reading
- Exposure to various perspectives through diverse book selections and reading conversations among peers
- The positive impact teachers have on students' reading lives

In the following sections, I share systems and structures for reading experiences and reading culture in secondary English classrooms. I invite you to consider how they contribute to growing reading as a process of learning and skill building, much like the writing and research processes. Readers need to cultivate their own reading habits and behaviors with the guidance of teachers and peers. The co-construction of reading routines between students and teachers is one way that secondary English teachers can design future-ready classroom spaces (Schlam Salman & Inbar-Lourie, 2023). Readers also need to develop an awareness of how various reading experiences can support them in developing literacy competencies, including future-ready skills, that are applicable to other academic, personal, and social spaces. Relevance and engagement frame the three following models for reading: independent reading, book clubs, and shared reading experiences.

Independent Reading

Independent reading is when teachers and students designate class time for reading a text of choice for a sustained period of time. While some English teachers have one unit dedicated to independent reading, I propose that independent reading is an ongoing process that lasts the entire school year. The main purpose of independent reading is to read for pleasure or personal interest and to share about one's reading life within the class reading community. Independent reading is something that consistently shifts and changes; teachers design systems that work for the class community. Figure 6.2 shows the components of independent reading.

Student Choice	Access	Sustained Reading
Partner Talk	Reading Response	Conferring
Book Talks	Recordkeeping	Reading Celebrations

FIGURE 6.2: Components of independent reading.

While independent reading is mostly solitary, there are components to an independent reading classroom routine that make reading participatory (Kelley & Jenkins, 2013) and a social practice (Gee, 1999; Street, 2016). These include partner talk, sharing book talks with peer groups or the whole class, sharing recommendations with peers in print or digital spaces, and conferring between students and teachers. Time is designated each day or within a week for independent reading. In addition to cultivating authentic reading habits, prioritizing time to sustain a volume of reading is one way that secondary English teachers can contribute to growing student achievement (Allington & McGill-Franzen, 2021). Since independent reading is designed to foster reading habits and behaviors through students reading texts of choice, an assignment or project may or may not be associated with reading time. Teachers make decisions about independent reading routines based on the students they have in their classes each year and what they need.

Think about the last thing you read (besides this book). Was there an adult choosing what to read for you? Was there an adult reading to you? Was there an adult present to stop and pose a question every few paragraphs? Most likely there wasn't. This is because reading after high school is independent reading (Gallagher, 2022).

While there are social aspects of reading in personal, social, and academic spaces like conversations about a text or a formal book club, the ways in which we approach reading as adults result from personal choices we make about how and why we read. In "real life," the reader is at the center of reading experiences, not another adult making choices about what to read and how to think about it. Meaning-making resides within the reader (Rosenblatt, 1978).

As I conveyed in the introduction (page 1), I don't write this to judge the work of English teachers or suggest that reading aloud and shared reading with discussion aren't important. The opposite is true. I know this through my own experiences with reading aloud and shared reading as an English teacher. They were some of the most precious times with my students. Also, bodies of research suggest that reading aloud and shared reading are instructional practices that prepare students to approach independent reading (Roessingh, 2020; Stoetzel & Shedrow, 2021).

I invite you to think about if and how the reading experiences students have in English class prepare them for reading beyond high school.

- Is there a balance of reading aloud or shared reading and independent reading experiences?
- Does the curriculum include mostly texts that students are required to read or want to read?
- Do students have opportunities to choose what they read?
- Are there authentic purposes for reading?
- Do students manage their own reading time and reading habits?
- Are there explicit connections between reading and future-ready skill development?

Consider the balance between shared reading experiences with explicit instruction and independent reading experiences for application of learning. Students need both opportunities for learning. In the following sections, we address the key actions to support independent reading activities.

LAUNCH INDEPENDENT READING

Making time for students to choose texts for independent reading is some of the most important work you will do in your reading community all school year. Beginning this process during the first days of school and continuing consistently thereafter signals the following to students.

- Reading is a *priority* in your class community.
- Their personal *choices* about reading are important.
- *Time* for reading in school is valued.

There are several ways in which you can prepare for launching an independent reading routine.

- **Connect with a librarian:** Contact your school librarian to make an appointment to bring your class to the library to select books. Plan to integrate library visits into your routine throughout the year so students have a consistent access point for selecting books. You may also contact a librarian at the public library in your community to share about independent reading in your class. You may be able to distribute public library card applications to students. A public library card typically avails students to print titles in the physical library as well as digital texts via an online platform. Consult with school administration about connecting with a public librarian and notify caregivers about the benefits of a public library card.

- **Read middle-grade and young adult books:** Read what your students read. See the reproducible "Middle Grade and Young Adult Book List" (page 226) for a list of fan favorites among middle and high school teachers that I have read with. The more you read, the better you will be able to recommend books to your students and share book talks to alert students to new titles.

- **Prepare to learn the identities of your students and who they are as readers:** Knowing about your students' identities impacts how you support them as readers throughout the year. It can help with recommending books, making decisions about how you invite students to respond to reading, and developing questions for students about the connections they are making or not making to their reading. See chapter 2 (page 29) for ways that students can share their identities. You may also share a reading survey with students to focus on their reading lives.

- **Develop a system for students to manage their reading materials:** Teacher and student management are essential to the functioning of independent reading in a classroom. Choose a system that works for you and students. Your system may change from year to year depending on your students and what they need. In my classroom, students brought their books and reading notebooks in a gallon-size bag to school and home each day. Keeping the two items together was helpful. Some students may prefer to read digitally and will access texts on a school-issued device or personal Kindle or iPad. Some teachers keep reading notebooks in bins in the classroom, but books and reading material travel with the students. Material management can be a challenge, but it's part of how students learn organization. If there are a few students who chronically forget to bring their materials to class, consider accessing a digital copy of what they are reading or have more than one copy of the print material in the classroom. While it may be frustrating when students forget their materials, I don't recommend letting it become contentious. Students may live in multiple homes, have various ways of getting to school, or may be challenged by organization. The most important part of independent reading is reading. Let the skill development be a work in progress.

MAKE INSTRUCTIONAL PLANS THAT INCLUDE INDEPENDENT READING

No matter the age of the readers, read-alouds can coach students for independent reading. Literacy instruction in general is stronger when you include read-alouds as a method to see how students engage with reading (Stoetzel & Shedrow, 2021).

Consider launching independent reading with a series of read-alouds. You may then circle back to read-alouds during or between units of study to continue cultivating independent reading. Modeling thinking and response strategies with short texts supports students in learning how to monitor their meaning-making while independently reading. A read-aloud also provides an opportunity for teachers to coach students to think about perspective when reading so students reflect on their own relationship with the texts they are reading. Consider using Bishop's (1990) metaphor of books as mirrors and windows in your dialogue about reading and perspective.

Use the revolving literacy lesson plan (see chapter 3, page 73) to design your series of introduction lessons. When using the revolving literacy lesson plan, a read-aloud followed by independent reading may take place over two days. The explicit instruction portion of the lesson that includes the interactive read-aloud may occur on day 1. Students then apply their learning from the read-aloud during the independent practice portion of the lesson on day 2. Teachers spend time conferring with students about their reading on day 2. An interactive read-aloud is a way to build in explicit instruction with independent reading throughout the year in ways that can complement designated units of study in reading and writing. Teachers can model ways to think about ideas, information, and perspectives.

Consider the skills, thinking routines, and curricular topics that are in your scope and sequence. Choose picture books and short excerpts of text to serve as mentor texts in a series of minilessons. After each minilesson with a mentor text, students can practice what was taught in their independent reading. Structured time early in the year allows all students to begin their new reading journey in a supportive space together before they venture off on their own independent reading journeys. After the initial launch of independent reading, consider revisiting a read-aloud routine once per quarter (for example, in August or September, November, January, and April).

CHOOSE A SCHEDULE FOR INDEPENDENT READING

In the previous section, I suggest planning instructional time focused on independent reading at designated times throughout the school year. In between, independent reading is the sacred time when students read. Students may write reading responses periodically, but the purpose of this reading structure is to provide sustained time for reading texts of choice. Choose a schedule for independent reading that works for you and your students. Not all schedules are the same; they are unique to the culture and preferences within the classroom. You also may choose an independent reading schedule to start the year and then change the schedule as the year progresses based on responses from students. Here are three options for an independent reading schedule.

1. Students read for ten minutes daily at the beginning or end of the period. Teachers plan lessons that are timed for ten minutes instead of a forty- or forty-five- minute period.
2. Designate one day of the week to forty or forty-five minutes of independent reading. Some students and teachers have shared preferences for Monday, Wednesday, and Friday.
3. Students read for twenty minutes during two days of the week (for example, on Tuesday and Thursday).

You may also encourage students to read at home. While we can't control what students do outside of school, we can prioritize time for them to read while in school.

PLAN FOR STUDENTS TO ACCESS READING MATERIAL

Access points for books and reading material vary within school communities and classrooms. Places to access books and reading material include schools, classrooms, and public libraries; e-reader platforms like SORA, E-Destiny, and Follett; websites; home libraries; and bookstores. *Access* also refers to how readers gain book recommendations and participate in a reading community. Access points may include a librarian, a teacher, a reading partner, a friend or classmate, a class book recommendation board or online space, websites like Amazon or Goodreads, or social media sites with specific book threads like Instagram (www.instagram.com; #bookstagram) and TikTok (www.tiktok.com; #booktok).

Another aspect of access is time. Students should have time in school to select books; engage in conversation about their reading with partners, peers, and adults; and make plans for future reading. Teachers are then better able to support students in developing authentic reading habits and routines.

ESTABLISH INDEPENDENT READING ROUTINES

The schedule for independent reading is an important part of your classroom routine. The following are other independent reading routines to integrate as you see fit.

- **Goal setting:** Part of what makes independent reading necessary in secondary English classrooms is students' reflection and self-management throughout the process. These processes are part of students' preparation for postsecondary experiences when they don't have teachers and classroom structures to guide them as intimately and often. Goals may connect to reading habits (frequency or duration of reading), reading behaviors (stamina or attention while reading), reading engagement (genres read or platforms used), or reading skill development (level of understanding or the strategies for meaning-making).

- **Partner talk:** Students have a reading partner that they discuss their independent reading with. There may be an established protocol for discussion, or the students can have authentic conversations without structure. Partner talk is a way for students to learn about what their peers are reading and for readers to continue to make meaning of their reading through discussion.

- **Book talks:** The teacher and students share book talks with the class. A book talk is a brief summary and recommendation of a book so others may decide whether they'd like to add the title to their to-read list. Book talks may also be informal and occur regularly as readers want to share. They are meant to be concise. Frameworks for book talks include the following.
    + Students can use the following sample framework. "I am reading [insert title and author]. It's about [share the topic, theme, or primary plotline]. If you're interested in [share topic or theme], then you should check it out."
    + Students could also use the following sample framework. "I am reading [insert title and author]. The genre is [insert genre]. Something that interests me is [insert point of interest]. If you like [share genre, topic, or theme], then you should check it out."

- Students can also present a ten-word book talk. This activity is challenging (and fun!) because it invites the reader to consider what is most important or universal in what they are reading. The reader sums it up in exactly ten words. Here is an example of a ten-word book talk about *Outliers: The Story of Success* by Malcolm Gladwell (2008): "Success is shaped by extraordinary factors in high achievers' lives."

- **Reading conferences:** A reading conference between the teacher and a student lets teachers gauge how students are progressing in their reading lives. Reading conferences typically occur during the guided or independent practice portion of the revolving literacy lesson plan. Keep in mind that in the guided or independent practice portion of a reading lesson, students may be working with a partner, group, or teacher (if guided) or may be working alone (if independent). Guided practice does not refer to guided reading where students are reading a leveled text in a small group with the teacher. Teachers may schedule reading conferences so they can talk with all readers throughout the course of a week or two. I have to acknowledge the complexity of a reading conference. Although they are short, they are mighty—mighty in how they can help teachers know readers and how they require management and flexibility at the same time.

HOLD STUDENTS ACCOUNTABLE

Accountability is probably what I talk with secondary teachers most about when it comes to independent reading. They often have questions like, How am I supposed to grade reading for pleasure? If the book isn't one we are reading together, or I don't know the book, how am I supposed to grade their work? These are valid concerns. Even if educators are excited about the prospects of independent reading, the management and accountability may be deterrents. There may be some classes where reading thrives and students are able to share details and insights about what they are reading whether the teacher monitors it or not. Avid readers are avid readers. What is more common is a class with avid readers, compliant readers, and avoidant readers. They are all readers; they just need different types of guidance.

If you are not comfortable dedicating class time to something that students are not going to earn a grade for, there are ways to build a grading system into authentic reading work. You may consider grading for completion or specific elements of reading responses. What follows are ways to build in accountability for reading.

- **Reading response journal:** Students are responsible for writing reading responses throughout the quarter or semester about their independent reading. You may provide a menu of items for students to choose from. Students should submit their responses for credit.

- **Blog or vlog as you read (recordkeeping):** Students can write a blog entry or record a vlog entry each time they come across an event or idea they connect to or want to share with others. They can create a space within the blog or vlog site for others to post comments, opening up opportunities for online interaction with other readers. For vlogs, video entries can also be uploaded to a class YouTube channel or Instagram page.
  + *Snapchat, TikTok, or Instagram Story*—Students can assume the role of a character and create a Snapchat or Instagram story that illustrates how the character experiences the world.
  + *One-pager*—Students create an illustration that represents what they are reading. In addition, they provide summary points, analysis of events, and impactful excerpts from their reading. The one-pager appears like a collage of images and words on the page.
  + *Written book recommendations*—Invite students to write a reading recommendation each time they finish reading a text. Post recommendations on a shared class website or Padlet so classmates can use it as a resource when deciding what to read next.

My advice to you is to be intentional about when and how often you ask students to submit independent reading work for a grade. While accountability is important, a main purpose of independent reading is to foster authentic reading habits and routines so students can reap the benefits of reading, as outlined at the start of this chapter. It may take some getting used to if you have not had an independent reading routine. It's something that requires practice in letting go. It was hard for me at first, but when I observed how students' attitudes and behaviors toward reading started to turn in a positive direction when I remained flexible, it was clear to me that independent reading, without full accountability all the time, was a necessary component in the secondary English classroom.

STAY COMMITTED AND SUSTAIN A CELEBRATORY CLASSROOM READING CULTURE

The school year is long. Staying committed and enthusiastic about independent reading can be challenging. There is curriculum to teach. Meetings to attend. Assessments to administer. Announcements to make. Holiday breaks. It's easy to say, "We'll just skip it today." Again, I understand. What we choose to spend time on in the classroom signals what is important to students. Reading culture events help keep independent reading relevant and create an ongoing commitment to developing future-ready skills associated with independent reading routines. Maintain reading as a priority through these culture-building events.

- **Start class with a book talk:** Have students regularly present book talks with the whole class or in partnerships. Use the suggested book talk frames from the previous section.
- **Establish First Chapter Fridays:** Every Friday, introduce a new book to students by reading the first chapter or the first few pages aloud. Reading the beginning of a new book each week exposes students to a variety of titles they may choose to read in the future. You may collaborate with colleagues in selecting books to ease your workload.
- **Showcase book fandom on social media pages:** Create a personal, professional, or class Instagram or TikTok account. Periodically show students, via a digital board in front of the room, what book fandom looks like on #Bookstagram and #BookTok. Educate students on how readers form reading communities on social media by sharing book recommendations and comments about books they are reading. Viewing book fandom may inspire students to read new titles or find a new social media niche.

FACILITATE A DISCUSSION OF THE WEEK

Another way to foster independence in reading is through a protocol called discussion of the week, which invites students to find the relevance in their reading. The premise of discussion of the week is making connections. Each week, students are invited to recall and reflect on the reading, writing, or thinking they have done in English class or another class within that week. They choose one topic to focus on in their discussion of the week response and are invited to make a connection between that topic and something else they have seen or read within the past couple of weeks. This can be a text of any kind (news, sports articles, opinion pieces, blog posts, memes, and so on), a video on YouTube or TikTok, an Instagram posting, a TV show, a movie, a book, and so on. Adapt the following suggested text to introduce discussion of the week to students.

> To learn even more about our world and to make connections between what you think about and are interested in at home and at school, you will have a weekly discussion on [insert digital platform]. You will share insights through writing your own response. You will learn the insights of others and engage in digital dialogue. This is your opportunity to make your learning matter and to see what you learn come alive in different contexts.

Students write to explain the connection they're making between the school reading, writing, or thinking experience and the personal media they've selected. They post their writing to a class online platform. Students briefly summarize both sources and then explain how they connect. Students provide digital links to the personal media source where applicable. Here are guiding questions to support students in articulating their connections.

- Is the connection based on similarities between the two experiences or sources?
- Is the connection about drastic differences in information or opinion?
- Does the connection spark interest in a new topic or idea?
- Does the connection spark an emotion, reaction, or feeling?
- Does the connection remind you of something else in your life?
- Is there a teacher or peer who may appreciate the connection and who you want to share it with?

After students post their discussion of the week submission, they respond to at least two other postings in the class. They can visit the source links provided and include references in the reply postings. Students may post their discussion of the week on an online platform of your choice. This may depend on the digital tools available and approved in your school community. There are tools in the Google Suite like Blogger (www.blogger.com), Docs (http://docs.google.com), and Sites (http://sites.google.com) that allow multiple collaborators or comment features. You may replace the written reply portion of the discussion with partner conversations intermittently so students have opportunities to practice sharing responses to reading through conversations.

This design is based on ecological views of learning and development, particularly on interest-driven learning, that require self-regulating, defining goals, and reflecting on how well one is doing (Barron, 2006). There is evidence of benefits of interest-driven learning over time (Renninger & Hidi, 2017): It increases attention, leads the learner to generate questions, and sustains engagement. Interest-driven learning can also catalyze a series of choices over time that help launch pathways to future jobs, educational opportunities, and careers. For example, interests can support academic resilience in overcoming challenges in processing text or persevering in difficult tasks (Darling-Hammond et al., 2020). While some students may engage with complex and challenging texts for discussion of the week, their interest in the topic or text may help cultivate the independent aspect of the work. See the reproducible "Discussion of the Week" (page 227) for a sample outline of discussion of the week for students.

USE NONFICTION ROUNDTABLES TO RAISE CITIZENS WHO READ

Another option for fostering an independent reading routine is for students to explore nonfiction. The name *nonfiction roundtable* is a play on the term roundtable discussion. At a roundtable discussion, a group of people gather to discuss a specific topic or list of topics. In the secondary English classroom, a nonfiction roundtable discussion is when a group of students read a nonfiction article independently and come together to discuss it and evaluate its importance.

Integrating nonfiction to foster independent reading contributes to building students' knowledge about the world around them. Research on reading has long demonstrated that comprehension depends on prior knowledge about the topic, which permits sense-making as much as decoding skills (Pearson, Cervetti, & Tilson, 2008). Darling-Hammond and colleagues (2020) suggest that when students have not had particular experiences or acquired certain background knowledge, teachers can create experiences for them to develop that knowledge.

To determine what students read at these roundtables, teachers curate current event, informational, and opinion articles to create weekly text sets. At the beginning of the week, students choose an article from the weekly text set that they are interested in reading. Students read the selected article throughout the week and respond through annotation or response notes to prepare for the roundtable discussion at the end of the week. The roundtable discussion happens with peers who selected the same text to read. See the reproducible "Reading Response Tool: Why Do We Read? Protocol" (page 228) for a reading response tool.

Teachers may group students by choice in text selection, areas of interest, proficiency level, personality types, or any existing reading partnerships. Groupings will change as student choices change.

At the end of the week, the roundtable group comes together to discuss the article they chose to read. They share points of interest, questions, wonderings, and connections. A goal for the group is to evaluate the importance of the content in the article they read. A goal for individual readers is for each student to establish what they learned or realized from reading and engaging in discussion with peers. Readers may also connect their learning to another academic area or a personal or social space.

WRAP-UPS FOR INDEPENDENT READING

Independent reading can be overwhelming. No matter how many systems and routines you put in place, there are still elements that aren't controlled. As secondary literacy educators, we strive for students to make choices and manage aspects of their own learning. Even though we want this, it still can be unsettling not to make all the decisions for what goes on in the classroom. Teachers not having complete control is part of a revolving literacy classroom: Teachers and students share the control and the decision making.

I aim to provide you with options for independent reading so you can create a plan you are comfortable implementing and that your students can connect to. You may start with a system like nonfiction roundtables for the first semester and then move into daily independent reading during the second semester. Or you may opt to engage students in discussion of the week during your first year of creating more independence and choice in reading. I encourage you to take parts of each of these systems to create a plan that is relevant and engaging for your students. Choice and active reading are pillars for planning. As we end this section of the chapter, I invite you to reflect on the independent reading options and how you may design a system that is conducive to your classroom space.

Stop and Think

How do you plan to integrate independent reading into your work with students?

Independent Reading Structure	Benefits for Students	Potential Challenges for Students
Daily or Weekly Independent Reading		
Discussion of the Week		
Nonfiction Roundtable		

Visit **go.SolutionTree.com/literacy** *for a free reproducible version of this reflection.*

Stop and Think

Use this planning page for independent reading in your classroom. Refer to the structures outlined in this section of the chapter for practical strategies designed for each component of the process.

Independent Reading Plan	Notes and Next Steps
Preparing to launch: How will you get started?	
Scheduling: When will you make time for independent reading?	
Managing materials: What is the procedure for students managing materials (books, e-readers, notebooks)?	
Accessing reading material: When and where will students access reading material and the reading community?	
Establishing routines: How does the reading community function together? Are there book talks? Do students share about their reading with reading partners? Are there reading conferences?	
Recordkeeping: How will the teacher keep track of students' reading lives? How will students keep track of their reading lives?	
Accountability: How do students demonstrate their commitment to and understanding of their reading?	
Communication: How will all stakeholders—students, teachers, administrators, parents and caregivers—know about the importance of independent reading?	
Staying committed: How will you maintain enthusiasm for reading? How will reading culture continue to grow throughout the school year? How are reading recommendations shared?	

Visit ***go.SolutionTree.com/literacy*** *for a free reproducible version of this reflection.*

Book Clubs

In the previous section about independent reading structures, I shared ways to integrate independent reading into units of study in English class. What students read and discuss during independent reading time may or may not be related to a unit of study. I suggest that book club units of study, which have different iterations, be part of the secondary English curriculum. Teachers deliver explicit instruction in areas of reading, group collaboration, and future-ready skill development (refer to the explicit instruction portion of the "Revolving Literacy Lesson Plan Thinking Map" in chapter 2, page 83). Students apply their learning while reading their book club books and working with their book club members (refer to the guided or independent practice portion of the "Revolving Literacy Lesson Plan Thinking Map" in chapter 2, page 83).

Book club units of study offer myriad benefits to student learning, literacies, and future-ready skill development, as well as curriculum design.

- Book clubs support the participatory nature (Kelley & Jenkins, 2013) of literacy development. Students collaborate to design reading schedules, formulate questions, lead inquiry discussions, and develop meaning through discussions.
- Book clubs align with research about literacy as a social practice (Gee, 2010; Street, 2016). Students define and engage in discourse (Gee, 1999) about texts and topics of interest. New literacies, or understandings, among student groups emerge as a result of the social experience of making meaning of the text.
- Book clubs offer students choice in reading. Choice is important to engagement and learning (Darling-Hammond et al., 2020; Wolpert-Gawron, 2017). Book clubs also offer choice to teachers. While students have choice in what they read for the unit, teachers select the books that students will pick from.
- Book clubs offer students agency in their learning. Students work together to design conditions for learning and reading schedules. Students and teachers work together to decide when book club discussions will happen and the focus for conversations. Student groups collaborate, as do students and teachers; both are attributes of a future-ready classroom (Schlam Salman & Inbar-Lourie, 2023).
- Articulating book club units of study across the grade-level continuum of English curriculum exposes students to different genres. Students also

CHAPTER 6: Teaching Readers in the Revolving Literacy Classroom

learn what it is like to participate in a book club or a group of learners working toward the same goal over time by getting instruction in club work in multiple grade levels.

In the following sections, I outline key elements of planning for book clubs, facilitating them in the classroom, and wrapping them up. The key elements are universal to book club design and are applicable to multiple grade levels. I invite you to reflect on your own classroom and context as you read. Think about how you could integrate the ideas and resources in this chapter and modify or adapt that material to fit your context.

BEHIND THE SCENES: PLANNING FOR A BOOK CLUB UNIT

Book club units of study are typically designed around a specific genre or theme. Questions to consider when deciding on a genre or topic are as follows.

- What genres or topics would students connect to most at their ages and stages of development?
- What genres or topics are covered in the grade levels before and after my grade level? How can I present genres and topics in a way that is well-articulated for students?
- Is there a genre or topic that students within the grade are typically interested in?
- How can I balance the genres and topics of shared texts and book clubs?
- What genres or topics are students typically overexposed and underexposed to in other reading experiences?
- Are there topics in other disciplines to align book club content with?

There isn't one right way to design the book club progression. School communities, groups of students, and content curricula vary by district and state or province. Table 6.1 (page 196) illustrates an example of a secondary English progression of book club units by genre with sample rationales.

Table 6.2 (page 197) illustrates an example of a secondary English progression of book club units by topic with sample rationales. Genres, topics, and rationales may be dependent on your context.

TABLE 6.1: A Sample Book Club Unit Progression by Genre With Sample Rationales

	Grade 6	Grade 7	Grade 8	Grade 9	Grade 10	Grade 11	Grade 12
Genre	Fantasy and Sci-Fi	Historical Fiction	Dystopian Fiction	Realistic Fiction	Narrative Nonfiction—Memoir or Autobiography	Thriller or Mystery	Nonfiction—Self-Help or Social Psychology
Sample Rationale	High interest, may connect to media interests Connection to ancient history in social studies	Exposure to a complex genre that may be new for readers Connection to early American history in social studies	High interest, may connect to media interests Early teenage years—contemplate how societies are formed and governed	High interest, social issues may mirror early high school years	Exposure to high-impact figures in society Learn from the mistakes and influences of others as students prepare for final years of high school	High interest Suspense keeps readers interested	High interest Preparation for life after high school Exposure to popular genre in adult reading

TABLE 6.2 A Sample Book Club Unit Progression by Topic With Sample Rationales

	Grade 6	Grade 7	Grade 8	Grade 9	Grade 10	Grade 11	Grade 12
Topic	Technology and Human Relationships	Friendships and Social Issues	War-Story Memoirs	Identity	Influencers	Decision Making	Habits for Success
Sample Rationale	High interest, may connect to media interests Reflect on how technology influences humans Reflect on the relationship between human relationships and advances in technology	Relevant to where students are in their social development; many make new friends in the early years of middle or junior high school	Reflection on the perseverance of others and the power of empathy; Connection to study of wars in social studies	Relevant to where students are in their personal development as they begin their high school years: Who am I and who do I want to be?	Exposure to high-impact figures in society Learn from the mistakes and influences of others as students prepare for final years of high school: Who am I in relation to others? Who do I want to be?	Reflection on how people make decisions as students age into adulthood and get ready for postsecondary experiences *This may be a nonfiction book club or fiction books with iconic characters that are forced into decision making	Relevant to preparing for postsecondary experiences Exposure to popular genre in adult reading

From here, let's look closer at determining book club choices, designing the instructional work of the unit, and selecting a mentor text for instruction.

SELECT THE BOOK CHOICES

Once you decide on the genre or topic of the book club, you can then select the books that students will choose from. Often, secondary English teachers express to me that they love the book club option for choice in reading in the curriculum because both teachers and students have choice in the planning. To give students relevant and engaging choices, there is work to be done behind the scenes to prepare for this unit. A common question is, "How do I know which books to pick?" Choice can sometimes be overwhelming. Here are some strategies that may help in the process.

- Read several books within the genre or topic you select for your book club unit. You may consider planning a book club unit during the year prior to implementation to give you enough time to read and select books.
- Divide and conquer. Work with your grade-level colleagues to each read a few titles and then share positive reflections and potential challenges of each text during your decision-making process.
- Ask a school or public librarian. A librarian may be able to give you a text set within the genre or topic of the unit. A librarian may also be able to summarize each text and provide you with insight about selections for the age of students you teach.
- Consult English teacher social media groups. Other teachers may already be doing the work you plan to do and may post book title suggestions. Using social media as a starting point can be helpful; be sure to read or read about suggested material to ensure books are appropriate for your students.
- Peruse websites like Amazon, Barnes and Noble, and Goodreads. Part of the algorithms of these sites is to pair similar books together as you search. If you read one book within a genre or topic that you plan to include in the unit, follow the cyber trails toward similar books. As with using social media, be sure to read or read about suggested material to ensure books are appropriate for your students.

When selecting books, it is important to plan for different types of readers in the classroom. Offer a diverse selection of books within your text set. Keep the following in mind when balancing your text set: contemporary texts, classic texts, length of book, text complexity, character and author diversity, variation of genre elements (for example, setting in historical fiction), and book format (prose, verse, highly illustrated, graphic novel).

DESIGN THE INSTRUCTIONAL WORK OF THE UNIT

As I previously shared, a book club unit of study provides explicit instruction in areas of reading, group collaboration, and future-ready skill development. Students apply their learning while reading their book club text and working with their book club members. Curriculum design varies by school district. Your team may purchase a book club unit of study that has teaching points and resources already written and curated, or teachers within your department may write curriculum units. Whether using a purchased or homegrown curriculum, I suggest using the revolving literacy unit framework to design the focus areas and rationale for the book club unit of study.

The revolving literacy framework unit planner can help illuminate the focus areas for instruction during minilessons as you reflect on what students need to learn related to literacy development. You may teach students strategies for reading or club collaboration, about aspects of the genre or topic, and how to reflect on future-ready skill development. Table 6.3 provides examples of lesson objectives (see chapter 3, page 73, for the revolving literacy lesson plan) in areas of instruction for book clubs.

TABLE 6.3: Examples of Lesson Objectives for a Book Club Unit of Study

Instructional Focus	Objective
Reading	Readers will be able to notice how themes develop throughout a story by reflecting on shifts in a character's thoughts or behaviors from the beginning to the end of the story. Readers will provide evidence from the text to support their assertions.
Genre or Topic	Readers will be able to identify how things in a society go awry at the start of a dystopian novel to establish the setting of a dystopian world.
Club Collaboration	Readers will be able to design a weekly reading schedule that all book club members can follow and be prepared for discussion.
Future-Ready Skill	Readers will be able to identify how they have practiced resilience or flexibility in their self-management in preparing for book club meetings.

SELECT A MENTOR TEXT FOR INSTRUCTION

You will want to select a mentor text or series of mentor texts to use for instruction. The mentor text serves as an example for students to learn from while you provide instruction. Mentor texts are tools to center discussions among the whole class in preparation for reading and book club discussions. Students learn from what the teacher models with the mentor text and apply it to their own reading and thinking.

The mentor text should be a text that mirrors the genre, topic, or attributes of what the students are reading. It can be a novel, a short story, text excerpts, or a series of picture books that illuminate the work of the unit. If you select a novel, it is not necessary for you to read the entire book to the class. You can select excerpts from the text to showcase for instruction. Mentor texts should be engaging and appropriate for whole-class study. Table 6.4 provides examples of mentor text and book club book choice pairings.

TABLE 6.4: Mentor Text and Book Club Book Choice Pairings

	Focus	Mentor Text	Book Club Choices
Middle School	Fantasy	*Harry Potter and the Sorcerer's Stone* by J. K. Rowling	• *The Girl Who Drank the Moon* by Kelly Barnhill • *The Lion, the Witch, and the Wardrobe* by C. S. Lewis • *Tristan Strong Punches a Hole in the Sky* by Kwame Mbalia • *The Lost Hero* by Rick Riordan • *The Hobbit* by J. R. R. Tolkien
	Social Issues Friendships	*Seventh Grade* by Gary Soto (short story)	• *When Stars Are Scattered* by Victoria Jamieson • *Song for a Whale* by Lynne Kelly • *The Fort* by Gordon Korman • *Show Me a Sign* by Ann Clare LeZotte • *The Stars Beneath Our Feet* by David Barclay Moore • *Dear Sweet Pea* by Julie Murphy • *Some Places More Than Others* by Renee Watson
High School	Narrative Nonfiction	*It's Trevor Noah: Born a Crime—Stories From a South African Childhood* by Trevor Noah	• *Enchanted Air: Two Cultures, Two Wings* by Margarita Engle • *Almost American Girl* by Robin Ha • *Becoming: Adapted for Young Readers* by Michelle Obama

High School	Narrative Nonfiction	*It's Trevor Noah: Born a Crime—Stories From a South African Childhood* by Trevor Noah	• *No Summit Out of Sight: The Youngest Person to Climb the Seven Summits* by Jordan Romero • *They Called Us Enemy* by George Takei • *Educated: A Memoir* by Tara Westover
	Identity	"How to Transform an Everyday, Ordinary Hoop Court Into a Place of Higher Learning and You at the Podium" by Matt De La Pena (short story), from *Flying Lessons and Other Stories*, edited by Ellen Oh	• *My Family Divided* by Diane Guerrero • *Free Lunch* by Rex Ogle • *Patron Saints of Nothing* by Randy Ribay • *I'm Not Your Perfect Mexican Daughter* by Erika L. Sanchez • *This Mortal Coil* by Emily Suvada

ONSTAGE: IMPLEMENTING A BOOK CLUB UNIT WITH STUDENTS

There are numerous ways to implement a book club as part of classroom activities. In the following sections, we look at how to introduce a unit of study and put those activities at the center of the work.

SHARE BOOK CLUB CHOICES WITH STUDENTS THROUGH A BOOK TASTING

A book tasting is an engaging way to introduce all the book club choices to students so they can make an informed choice for book club reading based on their interests. Book tastings are designed similarly to how one would engage in a food tasting—sample a small portion and decide on a first impression. As students sample portions of multiple books throughout the book tasting, they can then decide on what book they want to read in their book clubs. An aspect of reading development is getting to know yourself as a reader through encountering an abundance of books and making personal choices about reading (Allington & Gabriel, 2012; Wilhelm & Smith, 2016).

Plan for students to sit at tables in your classroom or in a library space. Each table gets one copy of each of the book club choices. If there are five books to choose from, then there should be five students at each table. Give each student a book tasting "menu" as shown in figure 6.3 (page 202). Print copies of this book-tasting menu, fold them, and distribute them to students to record their initial thoughts about each book.

Book Tasting!
What do you fancy?

Book Title	Author	First Impression			Explain Your Rating
		🙂	🤔	☹️	
		🙂	🤔	☹️	
		🙂	🤔	☹️	
		🙂	🤔	☹️	

Reflection:
What did you think about as you sampled the books at your table?
How can this influence the ways you engage students in reading?

Menu Option

Book Title:
_____

Author:
_____

Genre:
_____

My First Impression: 🙂   🤔   ☹️

Explain your first impression of this book:
_____
_____
_____

What are you wondering about this book?
_____
_____
_____

Welcome to a
Book Tasting!

Name: _____

Date: _____

Source: Radice, 2023, p. 57.

FIGURE 6.3: Book-tasting menu.

*Visit **go.SolutionTree.com/literacy** for a free reproducible version of this figure.*

Each student starts with one of the book club choices. Students have five to seven minutes to sample the book they have in hand and jot down thoughts in their menu recording sheet. After the allotted time, students rotate the books, and each student receives another book club option. Repeat this process with as many tasting rounds as there are book club choices. Teachers may also provide intriguing quotes and information about the authors along with the books to hook readers' interest. By the end of the book tasting, students should have sampled all the books. Then, they rank the books in order of preference on what to read. You may inform students that if and when they finish one book, they may choose to read another one of the books from the menu. Collect students' preferences and consider them when organizing book club groups.

INVITE BOOK CLUBS TO GET ACQUAINTED

Students learn collaboration and leadership skills throughout a book club unit. Students are accountable to themselves for reading and responding to reading; students are also accountable to each other. They need to be prepared for book club discussions by practicing routines and protocols for conversations. They need to learn how to engage in formal and informal talk about reading and other points of interest that emerge from conversation. Positive relationships among club members are helpful to the work. Before students begin reading, dedicate instructional time to teaching students how to generate positive and productive work environments, a skill that transcends into other academic, personal, and professional spaces.

- **Design a team challenge:** Design a task where book club members need to work to accomplish something together, like a game or building a tower out of cards. Think of minute-to-win-it challenges.
- **Establish meeting agreements:** Meeting agreements are ways that book club members stay accountable to one another and respect individual learning styles. Ask students to reflect on the following question: *What is important to you as you establish the reading community within your book club?* The agreements become the road map for club meetings. Club members should have a copy of their meeting agreements readily accessible in a reading notebook or digital space. See figure 6.4 (page 204) for an example of book club members sharing ideas for meeting agreements.

\multicolumn{5}{l}{**Meeting Agreements:** Please write what is important to you as you collaborate with your book club members in virtual space under your name in the chart.}
When collaborating, it's important to me that . . .			
Fay	**Donna**	**Jenna**	**Casey**
• Respect • Think before you speak • Be kind to one another • Be a good listener • Do your part • Stay focused on completing your work	• People are respectful and listen to others • Be prepared with the reading and materials • Everyone participates • Follow the rules and format for discussion • Stay on topic	• Respect and listen to each other • Understand rules and routines • Show kindness • Be prepared with the reading	• Respectful listening • Give everyone time to share their ideas • Kind disagreements • Read the assigned chapters each week • Complete the work so all members share responsibility

FIGURE 6.4: Book club meeting agreements.

TEACH BOOK CLUB GROUPS HOW TO DESIGN A READING SCHEDULE

Designing a schedule for reading and discussion is one of the most valuable processes students participate in within a book club unit. Teachers provide guidelines for students, such as how long the unit will last, how to manage time and develop realistic expectations, and when club meetings will occur within a week. Club members work together to build their own reading schedule based on meeting agreements, the number of pages in the club book, and the duration of a unit or parts of the unit.

Figure 6.5 illustrates a sample weekly schedule designed by a teacher. Students can use the teacher's schedule to make their reading plans.

Monday	Tuesday	Wednesday	Thursday	Friday
Minilesson	Minilesson	Minilesson	Minilesson	Minilesson
Independent reading (book club book) with conferring and response work	Independent reading (book club book) with conferring and response work	Independent reading (book club book) with conferring and response work	Independent reading (book club book) with conferring and response work	Independent reading (book club book) with conferring and response work
	Longer book club talk			Longer book club talk

FIGURE 6.5: Weekly class schedule during a book club unit.

Provide students with a monthly calendar to put in their reading notebook, folder, or digital space. Students may also use a digital calendar or the calendar application on their phones.

ESTABLISH PRACTICES FOR RESPONSES AND REFLECTION

Key elements like choice-in-response formats and journaling (Jocuis & Shealy, 2018) are important to planning and facilitating book club units. Writing about reading and student-directed discussions in response to reading are foundational to the work (Jocuis & Shealy, 2018). Decide on where students will write reading responses. Do you and your students prefer print or digital materials? Do students have choices on where and how to write their responses and organize their materials? Students will often respond to focus areas of instruction in their reading responses, but it is also important to provide students with opportunities to reflect on their club work and the future-ready skills they are developing through their independent and collaborative work.

BE PREPARED TO ADDRESS CHALLENGES

As with independent reading, the reality of this work is that there will always be challenges, no matter how many benefits and positive research implications there are. Challenges are part of the learning for teachers and for students. View challenges as opportunities. Figure 6.6 is an *If . . . Then . . .* chart I designed with and for secondary English teachers to help troubleshoot the typical challenges that arise during book club units.

If	Then
Student is resistant to participating in club meetings.	• Have a conversation with the student to discuss the resistance. • Evaluate the book club grouping: Do all feel comfortable? • Support the student in making plans for reading to help with preparedness. • Provide choices for how club members may participate—conversation stems, direct questions, or a book club game.
Student is not reading.	• Have a conversation with the student to discuss why reading is not happening. • Support the student in making plans for reading to help with preparedness. • Provide scaffolds for reading, if necessary. • Evaluate the book choice for the student.

FIGURE 6.6: Addressing challenges of book clubs assess and evaluate literacy development.

continued ▶

If	Then
Club members are reading at different paces.	• Be patient, as this may take time to figure out as you get to know your students as readers. • Speak with students individually who are reading at a quicker pace than others. They should participate in discussion related to the reading schedule that was agreed on and not share events that happen beyond the chapters being discussed. • Students reading at a quicker pace may read two books—a book club book and an independent reading book. They can stick to the reading schedule for their book club and read their independent reading book when they finish agreed-on sections of reading.
Club talk is shallow or students appear bored.	• Share a video or meme related to club work to start club discussions. • Provide conversation stems that address specific aspects of reading discussion. • Play a book club conversation game.
Club members are off task during club time.	• Provide an explicit task during club time to recalibrate focus and attention to club work. • Ask students to engage in self-reflection about productivity and submit it to the teacher.

All components of literacy development—language, future-ready skills, identity, community, and multimodal meaning-making—are integrated into a book club unit. Be intentional about assessing students throughout and at the conclusion of the unit. There are different skill areas that students cultivate through their independent and collaborative work. Figure 6.7 lists ideas for formative and summative assessments.

Formative Assessment: Monitoring Student Progress Throughout the Unit of Study	Summative Assessment: Evaluating Student Progress at the Culmination of the Unit of Study
Reading conferences: Anecdotal notes from conversations between the teacher and student	Literary or literary argument essay related to areas of study during minilessons
Reading responses	Choice project from a choice project board including multimodal response options
Drawings in response to reading	Reading response journal: Students select their most insightful reading responses from the unit and write a final reflection in response to those insights. Students submit the collection of responses and final reflection.
Conversation maps: Recording student responses during book club meetings	Formal reflection on how a student developed as a reader and learner with specific nods to choice and identity, community work in their book club, and how they will transfer skills to other academic and personal spaces

Anecdotal notes about reading routines and behaviors	Personal essay in response to reading (for example: *Write a narrative in response to the following question: Is your book club book a mirror or window? Write a formal essay to explain using evidence from the text.*)
Student reflections on future-ready skill development and reading (submitted via writing or video)	Socratic seminar: Book clubs formally prepare to host a Socratic seminar within the class to address the universal themes related to the text they read
Reading recommendation or book review write-up or video submission	

FIGURE 6.7: Formative and summative assessments for book club units.

WRAP-UP FOR REFLECTING ON BOOK CLUB IMPLEMENTATION

This work is rooted in previous research and theory about reader's response, literature circles, and grand conversations (Eeds & Wells, 1989; Rosenblatt 1968, 1995). Key elements to book club design like choice-in-response formats, text selection variety, student-directed discussion, teacher-as-facilitator roles, journaling, and student self-evaluations (Jocuis & Shealy, 2018) are important aspects of revolving literacy work in secondary English classrooms. Use the following reflection to consider all you have read about book clubs and the ways in which they put students at the center of literacy practices and learning.

Stop and Think

Reflection Question	My Thoughts	Next Steps
How might your current curriculum benefit from incorporating a book club unit?		
If you currently implement a book club unit, reflect on a part of the process outlined in this section that you find impactful. What new learning is emerging?		

continued ▶

Reflection Question	My Thoughts	Next Steps
Review the sample book club progressions across grades. What kind of book club would fit within your grade level and why?		
Think about the current shared texts and their themes. How might replacing a shared text unit with a book club unit accomplish similar goals in reading with an added focus on future-ready skill development?		

Visit **go.SolutionTree.com/literacy** for a free reproducible version of this reflection.

Shared Reading Experience

The shared reading experience is typically the most common structure for reading in secondary classrooms. *Shared reading* is an interactive read-aloud where students join in or share the reading of a text while guided and supported by the teacher.

Texts for shared reading are typically chosen by the teacher for an instructional purpose. Some texts have rich characters to analyze and discuss their development. Some texts offer multiple perspectives for readers to empathize and sympathize with. Some texts offer content to readers that aids in critical thinking and problem solving. Some texts are windows into different times and places and give readers a peek into what life was like during a certain era. Teachers select texts with intention to teach standards and meet students where they are in their academic, social, and emotional development. Shared texts serve as anchors for discussion and written responses. Students learn strategies in ways that are guided and scaffolded.

Shared reading experiences hold instructional, cultural, and communal value. They should be part of a varied approach to reading in the secondary English classroom to ensure that students have multiple opportunities to participate in guided and scaffolded reading instruction. Shared reading should be in addition to opportunities where students make choices about what they read, how they read, and the ways in which they respond. Students need to be actively involved in the meaning-making process across all structures.

COMMIT TO RELEVANCE IN SHARED READING

The learning sciences point to the importance of drawing on students' prior experiences (Darling-Hammond et al., 2020) and scaffolding to help students understand a task's relevance (Nasir, Rosebery, Warren, & Lee, 2014). Choosing a shared text can be challenging in that not all students have the same personal prior experiences for relevance. Use the shared reading experience to bridge relevance between school experience and occurrences in society and local communities. As I shared in chapter 1 (page 15), revolving literacy educators remain flexible. They are responsive to the world students live in and strive to build connections between school and other spaces. Select texts that are representative of the students within the classroom and that have common themes that adolescents can connect to.

Teachers of the humanities will often say that reading literature is about analyzing and contemplating the human experience. While this is true, I invite you to consider a follow-up question: *Which human experience does shared literature capture?* While there are common threads to the tapestry of humanity—love, loss, triumph, conflict, growth, tragedy, success—people experience those threads differently. Honor the diversity in the classroom and in your school community by considering the student population in your shared text selections. There are texts that students can and can't connect with. There is, however, value in a lack of connection to characters or events; this is how readers develop empathy and awareness of differences between themselves and others.

BALANCE CLASSIC AND CONTEMPORARY LITERATURE

Goodreads is an online social hub of reading resources. Readers engage in digital dialogue about reading. Readers can access book reviews. There are hundreds of book lists to aid viewers in their reading searches. There are several iterations of high school English class book lists; most have the same titles but in different orders depending on the specificity of the list title. Here are the first ten books on a list of required books in high school English class and "shelved" the greatest number of times on a high school list on Goodreads.

1. *The Great Gatsby* by F. Scott Fitzgerald—published 1925
2. *To Kill a Mockingbird* by Harper Lee—published 1960
3. *Romeo and Juliet* by William Shakespeare—published 1597
4. *Of Mice and Men* by John Steinbeck—published 1937
5. *Lord of the Flies* by William Golding—published 1954

6. *Macbeth* by William Shakespeare—published 1607
7. *1984* by George Orwell—published 1949
8. *Animal Farm* by George Orwell—published 1945
9. *The Catcher in the Rye* by J. D. Salinger—published 1951
10. *The Scarlett Letter* by Nathaniel Hawthorne—published 1850

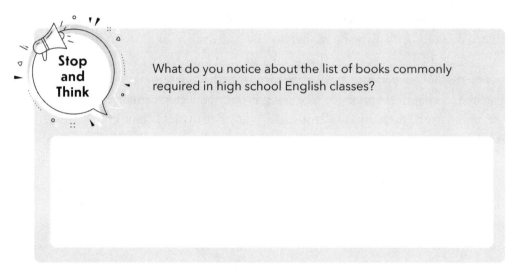

Stop and Think: What do you notice about the list of books commonly required in high school English classes?

Visit **go.SolutionTree.com/literacy** for a free reproducible version of this reflection.

The New York State Education Department (2017) Next Generation English Language Arts Standards include explicit guidance for teachers when selecting texts for curriculum:

> When choosing texts to meet the standards, teachers should provide a balance of classic and contemporary literature (both full length and shorter work) . . . Texts should reflect a global and diverse variety of authors, time periods, genres, and cultural perspectives.

Classic literature offers rich opportunities for language study, analysis, and critical thinking, as well as a study of the time period and place where stories are set. It is important that literacy educators balance the exposure students have in shared texts and library choices. Contemporary literature is representative of the time in which students live. Students may make personal and societal connections to what they read. Diversity in authorship is also important. "Writers are their times," as the editors of *The New York Times* (2021) book review write. "Books don't exist in a vacuum. . . . They are shaped by the context of the writer's own world" (*The New York Times*, 2021). If contemporary writers write in response to their own world, it is important to expose students to literature written in recent times. Students will have a frame of reference when reading.

Consider using the following questions to guide your text selection process.

- Will the content of the text interest my students? What are potential areas of learning? What might students connect with?
- What identity component is represented and is it portrayed without generalizing, stereotyping, or misrepresenting? If so, does the author acknowledge it?
- Who is the author? What positions the author to tell an authentic story?
- Is the story interesting and relevant to students?
- When was the book published? How does or doesn't the publication date impact the content and message?
- What do current students need to know about the time period in which the book was written or takes place?
- Whose voices are amplified in the text? Whose voices are quieted?

You may consider using the identity reflection tools outlined in chapter 2 (page 29) to guide your text selections of classic and contemporary literature.

Is there a balance of classic and contemporary literature in your current curriculum?

What are your thoughts about balancing classic and contemporary literature?

Visit **go.SolutionTree.com/literacy** *for a free reproducible version of this reflection.*

TEACH THE READERS AND READING, NOT TEXTS

Similar to teaching strategies related to the writing and research processes, teach strategies for navigating complex texts through shared reading experiences. Secondary English teachers need to be teachers of *readers and reading*, not just designated texts in the curriculum. Textual content is secondary to the competencies students need to develop for reading in various personal and academic contexts as well as for postsecondary pathways.

Teach students how to actively read, think, and reflect. What follows are protocols for coaching students to engage in metacognition, allowing for more strategic learning and deeper conceptual understanding (Darling-Hammond et al., 2020).

- **Why do we read?** Readers read for various purposes and respond in different ways. Readers read to think, wonder, discover, feel, and connect. Figure 6.8 illustrates the protocol to share with students.

- **Read, think, wonder!** Readers need to identify literal and figurative meaning from text, decipher why the text is important, and identify points of confusion or areas for future learning. Figure 6.9 provides a protocol for doing so. A reproducible, "Read, Think, Wonder," is on page 229.

- **Chunking text to discover meaning and significance:** Teach students that reading complex texts in chunks, or small sections, helps to develop understanding and discover how meaning is constructed throughout the entire text. Using the protocol in figure 6.10 (page 214), readers can chunk text in fiction (by chapter or scene) and nonfiction (by section or heading).

Text:	
Read to **Think**: Share what you are mostly thinking about while reading the text you chose. *What ideas keep repeating? What are you reminded of?*	
Read to **Wonder**: Share what you are wondering about while reading the text you chose. *Are you curious? Are you confused? Is there a specific question that comes to mind? What do you want to know more about?*	

Read to Discover: Share any new discoveries you made while reading. *Did you discover something new that you didn't know before? Did you discover that your own ideas or perspectives have changed? Did you learn something about yourself?*	
Read to Feel: Share how you feel in response to reading. *Why do you think you feel this way? Why or why didn't you have a personal reaction?*	
Read to Connect: Find a text or video related to the topic you read about to deepen your understanding of the content or to learn even more.	Title: Link (if applicable): *Why did you choose this text? What connections are you making?*

FIGURE 6.8: Why do we read protocol.

*Visit **go.SolutionTree.com/literacy** for a free reproducible version of this figure.*

I'm reading:		
Read, Think, Wonder		
Read: What does the text say?	**Think:** What does this text mean to me? What does this text mean to me in other contexts?	**Wonder:** What questions do I have? What do I want to learn more about after reading?

FIGURE 6.9: Read, think, wonder protocol.

*Visit **go.SolutionTree.com/literacy** for a free reproducible version of this figure.*

Name:				Date:
Focus for Reading				
	What is most important?			
Section of text	**Word?**	**Phrase?**	**Sentence?**	**My thinking**

FIGURE 6.10: What is most important chunking text protocol.

*Visit **go.SolutionTree.com/literacy** for a free reproducible version of this figure.*

Connection Between Reading Structures and Literacy Development

Offer students a variety of reading structures that position them as active learners. In this chapter, we explored independent reading, book clubs, and shared reading experiences (see figure 6.1, page 178). There is an incremental progression of choice and independence among the three structures.

- In independent reading experiences, students have free choice and may discuss their reading with a partner.
- In book club experiences, teachers choose the options and students choose from that set of options. Students read independently and among their book club members. Book club discussions are sporadic.
- In shared reading experiences, the teacher chooses the text. The text is mostly read to students, or there is a lot of whole-class discussion.

Students have opportunities to cultivate all components of literacy development through each of these reading structures. Table 6.5 summarizes the connection between the reading structures and components of literacy development.

TABLE 6.5: The Connection Between Reading Structures and Literacy Development Components

Components of Literacy Development	Independent Reading	Book Clubs	Shared Reading
Language	**Receptive language skills:** *Reading* for understanding, meaning-making, and pleasure *Listening* during partner talk, reading conferences, and book talks **Expressive language skills:** *Writing* about or *visually representing* reading in responses and reflections *Speaking* during partner talk, reading conferences, and book talks	**Receptive language skills:** *Reading* for understanding, meaning-making, interest, and discussion *Listening* during explicit instruction and book club meetings **Expressive language skills:** *Writing* about or *visually representing* reading in responses and reflections *Speaking* during book club meetings	**Receptive language skills:** *Reading* for understanding, meaning-making, analysis, and critical thinking *Listening* during explicit instruction, read-alouds, whole-class discussion, and partner talk *Viewing* if support or supplemental material is used (a scene from a play, a documentary to pair with nonfiction) **Expressive language skills:** *Writing* about or *visually representing* reading in responses and reflections *Speaking* during book club meetings
Identity	Students choose texts to read that represent their interests, passions, and life circumstances. Texts may act as mirrors and windows (Bishop, 1990) in reflecting identities.	Students choose a text to read that they are interested in and that may represent aspects of their identities. The text may act as a mirror or window (Bishop, 1999). Students construct an identity around being part of a book club, a group of people to be accountable to.	Students reflect on finding aspects of their identities or nonidentities in shared texts. This may influence the way students develop perspective about themselves and the world in which they live. Discussions may also influence the way students make connections and reflect on their own thinking and behavior. The text may act as a mirror or window (Bishop, 1999).

continued ▶

Components of Literacy Development	Independent Reading	Book Clubs	Shared Reading
Community	Students belong to a reading community within their classroom. Students share their thoughts about their reading with each other and with their teacher. Reading culture building establishes community. Students may venture to social media platforms to participate in online reading communities.	Students belong to a book club, a small reading community within their larger class reading community. Students establish meeting norms and agreements so the book club functions well. Students learn strategies for participating in an academic team.	Students read within a whole-class community. Discourse and discussion routines emerge from the shared experience. Students develop responsibility to the larger group for participation. A text may influence the way students think about or perceive community groups. The larger reading community may influence the reading lives of individual students as a result of the shared experience.
Future-Ready Skills Each structure for reading offers the potential to foster most of the highly ranked future-ready skills when intentionally embedded in planning. In this table, I emphasize which future-ready skills are unique to each reading structure.	The future-ready skills emphasized by an independent reading structure are: • Lifelong learning strategies • Motivation and self-awareness • Leadership and social influence • Resilience and flexibility • Motivation and self-awareness • Analytical thinking • Curiosity	The future-ready skills emphasized by a book club structure are: • Analytical thinking • Lifelong learning strategies • Leadership and social influence • Resilience and flexibility • Motivation and self-awareness • Empathy and active listening • Curiosity	The future-ready skills emphasized by a shared reading experience are: • Analytical thinking • Resilience and flexibility • Motivation and self-awareness • Empathy and active listening • Curiosity
Multimodal Meaning-Making	Students may read within and among different platforms. Students may choose to respond to their reading or create projects using different modalities. Students may participate in social media reading communities to enhance their reading lives.	Students may read within and among different platforms to support understanding of content material. Students may choose to respond to their reading or create projects using different modalities. Dialogue contributes to meaning-making of reading.	Media may be used to support and enhance understanding of a text or to act as the text (a scene from a play, a documentary, a scene from a movie or TV show). Students may choose to respond to their reading or create projects using different modalities. Dialogue contributes to meaning-making of reading.

Connection Between Reading Structures and Future-Ready Skills

Figure 6.11 depicts the connection between reading structures and future-ready skills, but as the job market, technology, and societal norms change, the elements and relationships of that figure may change. I encourage you to keep your own record of highly ranked future-ready skills and competencies and outline them across reading structures to help when planning units and lessons within the revolving literacy framework. Explicit instruction should incorporate strategies for reading and future readiness. Table 6.6 explains how reading structures support future-ready skill development to help with your curriculum planning.

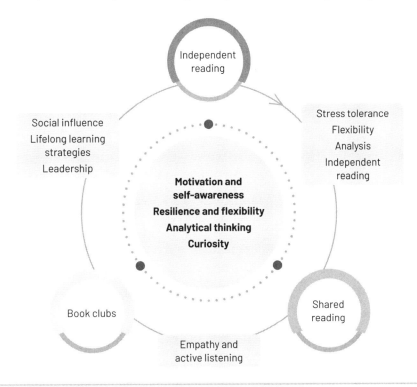

FIGURE 6.11: The connection between reading structures and future-ready skills.

TABLE 6.6: Explanation of How Reading Structures Support Future-Ready Skill Development

Reading Structure	Connections to Future-Ready Skills
Independent Reading Book Clubs	**Leadership:** Readers make personal reading plans. Readers choose their own texts and manage getting new texts when needed. Readers make plans for reading outside of school. They become leaders of their own learning.

continued ▶

Reading Structure	Connections to Future-Ready Skills
Independent Reading Book Clubs	**Social influence:** Readers share about reading with reading partners or in the class reading community. Readers also share and participate in reading communities via social media. Socialization around reading influences independent reading practices. **Lifelong learning strategies:** Readers manage reading records, reading reflections, and reading plans. Readers participate in a reading community where they share and receive reading advice and recommendations.
Book Clubs Shared Reading	**Empathy and active listening:** Readers learn empathy by engaging in conversation about experiences and information shared in text. Readers also learn empathy as they listen to the thoughts, ideas, and experiences from others in the group or class. Readers need to practice active-listening skills so they can participate in conversation and develop a true understanding of how others experience text. This supports the meaning-making process.
Independent Reading Book Clubs Shared Reading	**Motivation and self-awareness:** Readers need to stay motivated and engaged in all reading structures. Intrinsic motivation helps the learning process and aids in overall enjoyment of reading. Varying reading structures is an instructional strategy to foster student motivation. **Resilience, flexibility, and self-awareness:** Personal accountability is necessary in all reading structures. Readers need to be aware of when they are motivated and when they are not motivated. Readers also need to be aware of how their ideas and responses may impact others in the reading community. Readers manage personal plans for reading with independent reading and in book clubs. Readers should remain flexible so they discover personal reading plans and routines that work for them. **Analytical thinking:** Readers analyze text as they read in response to instruction and personal reflection. Readers share analysis in reading responses via writing, conversation, or video recording. **Curiosity:** Curiosity fuels the reading process. Readers select books for independent reading and book club work based on their curiosity and interest in text. Readers connect and engage with shared texts by developing and sharing questions for the teacher and peers to consider.

Reading Structures in the Revolving Literacy Framework

In this section, you will find a sample reading unit of study framework planning sheet and a sample lesson plan for the unit of study. I feature the launch of an independent reading unit of study where students connect or reconnect with their independent reading lives at the beginning of a school year or whenever you choose to begin your independent reading routine. I feature this unit because you can use many of the ideas for book clubs and for maintaining independent reading throughout the school year or an extended period. Also, secondary English teachers often inquire about a framework for launching independent reading.

UNIT OF STUDY FRAMEWORK

The purpose of the unit of study framework is to help secondary literacy educators ensure that they incorporate all components of literacy development into the unit of study. As I described in chapter 2 (page 29), use the framework template like a place setting on a dinner table. It holds each of the pieces needed for a literacy-focused unit: language, future-ready skills, identity, community, and multimodal meaning-making. It does not include specific lesson plans. Figure 6.12 is a sample unit of study plan for building and sustaining a reading life through independent reading.

Unit Summary: Making time for students to choose books and develop their reading lives is some of the most important work literacy educators do all year. Having a book in hand during the first days of school signals to students that reading is a priority in your class community, their choices about reading are important, and that time for reading in school is valued. Research suggests that the most important factors in a student's reading life are choice and access—the power to choose what to read and access to high-quality, high-interest books that are relevant and interesting (Flannery, 2023; Wilhelm and Smith, 2016; Allington and Gabriel, 2012).

While this unit of study is designed to help teachers launch independent reading, you can use and reuse the lessons throughout the school year as you stay committed to independent reading. This unit provides opportunities for students to reflect on their reading lives, set reading goals, learn strategies for accessing books, engage in reader response, and develop a personal set of tools for self-management of academic and personal tasks. Students will draw parallels between personal reading routines and future-ready skill development.

The purpose of this unit is for students to develop systems for independent reading and to reflect on their reading lives, set reading goals, learn strategies for accessing books, engage in reader response, and develop a personal set of tools for self-management of academic and personal tasks.

The unit serves as a road map for teachers. Not every lesson needs to be taught. Teachers can select lessons based on the reading identities and needs of students.

By the end of the unit, students will have a self-selected book for independent reading. Students will also have a notebook organized for goal setting, reading responses, reading reflections, and future-ready skill development reflections.

Keep in mind that independent reading is a continuous process. The end of this unit refers to the end of the launching period.

Language	Future-Ready Skills	Identity
• Students will read texts of choice. • Students will listen to partner talk and book talks to cultivate their reading lives. • Students will reflect on their process via writing or speaking.	• Analytical thinking • Lifelong learning strategies • Technological literacy • Resilience and flexibility • Social influence • Motivation and self-awareness	• Students choose a book they want to read based on interests, passions, and identities. • Students create personal responses to reading, drawing on the idea of books as mirrors and windows (Bishop, 1999).

FIGURE 6.12: Prioritizing independent reading—Building and sustaining a reading life unit plan.

continued ▶

Language	Future-Ready Skills	Identity
• Students will write and draw in response to reading. • Students may design multimodal responses to reading.	• Analytical thinking • Lifelong learning strategies • Technological literacy • Resilience and flexibility • Social influence • Motivation and self-awareness	• Students create personal plans for reading that are conducive to their lifestyle and learning preferences. • Students engage in ongoing reflection about their reading life and future-ready skill development.
Community	**Multimodal Meaning-Making**	
• Students participate in a whole-class reading community with designated reading time daily or weekly. • Teachers and students share reading lives with each other through conferences and book talks. • Students may belong to a schoolwide reading community where reading is valued and celebrated. There are reading culture events. • Students will have a reading partner to share their reading life with. • Students may participate in reading communities on social media like #Bookstagram and #BookTok to get recommendations and share comments about reading.	• Students may choose to read on a print or e-reader platform. • Students may read graphic novels or highly illustrated books. • Students may read digital material where reading includes digital text and media to make meaning. • Students may participate in reading communities on social media like #Bookstagram and #BookTok to get recommendations and share comments about reading. • Students may respond to reading in multimodal ways (writing, drawing, video creation, digital presentation, and so on). • Students may watch movies or video clips related to the content they are reading about or as an adapted version of the text they are reading.	

LESSON PLAN

In this section, I share a lesson plan for the unit on prioritizing independent reading by building and sustaining a reading life. This lesson may be taught early in the school year and then revisited quarterly as it focuses on personal goal setting and time management. The lesson plan shown in figure 6.13 is an example of how to plan a reading lesson that connects to future-ready skill development within the revolving literacy framework lesson plan.

Lesson Plan Thinking Map	
Connections for Learning	
Context: Why is today's lesson important to the work in the current unit of study?	This lesson invites students to think about reading in relation to other responsibilities they have in their lives and how to make time for reading. The lesson targets self-reflection, goal setting, and time management. Planning, organizing, time management, and reflection are skills that transcend reading. The skills apply to a variety of learning experiences in both academic and personal spaces. They are skills that students should refine in each grade level through age-appropriate experiences to help them exercise agency and practice feelings of self-efficacy.

Relevance: How does this lesson connect to future-ready skills, students' lives outside of school, or skills they may use in other areas of learning?	**Future-ready skills:** Lifelong learning strategies: Students take initiative to recognize personal, social, and academic events and responsibilities that may make it challenging to prioritize time for or attention to reading. Students participate in personal goal setting and develop a system to monitor their progress on attending to goals. Motivation and self-awareness: Students reflect on their motivation to read and maintain a reading routine. They self-assess what motivates them to read and what distracts them from reading. Being aware of personal motivation is helpful in many areas of life and productivity. **Connections:** This is a lesson to support students with managing their time and responsibilities, primarily outside of school. The lesson features conversation about distractions outside of school and how students can build a reading life beyond what they cultivate in the classroom. The lesson targets self-reflection, goal setting, and time management. Planning, organizing, time management, and reflection are skills that transcend reading. The skills are applicable to a variety of learning experiences in both academic and personal spaces.	
Connections for Literacy Instruction		
Language: Which domains of language are targeted in instruction and application of learning?	**Future-ready skills:** What future-ready skills are students developing?	**Identity:** How can students personally connect to this lesson?
Reading to discover mirrors and windows (Bishop, 1999) in self-selected texts Reading to discover new learning in self-selected texts Tracking thinking and personal responses to reading Writing and drawing responses to reading Speaking and listening during reading partner conversations	**Lifelong learning strategies:** Students take initiative to recognize personal, social, and academic events and responsibilities that may make it challenging to prioritize time for or attention to reading. Students participate in personal goal setting and develop a system to monitor their progress on attending to goals. **Motivation and self-awareness:** Students reflect on their motivation to read and maintain a reading routine. They self-assess what motivates them to read and what distracts them from reading. Being aware of personal motivation is helpful in many areas of life and productivity.	Students create personal reading plans that are conducive to their lifestyle and learning preferences. Students engage in ongoing reflection about their reading life and future-ready skill development.
Community: How are students participating in a community of learners within the classroom? How is their work contributing to a larger community outside of the classroom? How is the community influencing the work at hand?	**Multimodal meaning-making:** What modalities are students making meaning *from*? What modalities are students using to make meaning and demonstrate understanding?	

FIGURE 6.13: Making a personal plan for reading lesson plan.

continued ▶

Connections for Literacy Instruction	
Students share ideas for personal reading plans with their reading partner and the whole class community. Students use discussions from partnerships and the whole class to gauge ideas for their own personal plans for reading.	Teachers use an illustrated text as a mentor text for this lesson: "We All Know About Writer's Block. What About Reader's Block?" (Snider, 2019). Students create an illustration to capture their distractions and plans for reading. Students write personal reading goals.
Intention	
Objective (an intention for teachers): What is the goal for students to accomplish by the end of the lesson?	Students will acknowledge obstacles or distractions that may make it challenging to make time for reading outside of the classroom. Students will design a plan for reading readiness to establish a personal reading goal. Students will also determine how they will monitor their progress in working toward the goal.
Focus Statement (an intention for students): Ask students to state their objective in the first person as a way to take ownership of their learning.	*I will acknowledge the obstacles or distractions in my life that may make it challenging for me to read outside of school. I will then design a reading plan to establish a reading goal. I will also determine how I am going to monitor my progress and hold myself accountable.*
Standards: What standards does the lesson address?	[Insert your state's standards here.]
Explicit Instruction	
Tools and Texts: What resources and instructional materials are needed for this lesson? What is the teacher using to teach? What are students using or working with?	Students need an independent reading book, reading notebook (print or digital), plain paper, and color tools (markers, colored pencils). Teachers need the mentor text "We All Know About Writer's Block. What About Reader's Block?" (Snider, 2019), a reading notebook, plain paper, and color tools (markers, color pencils).
Whole-Class Instruction: Describe the lesson. What instructional strategy or strategies will you use? Why did you select the instructional technique? How does it help accomplish the goal of the lesson?	Check or highlight the method(s) used in this lesson: ☑ Think-aloud ☑ Demonstration ☑ Use of a mentor text ☑ Use of a demonstration text ☐ Show and explain ☐ Shared experience ☐ Media with active engagement **Describe the lesson:** The teacher introduces the concepts of writer's block and reader's block. They are experiences that challenge writers and readers in being productive (distractions, obligations, responsibilities). The teacher invites students to reflect on their own version of reader's block by asking, **"What challenges do you face when making time for reading?"** Teachers may choose to engage in a class discussion or invite students to share their experiences with a reading partner as they listen in to partner conversations. Read the graphic text "We All Know About Writer's Block. What About Reader's Block?" by Grant Snider (2019) with students. View each of the images (or the images you would like to share with students) and reasons for reader's block. Discuss ways to work around some of the obstacles that may be present in their lives. This discussion can support students in developing their own reading goals and plans.

Whole-Class Instruction: Describe the lesson. What instructional strategy or strategies will you use? Why did you select the instructional technique? How does it help accomplish the goal of the lesson?	Teachers share their own reason for reader's block. Teacher model thinking—how to acknowledge reader's block and how to develop a goal and plan for reading readiness. See following sample. 

	My Reader's Block:
	My eyes get tired after looking at a screen and working all day. I really want to read at night, but it is hard to transition from a screen to a book quickly.
	My Plan for Readiness:
	I plan to take a break before I start to read at night. I will not look at my computer, my phone, or the television for thirty to sixty minutes. I will do other things like draw, get a snack or eat a meal, talk with a family member, go outside, or exercise. Then, I will be ready to read.

Guided or Independent Practice: Describe what students are doing after the whole-class instruction. Share your conference or small-group instruction plan.	**Describe what students are doing after whole-class instruction. What scaffolds and supports are in place for students who are in need?**
	Students design their own reader's block reflection. Using plain paper and color tools, students illustrate their reader's block, similar to the illustrations in the mentor text. Illustrations may be put in students' reading notebooks or displayed in the classroom if students are comfortable.
	Students write about their reader's block and design a reading goal with a plan to make time for reading in their reading notebook.
	Students are encouraged to share their reading plans with a partner.
	Share your conference or small-group instruction plan. What scaffolds, strategies, or tools will you use to support students you meet with? What is the purpose for meeting with these students?
	Some students face challenges that need the support of an adult team to help them navigate. This activity is designed to think about planning skills that students can manage in ways that are appropriate for their ages and life circumstances.
	The teacher uses this time to conduct reading conferences to learn more about the reading lives of students. The teacher writes anecdotal notes about how students are personalizing plans for reading and creates a plan to follow up with those students who experience challenges with reading at home.

Reflection and Next Steps	
Daily Closure: How will you close the lesson to help future teacher or student planning? See table 3.2 (page 77) for closure options.	Students are invited to share their reading plans with a partner or the whole class. This is a lesson that can strengthen the reading community through sharing. Students may realize that there are peers with similar challenges or similar reading goals.
	You may choose to put students' drawings up in your classroom and use them to facilitate conversations about reading periodically. Students may also do this work in a personal reading notebook and revisit it to reflect on the plans they have made throughout the week, month, or school year.

continued ▶

Reflection and Next Steps	
After the Lesson: Evaluate the level of student engagement and the student work.	**Based on your observations, name areas where the lesson was successful and where students were successful.**
	Students were able to identify personal distractions and obstacles for reading (after-school activities, video games, taking care of siblings, social media, jobs, homework). Most students felt comfortable sharing with partners and the whole class.
	Students demonstrated understanding of the goal of the lesson. They acknowledged personal reader's block and created readiness plans. Some students needed support in thinking through a realistic plan for making time for reading outside of school.
	Based on your observations, what is needed in future instruction?
	Whole-group lesson: Revisit reading readiness plans next week and invite students to reflect on their progress. Students will share if they are actively working toward their goals and how they are managing their time.
	Conferences: Meet with Jake, Selma, and Ashley to discuss their reading plans. They may need additional support.
	Based on your observations, did students connect with the context and relevance of the lesson? Were they aware of how their work was part of a process to develop the named future-ready skill?
	Students were aware that goal setting and time management are universal active learning strategies. I asked them to discuss this with their partner. I will be better able to evaluate this when we revisit reading plans after students have had time to implement their personal plan.

Summary

Reading is perhaps the most remarkable, but intimidating, part of being an English teacher. Yes, intimidating. Sometimes frustrating. Some students love to read. Some students comply. Some students are avoidant or disengaged. For some students, reading is challenging. It's difficult to expect students to spend a lot of time on something they feel they are not good at. It may feel like you are in the middle of a juggling act sometimes.

Reading is also abstract. We, as teachers, can't see what is happening in students' minds as they read. In secondary English classes, we have to trust that the eye movement we see when observing students reading represents a connection between processing words on the page and thinking about what it says. Writing helps reading be more concrete, but we must be careful about overreliance on writing about reading. It can become inauthentic. Adults don't write essays or create Canva presentations after everything they read. For these reasons, it's important to do the following.

- Vary your approach to engaging students in reading.
- Provide choice and agency in the reading process.

- Design reading experiences that are relevant to students' lives inside the classroom, beyond the classroom, and in the future.
- Trust the process.

You are here. You are reading this book. You are thinking about how to motivate and engage the teenagers you teach. You are not giving up. I believe in you and the reading work you and your students can do together.

Which part of this chapter was most impactful for you as a literacy educator? Share your thinking.

Which reading structure is most prominent in your current curriculum? Share what you learned while reading about that structure that you want to bring back to your classroom.

Which reading structure needs to be developed in your current curriculum? What did you learn in this chapter that will help in your planning?

*Visit **go.SolutionTree.com/literacy** for a free reproducible version of this reflection.*

Middle Grade and Young Adult Book List

The following books are some teacher favorites. However, all school communities differ. Choose books that are most appropriate for your students and community

Middle Grade
- *A First Time for Everything* by Dan Santat
- *A Rover's Story* by Jasmine Warga
- *Dear Sweet Pea* by Julie Murphy
- *From an Idea to Google: How Innovation at Google Changed the World* by Lowey Bundy Sichol
- *In Your Shoes* by Donna Gephart
- *The Beatrice Prophecy* by Kate DiCamillo
- *The Fort* by Gordan Korman
- *The Midnight Children* by Dan Gemeinhart
- *The Remarkable Journey of Coyote Sunrise* by Dan Gemeinhart

Young Adult
- *Almost American Girl* by Robin Ha
- *Atomic Habits: An Easy and Proven Way to Build Good Habits and Break Bad Ones* by James Clear
- *Clap When You Land* by Elizabeth Acevedo
- *Dragon Hoops* by Gene Luen Yang
- *Free Lunch* by Rex Ogle
- *Parachutes* by Kelly Yang
- *Poisoned* by Jennifer Donnolly
- *Quiet: The Power of Introverts in a World That Can't Stop Talking* by Susan Cain
- *The Summer I Turned Pretty* by Jenny Hahn

Discussion of the Week

To learn even more about our world and make connections between what you think about at home and at school, you will have a weekly discussion on _____. This is your opportunity to make your learning matter and to see what you learn come alive in different contexts.

Your Post

Each week, please connect some aspect of your reading, writing, or thinking with **something else** that you have seen or read recently (within a week or two). This can be a text of any kind (news, sports article, opinion piece, blog post, and so on), a video on YouTube or TikTok, a TV show, a movie, a book, and so on.

Write to explain the connection you're making between your reading, writing, or thinking to the other media. Please provide a specific detail from your new source to help make the connection clear. Also provide a link to the source, if using online media. Here are some questions to consider.

- Is the connection based on similarities?
- Is the connection about drastic difference in information or opinion?
- Does the connection spark my interest in a new topic?
- Does the connection make me want to learn more about something?
- Does the connection spark an emotion?
- Does the connection remind me of something else in my life?
- Do I have a teacher or peer who may appreciate the connection, and who do I want to share with?

Your Reply

Please respond to at least two other posts in the class. Visit the provided link and include a quote or reference from the source in the post in your reply.

Reading Response Tool: Why Do We Read? Protocol

Students may use this reading response protocol to reflect on the intentions of reading and how intentions impact the way readers think about text.

Text:	
Read to **THINK:** Share what you are mostly thinking about while reading the text you chose. • What ideas keep repeating? What are you reminded of?	
Read to **WONDER:** Share what you are wondering about while reading the text you chose. • Are you curious? Are you confused? Is there a specific question that comes to mind? What do you want to know more about?	
Read to **DISCOVER:** Share any new discoveries you made while reading. • Did you discover something new that you didn't know before? • Did you discover that your own ideas or perspectives have changed? • Did you learn something about yourself?	
Read to **FEEL:** Share how you feel in response to reading. • Why do you think you feel this way? Why or why didn't you have a personal reaction?	
Read to **CONNECT:** Find a text or video related to the topic that you read about to deepen your understanding of the content or to learn even more.	Title: Link (if applicable): Why did you choose this text? What connections are you making?

Revolving Literacy © 2025 Solution Tree Press • SolutionTree.com
Visit **go.SolutionTree.com/literacy** to download this free reproducible.

Read, Think, Wonder

Students may use this reading protocol to make meaning throughout the reading experience.

I'm reading:		
Read, Think, Wonder		
Read: What does the text say?	**Think:** What does this text mean to me? What does this text mean to me in other contexts?	**Wonder:** What questions do I have? What do I want to learn more about after reading?

CONCLUSION

I've wanted to write this book since the early years of my teaching career. I'm glad I didn't. The revolving literacy framework is what guided my instruction as a middle-level English teacher and literacy specialist. It's what guided my instruction in special programs for high school students learning English as a new language and who were challenged by traditional learning models. The revolving literacy framework is what currently guides my instruction as a teacher of preservice teachers. It's what guides my literacy leadership and curriculum design projects. The revolving literacy framework has helped me make literacy learning relevant and engaging for students (and teachers!).

My own experiences wouldn't have been enough to convey how impactful revolving literacy work is. I have the pleasure of working with teams of secondary English teachers and administrators on curriculum development, scope and sequence design, independent reading initiatives, and reading culture building in various schools and communities. I am fortunate to work with secondary English teachers and administrators in a variety of professional development sessions where they are inspired by the revolving literacy framework and make their own plans for implementation. They share with me how their philosophies and instructional practices have transformed in response to the revolving literacy framework, student-centered decision making, and practical resources shared.

It is a good thing that I didn't write this book early in my teaching career. The guidance and resources in this book are a summation of how I, along with other secondary literacy educators, have approached revolving literacy work with success. They are responses to the list of questions I shared at the start of this book. There will always be questions. Questions and inquiry are how we learn, grow, and transform. The secondary English teacher role is evolving. I invite you to join in these efforts.

Let's circle back to something I wrote in the introduction to this book.

> The premise of *revolving literacy* is built on the Greek philosopher Heraclitus's notion that the only constant in life is change. Change is hard for people but change doesn't have to mean that something in education is necessarily *wrong*. Adolescents experience the world as it is and will enter into a world after high school that has many shades of gray. . . . What would be *wrong* is to not acknowledge that what it means to be literate is constantly evolving. Local and global communities demand ever-shifting skill sets of people in order to be productive and positive contributors to society.

Does it resonate differently now? Because of this notion of change and the challenges change can present, I am going to end with some advice for moving forward in this work.

- **Pick one thing:** Revolving literacy work is a marathon, not a sprint. Educators will come to this book from different philosophies and places in their professional work. For some, the ideas in this book will confirm and perhaps enhance what they already believe and are implementing in their classrooms and schools. For some, the ideas in this book will be new and may be the start of a journey. For some, the ideas in this book may be contrary to personal beliefs. I encourage you to pick one thing from this book that you are comfortable with that is different from your typical approach to try out. Focus on that one thing. Study it. Reflect on it. Ask your students for feedback. Let the one thing you try evolve into a second thing. You can do it.
- **Let go:** I admit—many secondary English teachers are often hesitant or apprehensive to start revolving literacy work. It's often about control. I get it. The seemingly challenging part of revolving literacy

work is that it is ever evolving. Teachers co-construct learning with students, giving them control of aspects of their learning. This is a goal of *future readiness*. But if we're being honest, we know that it's hard for us to give up control as teachers. Shared reading experiences keep the class together. The teacher decides on the schedule and timeline for reading and discussion. We know the classics. We read them in school. Our parents read them. They've been adapted into films, graphic novels, and remixes. Assigning students essays in response to one question or a list of prompts we provide makes it easier to teach and provide feedback. There is no denying this. However, student choice, voice, and agency in learning are how students learn, grow, and get ready for future academic spaces and postsecondary experiences. It's OK to not know everything that students read and write about.

- **Embrace balance:** *Homeostasis* refers to equilibrium in the body. There is a reason why we don't feel well when our body's homeostasis is interrupted. This is true for secondary English curriculum work. Balance how students engage in class between shared experiences, group experiences, partner experiences, and independent experiences. Balance the types of texts students have access to between classic, contemporary, and different formats. Balance the writing and research students engage in between some choice and some prescribed. Balance the reading experiences students engage in between some choice and some prescribed. After all, not everything in life is a choice. Approach teaching and learning in a way that preserves homeostasis in your planning.

- **Be patient and forgive yourself:** This work takes time. This work takes years to develop. You will learn from your students and colleagues what works well and what you need to revise. If something doesn't go as planned, celebrate that as an opportunity to figure out why. Ask your colleagues. Ask your students. Make a different plan for moving forward. Students are going to approximate in this work and so will you in the beginning.

- **Form a team of colleagues to plan with:** Team up with colleagues who are interested in revolving literacy work and plan together. Use the Stop and Think opportunities in this book as catalysts for planning-and-reflection conversations.

- **Share a firm belief that students need to belong to literacy communities that honor who they are and who they will become:** Young people spend a lot of time in school. School prepares them to participate in personal and social spaces, as well as future academic spaces. One of literacy and learning researcher Brian Cambourne's (1988) conditions of learning is *immersion*; young people need to be surrounded by interesting, engaging, and relevant literacy experiences. The literacy culture in your classroom and school provides access and membership to a larger community of readers, writers, and thinkers.
- **Keep learning and thinking:** As I shared at the start of this book, literacy educators need to remain flexible in order to be responsive to the communities students belong to and the postsecondary demands that young people are faced with. I encourage you to revisit the steps I shared earlier: Acknowledge change, reflect on personal understandings of what it means to be literate, learn, audit curriculum, reflect on instructional practices, and establish protocols for reflection. I hope this book has proven to be a resource for those steps.

When I first became an English teacher, a colleague who was a reading enthusiast asked me in late August as we were preparing for the new school year when my students were choosing independent reading books. My initial plan was to get started late in the fall. At that point, I wasn't quite sure how I was going to handle independent reading. My colleague looked at me and said, "If you don't make time for kids to put books in their hands that they choose right out of the gate, they won't know what's really important about reading and what's really important about English class."

From that day on, year after year, my students had a book of choice in their hands by the end of the first week of school. I figured everything else out after.

That is how I got started. How will you?

REFERENCES AND RESOURCES

Allington, R. L. (2014). How reading volume affects both reading fluency and reading achievement. *International Electronic Journal of Elementary Education, 7*(1), 13–26.

Allington, R. L., & Gabriel, R. (2012). "Every child, every day." *Educational Leadership, 69*(6), 10–15.

Allington, R. L, & McGill-Franzen, A. M. (2021). Reading volume and reading achievement: A review of recent research. *Reading Research Quarterly, 56*(1), 1–8.

Ames, C. (1992). Classrooms: Goals, structures, and student motivation. *Journal of Educational Psychology, 84*(3), 261–271.

Anderson, C. (2005). *Assessing writers*. Portsmouth, NH: Heinemann.

Anderson, M., & Jiang, J. (2018, May 31). *Teens, social media and technology 2018*. Pew Research Center. Accessed at www.pewresearch.org/internet/2018/05/31/teens-social-media-technology-2018 on March 30, 2023.

Baker, E. A., Pearson, P. D., & Rozendal, M. S. (2010). Theoretical perspectives and literacy studies: An exploration of roles and insights. In E. A. Baker (Ed.), *The new literacies: Multiple perspectives on research and practice* (pp. 1–22). New York: Guilford Press.

Barron, B. (2006). Interest and self-sustained learning as catalysts of development: A learning ecology perspective. *Human Development*, *49*(4), 193–224.

Bishop, R. S. (1990). Mirrors, windows, and sliding glass doors. *Perspectives: Choosing and Using Books for the Classroom*, *6*(3), ix–xi.

Blumenfeld, P. C., Puro, P., & Mergendoller, J. (1992). Translating motivation into thoughtfulness. In H. H. Marshall (Ed.), *Redefining student learning: Roots of educational change* (pp. 207–241). New York: Ablex Publishing.

Bransford, J. D., Brown, A. L., & Cocking, R. R. (2000). *How people learn: Brain, mind, experience, and school* (Expanded ed.). Washington, DC: National Academy Press.

Brophy, J. E., & Freiberg, H. J. (1999). *Beyond behaviorism: Changing the classroom management paradigm.* Boston: Allyn & Bacon.

Calderón, M., & Solo, I. (2017). *Academic language mastery: Vocabulary in context.* Thousand Oaks, CA: Corwin.

Cambourne, B. (1988). *The whole story: Natural learning and acquisition of literacy in the classroom.* Jefferson City, MO: Scholastic.

Cantor, P., Osher, D., Berg, J., Steyer, L., & Rose, T. (2018). Malleability, plasticity, and individuality: How children learn and develop in context. *Applied Developmental Science*, *23*(4), 307–337.

Clinton, K., Jenkins, H., & McWilliams, J. (2013). New literacies in an age of participatory culture. In H. Jenkins & W. Kelley (Eds.), *Reading in a participatory culture: Remixing* Moby-Dick *in the English classroom* (pp. 3–24). New York: Teachers College Press.

Couros, G., & Novak, K. (2019). *Innovate inside the box: Empowering learners through UDL and the innovator's mindset.* San Diego: Dave Burgess Consulting, Inc.

Darling-Hammond, L., & Adamson, F. (2014). *Beyond the bubble test: How performance assessments support 21st century learning.* San Francisco: Jossey-Bass.

Darling-Hammond, L., Flook, L., Cook-Harvey, C., Barron, B., & Osher, D. (2020). Implications for educational practice of the science of learning and development. *Applied Developmental Science, 24*(2), 97–140. doi.org/10.1080/10888691.2018.1537791

DeSilver, D. (2014, August 6). *Reshaping the workplace: Tech-related jobs that didn't exist (officially, at least) 15 years ago.* Pew Research Center. Accessed at www.pewresearch.org/short-reads/2014/08/06/reshaping-the-workplace-tech-related-jobs-that-didnt-exist-officially-at-least-15-years-ago on July 2, 2024.

Digital Marketing Institute. (2024, April 14). *Twenty surprising influencer marketing statistics.* Accessed at https://digitalmarketinginstitute.com/blog/20-influencer-marketing-statistics-that-will-surprise-you on November 14, 2024.

Drzensky, F., Egold, N., & van Dick, R. (2012). Ready for a change? A longitudinal study of antecedents, consequences and contingencies of readiness for change. *Journal of Change Management, 12*(1), 95–111. doi.org/10.1080/14697017.2011.652377

Duhigg, C. (2016, February 25). What Google learned from its quest to build the perfect team. *The New York Times.* Accessed at www.nytimes.com/2016/02/28/magazine/what-google-learned-from-its-quest-to-build-the-perfect-team.html on October 25, 2024.

Dweck, C. S. (2016). *Mindset: The new psychology of success* (Updated ed.). New York: Random House.

Eccles, J. S. (2005). Subjective task value and the Eccles et al. model of achievement-related choices. In A. J. Elliot & C. S. Dweck (Eds.), *Handbook of competence and motivation* (pp. 105–121). New York: Guilford Press.

Eccles, J. S., & Roeser, R. W. (2009). Schools, academic motivation, and stage-environment fit. In R. M. Lerner & L. Steinberg (Eds.), *Handbook of Adolescent Psychology: Individual Bases of Adolescent Development* (3rd ed., 404–434). New York: Wiley.

Eeds, M., & Wells, D. (1989). Grand conversations: An exploration of meaning construction in literature study groups. *Research in the Teaching of English, 23*(1), 4–29.

Fitzgerald, F. S. (1925). *The great Gatsby.* New York: Charles Scribner's Sons.

Flannery, M. E. (2023, August 30). *The joy of reading isn't dead yet.* Accessed at www.nea.org/nea-today/all-news-articles/joy-reading-isnt-dead-yet on November 30, 2024.

Freiberg, H. J., Huzinec, A. C., & Templeton, S. M. (2009). Classroom management—A pathway to student achievement: A study of 14 inner-city elementary schools. *Elementary School Journal, 110*(1), 63–80.

Gallagher, K. (2022, October 21). *Engaging adolescent readers* [Conference presentation]. New York State English Council Conference, Albany, NY, United States.

Gee, J. P. (1999). Critical issues: Reading and the new literacy studies—Reframing the National Academy of Sciences report on reading. *Journal of Literacy Research, 31*(3), 355–374. doi.org/10.1080/10862969909548052

Gee, J. P. (2004). *Situated language and learning: A critique of traditional schooling.* New York: Routledge.

Gee, J. P. (2010). A situated-sociocultural approach to literacy and technology. In E. A. Baker (Ed.), *The new literacies: Multiple perspectives on research and practice* (pp. 165–193). New York: Guilford Press.

Georghiades, P. (2004). From the general to the situated: Three decades of metacognition. *International Journal of Science Education, 26*(3), 365–383.

Gladwell, M. (2008). *Outliers: The story of success.* Boston: Little, Brown.

Golding, W. (1954). *Lord of the flies.* London: Faber and Faber.

Goodell, J. (2011, January 17). Steve Jobs in 1994: The *Rolling Stone* interview. *Rolling Stone.* Accessed at www.rollingstone.com/culture/culture-news/steve-jobs-in-1994-the-rolling-stone-interview-231132 on July 2, 2024.

Graham, S., Liu, X., Aitken, A., Ng, C., Bartlett, B., Harris, K. R., et al. (2018). Effectiveness of literacy programs balancing reading and writing instruction: A metanalysis. *Reading Research Quarterly, 53*(3), 279–304. doi.org/10.1002/rrq.194

Guthrie, J. T., & Wigfield, A. (2000). Engagement and motivation in reading. In M. L. Kamil, P. B. Mosenthal, P. D. Pearson, & R. Barr (Eds.), *Handbook of reading research* (Vol. 3, pp. 403–422). Mahwah, NJ: Lawrence Erlbaum Associates.

Hallett, R., & Hutt, R. (2016, June 7). *10 jobs that didn't exist 10 years ago.* Accessed at www.weforum.org/agenda/2016/06/10-jobs-that-didn-t-exist-10-years-ago on July 2, 2024.

Hattie, J. A. C. (2009). *Visible learning: A synthesis of 800+ meta-analyses on achievement.* New York: Routledge.

Hattie, J. A. C. (2012). *Visible learning for teachers: Maximizing impact on learning.* New York: Routledge.

Hattie, J., & Gan, M. (2011). Instruction based on feedback. In R. E. Mayer & P. A. Alexander (Eds.), *Handbook of research on learning and instruction* (pp. 249–271). New York: Routledge.

Heath, S. B. (1983). *Ways with words: Language, life, and work in communities and classrooms.* Cambridge, United Kingdom: Cambridge University Press.

Jenkins, H. (2009). *Confronting the challenges of participatory culture: Media education for the 21st century.* Cambridge, MA: The MIT Press.

Jocuis, R., & Shealy, S. (2018). Critical book clubs: Reimagining literature reading and response. *Reading Teacher, 71*(6), 691–702.

Johnston, V. (2016). Successful read-alouds in today's classroom. *Kappa Delta Pi Record, 52*(1), 39–42. doi.org/10.1080/00228958.2016.1123051

Kalantzis, M., Cope, B., & Cloonan, A. (2010). A multiliteracies perspective on the new literacies. In E. A. Baker (Ed.), *The new literacies: Multiple perspectives on research and practice* (pp. 61–87). New York: Guilford Press.

Kelley, W., & Jenkins, H. (2013). Define reading: A (sort of) historical perspective. In H. Jenkins, W. Kelley, K. Clinton, J. McWilliams, R. Pitts-Wiley, & E. Reilly (Eds.), *Reading in a participatory culture: Remixing* Moby-Dick *in the English classroom* (pp. 43–48). New York: Teachers College Press.

Kober, N., & Rentner, D. S. (2020). *History and evolution of public education in the US.* Washington, DC: Center on Education Policy. Accessed at files.eric.ed.gov/fulltext/ED606970.pdf on July 2, 2024.

Kohn, A. (2010). How to create nonreaders: Reflections on motivation, learning, and sharing power. *English Journal, 100*(1), 16–22.

Kolar, N. (2019, July 15). *Project Oxygen and Project Aristotle—What makes Google, Google?* Accessed at https://nathankolar.medium.com/project-oxygen-and-project-aristotle-what-makes-google-google-2a3fc79e5210 on October 25, 2024.

Lankshear, C., & Knobel, M. (2007). *A new literacies sampler*. New York: Peter Lang.

Lee, C. D. (2007). *Culture, literacy, and learning: Taking bloom in the midst of the whirlwind*. New York: Teachers College Press.

LePage, P., Darling-Hammond, L., & Akar, H. (2005). Classroom management. In L. Darling-Hammond & J. Bransford (Eds.), *Preparing teachers for a changing world: What teachers should learn and be able to do* (pp. 327–357). San Francisco: Jossey-Boss.

Lesaux, N. K., & Carr, K. C. (2024). *Science of reading: What is it? New York*: Author. Accessed at www.nysed.gov/sites/default/files/programs/standards-instruction/literacy-brief-1.pdf on May 7, 2024.

McBreen, M., & Savage, R. (2020). The impact of motivational reading instruction on the reading achievement and motivation of students: A systematic review and meta-analysis. *Educational Psychology Review*, 33, 1125–1163.

McCain, T., & Jukes, I. (2001). *Windows on the future: Education in the age of technology*. Thousand Oaks, CA: Corwin.

McCrimmon, J. (1984). *Writing with a purpose*. New York: Houghton Mifflin School.

Miller, D., & Sharp, C. (2018). *Game changer: Book access for all kids*. New York: Scholastic.

Mills, K. A. (2015). *Literacy theories for the digital age: Social, critical, multimodal, spatial, material and sensory lenses*. Bristol, United Kingdom: Multilingual Matters.

Motivation. (n.d.). In *Merriam-Webster's online dictionary*. Accessed at www.merriam-webster.com/dictionary/motivation on March 30, 2024.

Murray, D. (1982). *Learning by teaching: Selected articles on writing and teaching*. Portsmouth, NH: Heinemann.

Nasir, N. S., Rosebery, A. S., Warren, B., & Lee, C. D. (2014). Learning as a cultural process: Achieving equity through diversity. In R. K. Sawyer (Ed.), *The Cambridge handbook of the learning sciences* (pp. 686–706). New York: Cambridge University Press.

National Academies of Sciences, Engineering, and Medicine. (2018). *How people learn II: Learners, contexts, and cultures*. Washington, DC: The National Academies Press. https://doi.org/10.17226/24783

National Council of Teachers of English. (2019, November 7). *Definition of literacy in a digital age.* Accessed at https://ncte.org/statement/nctes-definition-literacy-digital-age on February 7, 2025.

National Council of Teachers of English. (2022, April 9). *Media education in English language arts.* Accessed at https://ncte.org/statement/media_education on November 14, 2024.

New London Group. (1996). A pedagogy of multiliteracies: Designing social futures. *Harvard Educational Review, 66*(1), 60–92.

New York State Education Department. (2017). *New York State Next Generation English Language Arts Standards* (Revised ed.). New York: Author. Accessed at www.nysed.gov/sites/default/files/programs/standards-instruction/nys-next-generation-ela-standards.pdf on March 14, 2024.

New York State Education Department. (2024). *Literacy briefs.* Accessed at www.nysed.gov/curriculum-instruction/literacy-briefs on April 3, 2024.

New York Times (2021, April 1). 11 new books we recommend this week. *The New York Times.* Accessed at www.nytimes.com/2021/04/01/books/review/11-new-books-we-recommend-this-week.html on April 12, 2021.

Odabaş, M., & Aragão, C. (2023, April 4). *School district mission statements highlight a partisan divide over diversity, equity and inclusion in K–12 education.* Pew Research Center. Accessed at www.pewresearch.org/social-trends/2023/04/04/school-district-mission-statements-highlight-a-partisan-divide-over-diversity-equity-and-inclusion-in-k-12-education on July 2, 2024.

Olthouse, J. M. (2013). Multiliteracies theory and gifted education: Creating "smart spaces" in the language arts classroom. *Gifted Child Today, 36*(4), 246–253.

Organisation for Economic Co-operation and Development. (2018). *The future of education and skills.* Accessed at www.oecd.org/en/about/directorates/directorate-for-education-and-skills.html on July 2, 2024.

Orwell, G. (1945). *Animal farm.* London: Secker & Warburg.

Pearson, P. D., Cervetti, G. N., & Tilson, J. L. (2008). Reading for understanding. In *Powerful learning: What we know about teaching for understanding* (pp. 71–112). San Francisco: Jossey-Bass.

Perry, K. H. (2012). What is literacy?—A critical overview of sociocultural perspectives. *Journal of Language and Literacy Education, 8*(1), 50–71.

Radice, L. (2023). *Leading a culture of reading: How to ignite and sustain a love of literacy in your school community.* Bloomington, IN: Solution Tree Press.

Radice, L. (2024, January 9). *Bringing AI to the classroom: Urgent questions for educators* [Blog post]. Solution Tree. Accessed at www.solutiontree.com/blog/bringing-ai-to-the-classroom-urgent-questions-for-educators on April 12, 2024.

Rafferty, A. E., Jimmieson, N. L., & Armenakis, A. A. (2013). Change readiness: A multilevel review. *Journal of Management, 39*(1), 110–135.

Renninger, K. A., & Hidi, S. (2017). *The power of interest for motivation and engagement.* New York: Routledge.

Research. (2024). In *Oxford English dictionary online.* Accessed at www.oed.com/dictionary/research_n1?tl=true on April 6, 2024.

Rideout, V., Peebles, A., Mann, S., & Robb, M. B. (2022). *Common sense census: Media use by tweens and teens, 2021.* San Francisco: Common Sense. Accessed at www.commonsensemedia.org/sites/default/files/research/report/8-18-census-integrated-report-final-web_0.pdf on July 2, 2024.

Roessingh, H. (2020). Read-alouds in the upper elementary classroom: Developing academic vocabulary. *TESOL Journal, 11*(1). doi.org/10.1002/tesj.445

Rosenblatt, L. M. (1968). *Literature as exploration.* Champaign, IL: National Council of Teachers of English.

Rosenblatt, L. M. (1978). *The reader, the text, the poem: The transactional theory of the literary work.* Carbondale, IL: Southern Illinois University Press.

Rosenblatt, L. M. (1995). *Literature as exploration* (5th ed.). New York: Modern Language Association of America.

Rubin, H., Estrada, L., & Honigsfeld, A. (2022). *Digital-age teaching for English learners: A guide to equitable learning for all students* (2nd ed.). Thousand Oaks, CA: Corwin.

Ryan, R. M., & Deci, E. L. (2000). Self-determination theory and the facilitation of intrinsic motivation, social development, and well-being. *American Psychologist, 55*(1), 68–78.

Scaccia, J. P., Cook, B. S., Lamont, A., Wandersman, A., Castellow, J., Katz, J., et al. (2015). A practical implementation science heuristic for organizational readiness: R=MC2. *Journal of Community Psychology, 43*(4), 484–501.

Schaeffer, K. (2021, November 12). *Among many U.S. children, reading for fun has become less common, federal data shows.* Pew Research Center. Accessed at www.pewresearch.org/fact-tank/2021/11/12/among-many-u-s-children-reading-for-fun-has-become-less-common-federal-data-shows on March 27, 2023.

Schlam Salman, J., & Inbar-Lourie, O. (2023). Exploring English language teachers' beliefs about future readiness: Developing pedagogical practices for the 21st century. *Language Teaching Research.* doi.org/10.1177/13621688231179515

Shakespeare, W. (1993). *Romeo and Juliet.* Mineola, NY: Dover. Original work published 1597

Snider, G. (2019, August 2). We all know about writer's block. What about reader's block? *The New York Times.* Accessed at www.nytimes.com/2019/08/02/books/we-all-know-about-writers-block-what-about-readers-block.html on July 2, 2024.

Steele, D. M., & Cohn-Vargas, B. (2013). *Identity safe classrooms: Places to belong and learn.* Thousand Oaks, CA: Corwin.

Steinbeck, J. (1937). *Of mice and men.* New York: Covici-Friede.

Stiggins, R., & Chappuis, J. (2005). Using student-involved classroom assessment to close achievement gaps. *Theory Into Practice, 44*(1), 11–18.

Stipek, D. J. (1996). Motivation and instruction. In D. C. Berliner & R. C. Calfee (Eds.), *Handbook of educational psychology* (pp. 85–113). New York: Macmillan.

Stoetzel, L., & Shedrow, S. (2021). Making the transition to virtual methods in the literacy classroom: Reframing teacher education practices. *Excelsior: Leadership in Teaching and Learning, 13*(2), 127–142.

Strauss, V. (2017, December 20). The surprising thing Google learned about its employees and what it means for today's students. *The Washington Post.* Accessed at www.washingtonpost.com/news/answer-sheet

/wp/2017/12/20/the-surprising-thing-google-learned-about-its-employees-and-what-it-means-for-todays-students on July 2, 2024.

Street, B. (1997). The implications of the "new literacy studies" for literacy education. *English in Education, 31*(3), 45–59.

Street, B. (2003). What's "new" in new literacy studies? Critical approaches to literacy in theory and practice. *Current Issues in Comparative Education, 5*(2), 77–91.

Street, B. (2016). Learning to read from a social practice view: Ethnography, schooling and adult learning. *Prospects: Comparative Journal of Curriculum, Learning, and Assessment, 46*, 335–344.

Taylor, D. (1997). *Many families, many literacies: An international declaration of principles*. Portsmouth, NH: Heinemann.

Unsworth, L. (2008). Multiliteracies, e-literature and English teaching. *Language and Education, 22*(1), 62–75.

U.S. Bureau of Labor Statistics. (2024, April 17). *Fastest growing occupations*. Accessed at www.bls.gov/emp/tables/fastest-growing-occupations.htm on July 2, 2024.

Wandersman, A., Duffy, J., Flaspohler, P., Noonan, R., Lubell, K., Stillman, L., et al. (2008). Bridging the gap between prevention research and practice: The interactive systems framework for dissemination and implementation. *American Journal of Community Psychology, 41*(3–4), 171–181. doi.org/10.1007/s10464-008-9174-z

Wilhelm, J. D., & Smith, M. W. (2016). The power of pleasure reading: What we can learn from the secret reading lives of teens. *English Journal, 105*(6), 25–30.

Wolpert-Gawron, H. (2017). *Just ask us: Kids speak out on student engagement*. Thousand Oaks, CA: Corwin.

Wolpert-Gawron, H. (2018, November 18). *Why choice matters to student learning*. KQED. Accessed at www.kqed.org/mindshift/52424/why-choice-matters-to-student-learning on July 2, 2024.

World Economic Forum. (2016, January). *The future of jobs: Employment, skills and workforce strategy for the fourth industrial revolution*. Geneva, Switzerland: Author. Accessed at www3.weforum.org/docs/WEF_Future_of_Jobs.pdf on July 2, 2024.

World Economic Forum. (2020, October 20). *Future of jobs report 2020*. Geneva, Switzerland: Author. Accessed at www3.weforum.org/docs/WEF_Future_of_Jobs_2020.pdf on July 3, 2024.

World Economic Forum (2023a, April 30). *Future of jobs report 2023*. Accessed at www.weforum.org/reports/the-future-of-jobs-report-2023/in-full/4-skills-outlook on July 3, 2024.

World Economic Forum. (2023b, April 30). *Future of jobs report 2023: Up to a quarter of jobs expected to change in the next five years*. Accessed at www.weforum.org/press/2023/04/future-of-jobs-report-2023-up-to-a-quarter-of-jobs-expected-to-change-in-next-five-years on July 3, 2024.

Yeager, D. S., & Walton, G. M. (2011). Social-psychological interventions in education: They're not magic. *Review of Educational Research*, *81*(2), 267–301.

Zahidi, S. (2023). *Preface: The future of jobs report 2023*. Accessed at www.weforum.org/publications/the-future-of-jobs-report-2023/in-full on November 7, 2024.

INDEX

A

Acevedo, E., 226
acknowledging change, 10
active listening. *See* listening
Adamson, F., 61
addressing challenges, 205–207
affirmations, 3
after the lesson, 85, 108, 159
    reading structures, 224
agency, 6, 13, 49, 74, 194
alignment, 11
Almost American Girl (Ha), 200, 226
Amazon, 185, 198
American College Test (ACT), 58, 62
analogy for the revolving literacy lesson, 75–76
analysis, 148
analytical thinking, 17, 26
    reading structures, 218
    teaching researchers, 148–149
    writing and, 99, 122
analyzing and evaluating information, 147
anchor standards, 55
Animal Farm (Orwell), 51, 210
AnswerGarden, 34

application, 49, 74
Aragão, C., 7
Armenakis, A. A., 29
artificial intelligence (AI), 8, 21–22, 99
    big data and, 27
    questions and considerations about, 9, 101–102
    use of, 148–149
    writing and, 199
    writing in the era of, 100–102
assessment
    as an ongoing component of the learning process, 58–59
    circular model, 60–62
    defined, 59
    formative, 60, 206–207
    ongoing, 49–50, 74
    summative, 206–207
    testing, 62–63
    three parts, 59–60
Atomic Habits (Clear), 226
auditing curriculum, 11
authenticity, 2, 9, 182
avoiding plagiarism, 147

B

Baker, E. A., 5, 16
balancing classic and contemporary texts, 50–51, 182, 209–211
Barnes and Noble, 198
Barnhill, K., 200
The Beatrice Prophecy (DiCamillo), 226
Becoming (Obama), 200
being alert to false information/sources, 147
being purposeful about what to teach, 58
Bishop, R. S., 32, 184
blogs, 188
book clubs, 3, 51–52, 194–195, 216
    addressing challenges, 205–207
    choosing a mentor text, 200201
    choosing books, 198–199
    designing the instruction work of the unit, 199
    establish practices for responses and reflection, 205
    examples of lesson objectives, 199
    implementing a unit with students, 201–207
    inviting students to get acquainted, 204–204
    planning for a unit, 195–198
    reading structures, 217–218, 194–195
    sample units, 196–197
    teaching students to design a reading schedule, 204
    wrap-up for reflecting on implementation, 207
book talks, 186–187, 189
book tasting, 201–203
    menu, 202
Brin, S., 21

C

Cain, S., 226
Cambourne, B., 234
career pathways, 3–4
The Catcher in the Rye (Salinger), 210
change
    acknowledging, 10
    examples of agreements, 34
    defining, 35
    committing to, 7–9
character, 6–7

ChatGPT, 100–101
choice, 9, 13, 48–49, 74, 180, 182, 192, 194
    builds ownership, 48
    increases engagement and motivation, 48
    prioritizing, 51
choosing a schedule for independent reading, 185
choosing an idea, 113–114
    stages of the research process, 132, 134
chunking text, 212, 214
circular model of assessment, evaluation, and reflection, 60–62
    example, 61
civics
    literature and, 6–7
    nonfiction roundtables, 191
Clap When You Land (Acevedo), 226
Clear, J., 226
Cloonan, A., 18
co-construction of learning, 73–74
college readiness, 3–4, 7
commitment to learning, 24–25
committing to change, 7–9
committing to relevance in shared reading, 209
community, 216, 234
    as a planning component, 31–33
    literacy and, 17
    reading, 180
    reading structures, 220–221
    reflection questions, 39
    research, 131–132, 144
    writing and, 83, 92–94, 104, 106, 124–126
comparing performance-based and revolving literacy lesson structures, 77
components of independent reading, 181
components of literacy development, 19, 215–218
    connecting writing to, 93–94
conducting interviews, 135
conducting observations, 135
connecting with a librarian, 182
connections
    between reading structures and future-ready skills, 217–218
    between reading structures and literacy development, 214–216
    between revolving literacy writing process and future-ready skills, 99

between teaching the research process and future readiness, 146
between teaching the research process and literacy, 139–140
between the research process and future-ready skills, 149
between writing and future-ready skills, 98–99
community, 144–145
components, 215–216
future-ready skills, 143
identity, 143–144
language, 140–143
multimodal meaning-making, 145
research and future-ready skill alignment, 148–149
Consistency Management and Cooperative Discipline model, 131–132
content and relevance, 76–77, 83
conventions and layout, 89
Cope, B., 18
core skills for workers in 2023, 20
core values, 9–10
    maintaining, 6–7
COVID-19 effects on identity, 35
crafting questions, 134
creating focus groups, 135
creative thinking, 17, 26
    teaching researchers, 148–149
    writing and, 99, 119–121
critical thinking skills, 17, 20
cumulative instruction.
    See systemic instruction
curiosity, 26
    reading structures, 218
    teaching researchers, 148
    writing and, 99, 119
curriculum
    auditing, 11
    being purposeful about, 58
    implications of teaching researchers, 149–153
    research unit vertical alignment discussion questions, 153
    vertical articulation of research units in grades 3–12, 151

D

daily closure, 76, 78–79, 85, 107, 159, 223
Darling-Hammond, D., 61, 74, 191
data tracking, 21–22
De La Pena, M., 201
Dear Sweet Pea (Murphy), 200, 226
declaring the relevance of the research, 137
defining literacy, 16–19
defining the language for your curriculum work, 34–35
    examples of agreements, 34
delineating and evaluating an argument, 147
demonstration text, 79–80, 106
designing a team challenge, 203
designing the instructional work of a book club unit, 199
    examples of lesson objectives, 199
developing a research question
    expressive language, 141
    stages of the research process, 132, 134
developing a thesis statement
    expressive language, 132, 136, 141
developing focused questions, 147
developing questionnaires or surveys, 135
digital navigation, 18
direct instruction. *See* explicit instruction
discussion of the week, 189–190, 227
diversity, 3–4
    defining, 35
    in authorship, 210–211
domains of language, 54–57
Donnolly, J., 226
drafting, 114–115, 121
Dragon Hoops (Yang), 226
Drzensky, F., 29
dynamic knowledge, 5

E

Eccles, J. S., 179
E–Destiny, 185
editing, 116, 121
Educated (Westover), 201
Egold, N., 29
email writing, 91
embracing balance, 233
Emerson College, 88
empathy, 28

reading structures, 218
teaching researchers, 148–149
writing and, 99, 121
Enchanted Air (Engle), 200
engagement, 1–4, 9
choice increases, 48
Engle, M., 200
English teachers are reading teachers, 24–25, 30, 178–180
establishing a purpose
language, 140
stages of the research process, 132
establishing a vision, 12, 36
example, 37
for revolving literacy work, 36–40
turn the vision into a mission statement, 40–41
establishing book club meeting agreements, 203–204
establishing how to facilitate learning, 47
agency and application, 49
choice, 48–49
ongoing assessment, feedback, and reflection, 49–50
systematic and explicit instruction, 47–48
establishing independent reading routines, 186–187
establishing new priorities, 12
establishing practices for responses and reflection, 205
establishing protocols of ongoing reflection, 11–12
establishing routines for independent reading, 186–187
Estrada, L., 17
evaluate to make meaning, 135
evaluating source materials
stages of the research process, 132, 134–135
evaluation, 74, 85
circular model, 60–62
ongoing, 49–50, 59
evidence of literacy learning, 142–145, 169–170
examples
agreements, 34
circular model of assessment, evaluation, and reflection, 61
establishing a vision, 37

lesson objectives of a book club unit, 199
lesson plan thinking map, 105–108
me maps, 46
mission statement, 40
question protocol, 42
reflection prompts, 138
standards, 55–57
turning your vision into a mission statement, 40
unit of study framework, 104, 154–155
vision for a revolving literacy unit, 37
explicit instruction, 47–48, 74, 76, 78–79, 84, 217, 222
exploring the idea, 114
expressive language skills, 17, 141–142, 215

F

facilitating a discussion of the week, 189–19
fan fiction, 91
feedback, 3
immediate, 60, 74
ongoing, 49–50
First Chapter Fridays, 189
A First Time for Everything (Santa), 226
Fitzgerald, F. S., 51, 209
flexibility, 17, 27, 99
reading structures, 218
teaching researchers, 149
writing and, 119–122
Flying Lessons and Other Stories (Oh), 201
focus statement, 84, 106
Follett website, 185
following a standard citation system, 147
forgiving yourself, 233
formal letter writing, 92
formative assessment, 60
forming a team of colleagues, 233
The Fort (Korman), 200, 226
Fourth Industrial Revolution, 8
Free Lunch (Ogle), 201, 226
From an Idea to Google (Sichol), 226
Future of Jobs Report (World Economic Forum), 5, 8, 19, 32, 98
future-ready skills, 5–10, 12–13, 83, 216
as a planning component, 31–32
as literacy, 19–21
connection with reading structures, 217–221

connection with writing, 92, 98–99–ready
language skills development, 54–57
literacy development, 17
newfound literacies, 15–19
reflection questions, 39–40
Skills on the Rise for Workers, 26–28
Stop and Think, 23, 25
teaching researchers, 143
understanding revolving literacy, 21–24
writing and, 104, 123, 125–126

G

Gallagher, K., 87–89
gathering information
receptive language, 140–141
stages of the research process, 132, 134–135, 147
Gee, J. P., 16
Gemeinhart, D., 226
general capacity, 29–30
generating and collecting ideas, 111–112, 119
expressive language, 141
stages of the research process, 132–133
genres of writing, 123, 125–126
Gephart, D., 226
getting concrete about the abstract future, 4
committing to change, 7–9
highlighting future readiness, 5–6
looking back and keeping forward, 4–5
maintaining core values, 6–7
The Girl Who Drank the Moon (Barnhill), 200
Gladwell, M., 187
global connectedness, 5
goal setting, 186
Golding, W., 51, 209
Goodreads, 185, 198, 209
Google, 21, 32
Blogger, 190
Docs, 34, 190
Forms, 34
Sites, 190
grading, 52
Graham, S., 92
The Great Gatsby (Fitzgerald), 51, 209
grouping students, 191
guided or independent
practice, 76, 78, 85, 107, 158
reading structures, 223

H

Ha, R., 200, 226
Hahn, J., 226
Hallet, R., 7
hard skills, 21
Harry Potter and the Sorcerer's Stone (Rowling), 200
Hawthorne, N., 210
Heraclitus, 10, 232
highlighting future readiness, 5–6
The Hobbit (Tolkien), 200
holding students accountable, 187–188
homeostasis, 233
Honigsfeld, A., 17
how to prioritize literacy components, 31
"How to Transform an Everyday, Ordinary Hoop Court into a Place of Higher Learning and You at the Podium" (De La Pena), 201
human relations, 20–21
Hutt, R., 7

I

I write, you write, I write, 136
I'm Not Your Perfect Mexican Daughter (Sanchez), 201
ideas, 89
identifying problems, issues, or inquiries to explore, 147
identity, 83
components, 43–44
defining, 35
fluidity, 22
literacy and, 17
reading structures, 215, 219–221
teaching researchers, 143–144
writing and, 92–93, 104, 124–126
identity audit, 43, 65
reflection space for, 43–44
immersion, 234
implementing a book club with students, 201
addressing challenges, 205–207
book tasting menu, 202
establish practices for responses and reflection, 205
inviting students to get acquainted, 204–204

sharing choice through a book
tasting, 201–203
teaching students to design a reading
schedule, 204
In Your Shoes (Gesphart), 226
Inbar-Lourie, O., 5, 131
independent reading, 13, 52, 180–181, 216
choosing a schedule for, 185
components of, 181
defined, 180
establish routines, 186–187
facilitating a discussion of the
week, 189–190
holding students accountable, 187–188
launching, 182–184
making instruction plans that
include, 184–185
plan, 193
planning to students to access reading
material, 185–186
reading structures, 217–218
staying committed and sustaining a
celebratory culture, 188–189
using nonfiction roundtables, 191
wrap-ups for, 191–192
industrial model of education, 4–5
innovation, 5
innovation-specific capacity, 29–30
Instagram, 185, 188
instructional plans that include independent
reading, 184–185
instructional practices
reflecting on, 11
intention, 76–77
intersection between cognition and
human relations, 20–21
inviting students to get acquainted, 204–204
iPads, 182
It's Trevor Noah (Noah), 200–201

J

Jamieson, V., 200
Jenkins, H., 16
Jimmieson, N. L., 29
job readiness, 3–4, 7
journaling, 133
reading response, 187–188

K

Kalantzis, M., 18
Kelley, W., 16
Kelly, L., 200
Kindles, 183
Kober, N., 6
Kohn, A., 48
Korman, G., 200, 226

L

language, 83, 140, 215
as a planning component, 31–32
evidence of literacy learning, 142–143
examples of standards, 55–57
expressive, 141–142
layering standards, 55
literacy and, 17
reading structures, 219–221
receptive, 140–141
skills development, 54–57
writing and, 92–93, 104
launching independent reading, 182–184
layering standards, domains of language, and
future–ready skills, 55
leadership skills, 17, 28
reading structures, 217
teaching researchers, 148–149
writing and, 99, 106, 121
learning and thinking, 234
learning new information, 11
Lee, H., 209
lesson plan, 81–82, 105
reading structures, 220
research in the revolving literacy
framework, 155–156
thinking maps, 105–108, 156–159,
220–224
lesson schedule, 80–81
revolving literacy, 81
lesson structure, 76–80
comparing performance–based and
revolving literacy, 77
letting go, 232–233
Lewis, C. S., 200
LeZotte, A. C., 200
lifelong learning strategies, 7, 26, 149

reading structures, 218, 221
writing and, 99, 119–122
The Lion, the Witch, and the Wardrobe (Lewis), 200
listening
    active, 17, 28, 148–149, 218
    examples of standards, 55–57
    reflection questions, 38
    writing and, 99, 121
literacies
    change as culture changes, 21–22
    connection to teaching the research process, 139–146
    core skills for workers, 20
    defining, 16–19
    future-ready skills as, 19–20
    intersection between cognition and human relations, 20–21
    newfound, 15–16
literacy analysis, 91
literacy development
    connection with reading structures, 214–216
looking back and forward, 4–5
Lord of the Flies (Golding), 51, 209
The Lost Hero (Riordan), 200

M

Macbeth (Shakespeare), 210
machine learning, 9
maintaining core values, 6–7
making instruction plans that include independent reading, 184–185
making strategic use of digital media, 147
Mann, H., 6
material management, 183–184
Mbalia, K., 200
me maps, 44–46, 66
    example, 46
    outline for, 45
    using sticky notes, 46
meaning making
    cocreating, 17
    multimodal, 17–18, 31, 33, 39, 83, 216, 220–221
    teaching researchers, 145
    writing and, 92, 94, 104, 106, 124–126
media literacy, 5

media with active engagement, 80, 106
Menti, 34
mentor texts, 79, 106
    choosing, 200–201
The Midnight Children (Gemeinhart), 226
Miller, D., 35
Mills, K. A., 15
mission statement, 40–41
    example, 40
Moore, D. B., 200
motivation, 27, 30
    choice increases, 48
    defined, 29
    reading structures, 218, 221
    teaching researchers, 149
    writing and, 99, 119–122
moving from issue to topic, 132
multimodal meaning making
    as a planning component, 31, 33, 83
    reading structures, 216, 220, 221
    reflection questions, 39
    teaching researchers, 145
    writing and, 92, 94, 104, 106, 124–126
Murphy, J., 200
Murray, D. M., 96
music, 18
My Family Divided (Guerrero), 201

N

narrowing ideas, 113, 119–120
    receptive language, 140
    stages of the research process, 132–134
National Academies of Sciences, Engineering, and Medicine, 49, 129
National Council of Teachers of English (NCTE), 16
new literacies
    change as culture changes, 21–22
    defined, 21
New York State Education Department, 47, 49, 55, 58, 210–211
New York State English Council, 89
The New York Times, 210–211
Next Generation English Language Arts Anchor standards (NY State Education Dept.), 55, 210–211
1984 (Orwell), 210
No Summit Out of Sight (Romero), 201

Noah, T., 200–201
nonfiction roundtables, 191
North Carolina State University, 88

O

Obama, M., 200
Objective, 84, 106
Odabaş, M., 7
Of Mice and Men (Steinbeck), 51, 209
Ogle, R., 201, 226
Oh, E., 201
Organisation for Economic Co–operation and Development, 6
organization, 89
Orwell, G., 51. 21–
Outliers (Gladwell), 187
Oxford English Dictionary, 129

P

Padlet, 188
Page, L., 21
Parachutes (Yang), 226
participating in the research community, 147
partner talks, 186
patience, 233
Patron Saints of Nothing (Ribay), 201
Pearson, P. D., 5
peer relationships, 3–4
picking one thing, 232
planning components, 31
    community, 33
    future-ready skills, 32
    language, 32
    multimodal meaning making, 33
    process-oriented instruction, 33–34
    student identities, 32–33
planning for a book club unit, 195–198
    sample, 196–197
planning for students to access reading material, 185–186
planning lessons, 73–75
    analogy for revolving literacy lesson, 75–76
    co-construction of learning, 73–74
    lesson plan, 81–82
    lesson schedule, 80–81
    lesson structure, 76–80
    Revolving Literacy Lesson Plan Thinking Map, 83–85
    revolving literacy lesson structure, 75
    Stop and Think, 82
Plymouth State University, 88
Poisoned (Donnolly), 226
presenting claims, findings, and evidence, 147
presenting research findings, 147
prevision, 96
print skills, 18
priorities
    establishing, 12
    tools for designing, 29–71
problem-solving skills, 17, 20
process-oriented instruction, 33–34
Project Aristotle, 21, 32
Project Oxygen, 21, 32
providing claims and explanation
    expressive language, 142
    receptive language, 141
    stages of the research process, 132, 136–137
psychological safety, 21

Q

question dump, 133
question protocol, 41–42
    example, 42
questions about student writing, 89
    about AI, 100–103
    are currency, 2–3
    balancing contemporary and canonical texts, 51–52
    curriculum, 58
    discussion of the week, 227
    how do students write, 95–97
    language skills development, 54
    reflection, 37–38
    to guide the text selection process, 211
    what do students write, 90–94
    why do students write, 89
Quiet (Cain), 226

R

RADaR process, 115
Rafferty, A. E., 29
read, think, wonder protocol, 212–213, 229

read-alouds, 184
reading, 12–13, 17
    book clubs, 13, 194–208
    conferences, 187
    connection between reading structures and future-ready skills, 217–218
    connection between reading structures and literacy development, 214–216
    curriculum models, 178
    Discussion of the Week, 227
    English teachers are reading teachers, 178–180
    examples of standards, 55–57
    independent, 13, 180–192
    Middle Grade and Young Adult Book List, 226
    Read, Think, Wonder, 229
    Reading Response Tool, Why Do We Read? Protocol, 228
    reading structures in the revolving literacy framework, 218–224
    reflection questions, 37
    shared reading experience, 208–214
    shared reading, 13
    Stop and Think, 192–193, 207–208, 210–211, 225
    teaching, 177–178
    to learn more, 133–134
reading structures, 218
    connection to future–ready skills, 217–218
    connection to literacy development, 214–216
    lesson plan, 220–224
    unit of study framework, 219–220
receptive language skills, 17, 140–141, 215
reciprocity between the classroom and students' lives, 1
reflecting on the stages of research, 147
    expressive language, 142
    stages of the research process, 132, 134, 137–138
reflection, 24–25, 74
    circular model, 60–62
    establishing protocols for ongoing, 11–12
    on instructional practices, 11
    on what it means to be literate, 11
    on writing, 107, 117–118, 122
    ongoing, 49–50
    prompts, 138

revision of curriculum, 30
    students, 59–60, 67–68
    teachers, 60
refocusing what is taught, 50
    being purposeful about what to teach, 58
    focusing on future-readiness and language skills, 54–57
    reconsidering the emphasis on shared canonical texts, 50–53
    shifting to a student literacy-driven model for planning, 53–54
relevance, 1–4, 9, 83, 179, 221
The Remarkable Journey of Coyote Sunrise (Gemeinhart), 226
Rentner, D. S., 6
reproducibles
    Connection Between Literacy Development Components and the Research Process Checklist, 169–170
    Connection Between Stages of Writing and Future-Ready Skills, 119–122
    Evaluating Sources to Make Meaning, 166
    Explanations of Each Stage of the Literacy Writing Process, 112–118
    Explanations of Each Stage of the Research Process, 163–164
    Explanations of Each Stage of the Revolving Literacy Writing Process, 136
    Future-Ready Skill Student Reflection, 67–68
    Identity Audit, 65
    Me Map, 66
    New Visions and New Priorities, 69–71
    Revolving Literacy Lesson Plan Thinking Map, 83–85
    Revolving Literacy Research Articulation Planning Tool for Grades 7–12, 171–172
    Revolving Literacy Research Articulation Planning Tool for Grades 7–9, 173–174
    Revolving Literacy Research Articulation Planning Tool for Grades 9–12, 175–176
    Revolving Literacy Writing Articulation Planning Tool for Grades 7–12, 123–124
    Revolving Literacy Writing Articulation Planning Tool for Grades 7–9, 125

Revolving Literacy Writing Articulation Planning Tool for Grades 9–12, 126
Skills on the Rise for Workers for 2023 to 2027, 26–28
Student Identity Question Protocol, 64
Summarize to Understand, 165
Synthesize to Share, 167–168
research unit vertical alignment discussion questions, 153
research, 12–13
   and its relevance, 129–130
   connection to literacy, 139
   defined, 129
   future-ready skills alignment, 148
   in academic, professional, and social spaces, 130
   in the revolving literacy framework, 153
   lesson plan, 155–159
   papers, 91
   progression, 51
   stages of the process, 131–137
   unit of study framework, 154–155
resilience, 17, 27
   reading structures, 218
   teaching researchers, 148–149
   writing, 99, 119–122
reskilling, 8
résumé writing, 92
reviews and critiques, 91–92
revising, 96, 115, 121
revolving literacy framework, 2, 10, 12
   defined, 22
   key planning components, 31–34
   lesson structure, 77–
   planning lessons, 73–85
   research opportunities planning tool, 162
   understanding, 21–24
   writing opportunities planning tool, 111
Ribay, R., 201
Riley, R., 7
Riordan, R., 200
Rolling Stone, 21
Romeo and Juliet (Shakespeare), 3, 51, 209
Romero, J., 201
A Rover's Story (Warga), 226
Rowling, J. K., 200
Rozendal, M. S., 5
Rubin, H., 17

S

safety, 43–44
Salinger, J. D., 210
Salman, J. S., 5
Sanchez, E. L., 201
Santat, D., 226
Scaccia J. P., 29
scaffolding, 60, 107
The Scarlett Letter (Hawthorne), 210
Schlam Salman, J., 131
Scholastic Aptitude Test (SAT), 58, 62
selecting book choices, 198–199
self-awareness, 27
   reading structures, 218, 221
   teaching researchers, 149
   writing and, 99, 119–122
sentence fluency, 89
Seventh Grade (Soto), 200
Shakespeare, W., 51–52, 209–210
shared canonical texts
   defined, 50
   moving to a student-literacy driven model, 53–54
   reconsidering the emphasis on, 50–53
shared experience, 80, 106
shared reading, 13, 208–209, 216
   balancing classic and contemporary literature, 209–211
   committing to relevance, 209
   reading structures, 218
   teaching readers and reading, not texts, 212–214
shared text-driven model, 92
sharing conclusions or findings
   expressive language, 142
   receptive language, 141
   stages of the research process, 132, 137
sharing research implications, 137
sharing text choice through a book tasting, 201–203
Sharp, C., 35
show and explain, 80, 106
Show Me a Sign (LeZotte), 200
Sichol, L. B., 226
signs and symbols, 18
silos of time, content, and space, 4
Snapchat, 188
Sobs, S., 21

social commentary, 92
social influence, 28
    reading structures, 218
    teaching researchers, 148–149
    writing and, 99, 106, 121
social media, 21–22, 189–190
    posting on, 91
social practices, 17
social-emotional learning, 7
soft skills, 21
Some Places More Than Others (Watson), 200
Song for a Whale (Kelly), 200
SORA, 185
Soto, G., 200
sound effects, 18
speaking
    examples of standards, 55–57
    reflection questions, 38
    stages of the research process, 131–132, 146
        choosing an idea and developing a research question, 134
        developing a thesis statement, 136
        establishing a purpose, 132
        gathering information and evaluating source material, 134–135
        generating ideas, 133
        narrowing ideas, 133–134
        providing claims and explanations, 136–137
        reflecting, 137–138
        sharing conclusions or findings, 137
standardized tests, 52, 62–63, 89, 106
standards, 55, 84, 123, 125–126
The Stars Beneath Our Feet (Moore), 200
staying committed to a reading culture, 188–189
Steinback, J., 51, 209
Stop and Think sections, 13
    newfound literacies in future–ready skills, 19, 23, 25
    planning lessons, 82
    teaching readers, 192–193, 207–208, 210–211, 225
    teaching researchers, 130–131, 138–139, 145–146, 150, 160–161
    teaching writing, 94–95, 97–98, 109–110
    tools for designing new visions and priorities, 30, 35, 41, 52–53
Street, B., 16

student identities, 182
    as a planning component, 32–33
    reflection questions, 38–39
student literacy-driven model, 53–54
    vs. a shared text-driven model, 53–54
student profiles, 41
    identity audit, 42–43
    me maps, 43–46
    question protocol, 41–42
studying media sources, 135
submitting and sharing writing, 116–117, 121
summarize to understand, 135
The Summer I Turned Pretty (Hahn), 226
sustaining a celebratory culture, 188–189
Suvada, E., 201
synthesize to share, 135
synthesizing information, 147
systematic instruction, 47–48, 74
systems thinking, 27
    teaching researchers, 148–149
    writing and, 99, 119–122

T

Takei, G., 201
T-charts, 132
teaching readers and reading,
    not texts, 212–214
teaching researchers, 127–129
    Connection Between Literacy Development Components and the Research Process Checklist, 169–170
    connection between teaching the research process and future readiness, 146–149
    connection between teaching the research process and literacy, 139–146
    curriculum implications, 149–153
    Evaluating Sources to Make Meaning, 166
    Explanations of Each Stage of the Research Process, 163–164
    research and its relevance, 129–130
    research in the revolving literacy framework, 153–159
    Revolving Literacy Research Articulation Planning Tool for Grades 7–12, 171–172
    Revolving Literacy Research Articulation Planning Tool for Grades 7–9, 173–174

Revolving Literacy Research Articulation Planning Tool for Grades 9–12, 175–176
revolving literacy research opportunities planning tool, 162
stages of the research process, 131–137
Stop and Think, 130–131, 138–139, 145–146, 150, 160–161
Summarize to Understand, 165
Synthesize to Share, 167–168
teaching students to design a reading schedule, 204
teaching writing, 87–89
  connection between writing and future-ready skills, 98–99
  Explanations of Each Stage of the Literacy Writing Process, 112–118
  in the era of AI, 100–102
  in the revolving literacy framework, 103
  questions about student writing, 89–98
  Revolving Literacy Writing Articulation Planning Tool for Grades 7–12, 123–124
  Revolving Literacy Writing Articulation Planning Tool for Grades 7–9, 125
  Revolving Literacy Writing Articulation Planning Tool for Grades 9–12, 126
  Stop and Think, 94–95, 97–98, 109–110
  unit of study framework, 103–108
team talks, 134
technological literacy, 21–22, 26
  teaching researchers, 148–149
  writing and, 99, 119, 121
testing, 62–63
texts
  balance of classic and contemporary, 9, 50–51
  defining, 35
  demonstration, 79–80
  mentor, 106
  mentor, 79
  moving to a student literacy-driven model, 53–54
They Called Us Enemy (Takei), 201
think-alouds, 79, 106
thinking maps, 156–158, 220–224
This Mortal Coil (Suvada), 201
TikTok, 185, 188–189
To Kill a Mockingbird (Lee), 209

Tolkien, J. R. R., 200
tools for designing new visions and priorities, 29–30
  assessment as an ongoing component of the learning process, 58–63
  creating student profiles, 41–46
  defining the language, 34–35
  establishing a vision, 36–41
  establishing how to facilitate learning, 47–50
  Future-Ready Skill Student Reflection, 67–68
  Identity Audit, 65
  key planning components, 31–34
  Me Map, 66
  New Visions and New Priorities, 69–71
  refocusing what is taught, 50–58
  Stop and Think, 30, 35, 41, 52–53
  Student Identity Question Protocol, 64
transferable skills, 5
Tristan Strong Punches a Hole in the Sky (Mbalia), 200
turning your vision into a mission statement, 40–41
  example, 40

U

U.S. Census Bureau, 32
understanding revolving literacy, 21–24
  as a relationship between school and students' lives, 22
unit of study framework, 103–104
  examples, 104, 154–155
  reading structures, 219–220
  research in the revolving literacy framework, 154
University of South Carolina, 88
Unsworth, L., 16
use of AI, 148–149
using color tools, 137
using questions to frame thinking, 132
using strong transitions, 137

V

van Dick, R., 29
vertical articulation of research units in grades 3–12, 151

viewing, 17
    reflection questions, 38
vision, 96
    establishing, 12
    tools for designing, 29–71
    tools for establishing, 36–41
    turning into a mission statement, 40–41
visually representing, 17
    reflection questions, 38
Vlogs, 188
voice, 89

W

Wandersman, A., 29
Warga, J., 226
Watson, R., 200
Westover, T., 201
When Stars Are Scattered (Jamieson), 200
whole-class instruction, 84, 222–223
    teaching researchers, 158
    writing and, 106–107
why are we doing this, 2–3
why do we read protocol, 212–213
word choice, 89
World Economic Forum, 5, 7–8, 19–20, 32, 98
wrap-ups
    for independent reading, 191–192
    for reflecting on book club implementation, 207
write it three times, 136
writing, 12, 17, 51
    Connection Between Stages of Writing and Future–Ready Skills, 119–122
    connection between writing and future–ready skills, 98–99
    examples of standards, 55–57
    Explanations of Each State of the Literacy Writing Process, 112–118
    in the era of AI, 100–102
    in the revolving literacy framework, 103
    invitations, 88–89
    planning tool, 111
    process in the revolving literacy framework, 97
    questions about student writing, 89–98
    reflection questions, 38
    Revolving Literacy Writing Articulation Planning Tool for Grades 7–12, 123–124
    Revolving Literacy Writing Articulation Planning Tool for Grades 7–9, 125
    Revolving Literacy Writing Articulation Planning Tool for Grades 9–12, 126
    Stop and Think, 94–95, 97–98, 109–110
    teaching, 87–89, 108–111
    unit of study framework, 103–108

Y

Yang, G. L., 226
Yang, K., 226
YouTube, 188–189

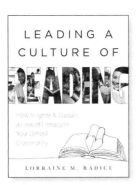

Leading a Culture of Reading
Lorraine M. Radice

Engaged students achieve better reading success. Grounded in current research, this book provides practical resources and strategies, including the use of technology and social media, that will help educators improve literacy culture in their schools.
BKG124

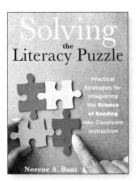

Solving the Literacy Puzzle
Norene A. Bunt

Using graphic organizers, assessments, and reflection questions, educators can unpack five core components of literacy instruction within the science of reading framework. This comprehensive guide prepares teachers to confidently implement effective literacy instruction in their classrooms.
BKG158

Their Stories, Their Voices
Kourtney Hake and Paige Timmerman

Kourtney Hake and Paige Timmerman share a step-by-step, build-your-own framework that helps students excel in writing and life, showing how personal narrative harnesses students' natural urge to tell stories.
BKG173

Digital Projects Playbook
John Arthur

Students in today's classrooms live in a digital world. Tap into the unique opportunities this offers with author John Arthur's collection of resource-packed projects designed to leverage students' digital skills and support their academic, cognitive, and creative development.
BKG171

Visit SolutionTree.com or call 800.733.6786 to order.

Quality team learning **from authors you trust**

Global PD Teams is the first-ever **online professional development resource designed to support your entire faculty on your learning journey.** This convenient tool offers daily access to videos, mini-courses, eBooks, articles, and more packed with insights and research-backed strategies you can use immediately.

 GET STARTED
SolutionTree.com/**GlobalPDTeams**
800.733.6786